Immortal Yearnings

Mystical Imaginings and Primordial Affirmations of the Afterlife

Immortal Yearnings

Mystical Imaginings and Primordial Affirmations of the Afterlife

Annamaria Hemingway

6th BOOKS

Winchester, UK
Washington, USA

First published by Sixth Books, 2012
Sixth Books is an imprint of John Hunt Publishing Ltd., Laurel House, Station Approach,
Alresford, Hants, SO24 9JH, UK
office1@jhpbooks.net
www.johnhuntpublishing.com
www.6th-books.com

For distributor details and how to order please visit the 'Ordering' section on our website.

ISBN: 978 1 78099 517 5

A CIP catalogue record for this book is available from the British Library.

Design: Stuart Davies

Printed in the USA by Edwards Brothers Malloy

CONTENTS

In the depth of your hopes and desires lies your silent knowledge of the beyond; and like seeds dreaming beneath the snow your heart dreams of spring.

Trust the dreams, for in them is hidden the gate to eternity.

Khalil Gibran, *The Prophet*

For my Brighton Boys,
Jay and Toby

Introduction

In her eyes a thought Grew sweeter and sweeter, a deepening like the dawn, a mystical forewarning.
Thomas Bailey Aldrich, *Pythagoras*

Throughout the evolution of human consciousness, mystical visions and divine apparitions reveal recurring and primordial affirmations of an alternate reality, providing a foundation for both the mythological beliefs of world religions and the spiritual development of humanity. The word *mystic* originates from the Greek *mysticos,* translated to mean "one who had been initiated into the secrets of the ancient Mystery Cults of Greece and Egypt." While such transcendent visionary states are universal and share many similar characteristics, they are not subject to any particular religious tradition, but are described as having a spiritual component. These *magical* and enigmatic experiences occur beyond the realms of everyday consciousness, dissolving barriers of time, space, and logic to reconnect us with an expanded state of *cosmic consciousness,* which radically changes perception of the deeper meaning of reality.

The deep insights generated through altered states also highlight parallels between ancient mystical religious beliefs and science. The physicist, Fritjof Capra, whose previous experience was limited to mathematical theories and diagrams, tells of his own awakening that took place one summer day at the ocean and led to a re-visioning of prior beliefs:

> I 'saw' cascades of energy coming down from outer space....I 'saw' the atoms of elements and those of my body participating in this cosmic dance of energy; I felt its rhythm and I 'heard' its sound, and at that moment I *knew* that this was the Dance of Shiva, the Lord of Dancers worshipped by the Hindus.[1]

The core element of such a vision is liberation from an ego-based identification, resulting in a spiritual epiphany that has a transformative effect. Such an illuminating shift in perception contains the archetypal affirmation of death and spiritual rebirth, culminating in a heightened sense of a transcendent merging with 'God' or a higher power in many different guises in what C. G. Jung referred to, as a fleeting awareness of *absolute knowledge*.

Mystical states are paradoxical in their nature, as they register in the psyche as sensations, feelings, and archetypal symbolic images, yet mystics, seers, and prophets from many different religious traditions struggle to find language that can adequately articulate the *ineffable* ecstatic essence of such inexplicable experiences.

Many believe that mystical states of consciousness can only be accessed by a select few illumined beings, such as saints and sages, who through intense spiritual practice and ritual, access these realms. However, the reality is that supernatural states of enlightenment can occur spontaneously to anyone, at any time, and that they can be triggered by a variety of stimuli, including: music, poetry, art, nature, meditation, and sudden trauma to the body as in a near-death experience, to name but a few.

Surveys carried out in the United States and the United Kingdom indicate that approximately one-third of the adult population in both these countries claim to have had some type of mystical encounter (Greeley 1975). A Gallup Poll conducted in 1976, also found a similar proportion of respondents reporting *otherworldly* sensations, often described as having religious or spiritual connotations. In 1994, The National Opinion Research Center of Chicago revealed that over two-thirds of Americans believed that they had undergone a mystical experience in which they felt connection to a higher spiritual presence.

Equally important as the realization that numinous visions do spontaneously manifest, is understanding the prime importance of such sudden leaps in intuitive wisdom in a world where we yearn to experience the nature of the *holy* and the *sacred* in our lives. Joy Mills writes:

> The central characteristic of the mystical experience—ineffable, noetic, fleeting, timeless—is the enveloping sense of oneness with a universe suddenly known and felt as luminous from within.[2]

One of the more widely known variations of a mystical vision is the near-death experience, which contains mythic motifs and archetypal dimensions and has a permanent transformative effect in the future life of a survivor of such a transcendent other-worldly encounter. Many return from euphoric near-death journeys with an unshakable belief in a continuum of consciousness following death and discover a new unique sense of purpose to our fleeting earthly existence. The power of these life-changing stories also brings hope and strength to the dying and the bereaved, in the calm assurance that death is merely a transition to be embraced and not feared.

Through exploring, interpreting, and evaluating the archetypal and symbolic dimensions of contemporary near-death experiences and comparing them to those of similar transcendent states, we can glean invaluable knowledge to escape from the allegory of Plato's darkened cave and emerge into the light of a divine legacy.

Notes

1 Fritjof Capra, *The Tao of Physics: An Exploration of the Parallels Between Modern Physics and Eastern Mysticism* (Boston: Shambhala, 1991), 11.

2 Joy Mills, "Nature of Mystical Experience," in *The Silent Encounter: Reflections on Mysticism*, ed. Virginia Hanson (Wheaton: Quest, 1974), 7.

Chapter 1

Archetypes, Symbols, and Alchemy: The Essence of Mystical Imaginings

For it is not that "God" is a myth, but that myth is the revelation of the divine life in man.
C. G. Jung, *Memories, Dreams, Reflections*

By their very nature, mystical visions are ineffable and beyond rational comprehension. Attempts to explore the transcendent value of such experiences, including the NDE, requires the ability to translate and interpret the primordial essence of archetypes and the mysterious quality of symbols that speak in the poetic timeless language of the soul.

Clearly defining the term ***archetype*** is difficult, as archetypal content is expressed through metaphor and so always contains a hidden meaning that defies all rational explanation. Archetypes can only be identified through the effects they manifest, and their origins remain unclear. Jolande Jacobi writes:

> The origin of an archetype remains obscure, its nature unfathomable; for it dwells in that mysterious shadow realm, the collective unconscious, to which we shall never have direct access, and whose existence and operation we can have only indirect knowledge, precisely through our encounter with archetypes, i.e., their manifestations in the psyche.[1]

Put simply, archetypes comprise of sets of images that have been indelibly stamped on the human psyche; an example would be the alternating darkness of night and the light of day. For ancient cultures, recurring images, such as the daily journey of the sun, were preserved in myths and provided spontaneous analogies for death and rebirth.

The ancient Greeks sought to determine *a priori* causes to explain the world in which they lived. Heraclitus, the pre-Socratic philosopher, renounced his kingdom in order to seek knowledge. The great body of his work was lost. However, fragments survive that illustrate how his thinking was not only philosophical, but also poetic and prophetic. Heraclitus believed that the core essence of matter was *energy* and *wisdom* that governed and permeated all things and he likened the cosmos to a regenerative alchemical eternal fire:

> All things change to fire,
> and fire exhausted
> falls back into things.[2]

Aristotle sought to determine philosophical answers from a more theoretical standpoint, concluding that philosophical insights could be gained through expanding the powers of perception. Pythagoras viewed mathematical reason and logic as providing a language that explained the prophetic cosmic principles of the universe, and he coined the word 'philosopher' to mean the lover of wisdom.

The famous Platonic dialogues expanded the ideas of Socrates, who instilled Plato with a quest for enlightenment. Plato developed the concept of 'forms' in which qualities, such as beauty, have an eternal essence containing primordial *forgotten* knowledge and so represent an early understanding of unconscious contents. He writes:

> [W]hen we perceive something, either by the help of sight, or hearing, or some other sense, from that perception we are able to obtain a notion of some other things like or unlike which is associated with it but has been forgotten . . . and learning is

simply recollection.[3]

It is evident to see that there is a relationship between Plato's concept of 'forms' and the archetypes, for both relate to the idea of an image that is formed, but exists outside of everyday consciousness. However, 'forms' were deemed absolute and eternal, existing before all experience. Archetypes differ, as they are not static inherited memories, but rather alive and fluid, with their dynamic force reflecting the changing images of life that can dissolve and then, out of the old, be created anew.

The word *archetype* means 'image' or 'copy' and so archetypes can be viewed as imprints of primordial affirmations and patterns residing in the collective unconscious of humanity. Archetypal energies also possess paradoxical bipolar aspects, integrating all possibilities from the past and the future—like the mythical Janus head—archetypes look both forwards and backwards.

The notion that the psyche contained material unavailable in conscious awareness was speculated upon for thousands of years by a great many early Greek philosophers, including Dionysius and Plotinus. The mystical traditions of India recorded in the Holy Scriptures of the *Vedanta,* also pursued such thought, as did mystics from the Middle Ages, including Meister Eckhart and Boehme. By the late nineteenth century, debates on the unconscious realms were of paramount speculation and interest.

Sigmund Freud pursued his research into the concept and contents of the unconscious and he coined the word *psychoanalysis*. The expression is a combination of two Greek words that have very different connotations. *Psyche* denotes the rich emotional aspect of the soul that is totally human, and devoid of scientific attachment, while *Analysis* implies a form of sterile evaluation. In English terminology, a stronger emphasis is placed on *analysis.* However, in German, the language that Freud wrote in, importance was placed on the psyche or soul. Bruno

Bettelheim writes:

> By coining the term "psychoanalysis" to describe his work, Freud wished to emphasize that by isolating and examining the neglected and hidden aspects of our souls we can acquaint ourselves with those aspects and understand the roles they play in our lives. It was Freud's emphasis on the soul that made his analysis different from all others. What we think and feel about man's soul— our own soul—is all important in Freud's view.[4]

Freud was greatly interested in mythology. As a child, he became enthralled by the family Bible, which also included images and illustrations of Egyptian gods from biblical times. His Vienna consulting rooms were full of ancient antiquities and he used these captivating images and the power they held as inspirational tools in his heroic quest to discover universal truths of human nature. He was particularly drawn to the symbolism of *Oedipus*, and from this myth, he formulated his famous *Oedipus complex* theory that centered on unconscious impulses and emotions stemming from the early relationships a child had with its parents.

The myth of *Amor and Psyche* also greatly fascinated Freud. Perhaps this was because Psyche was described as having wings that resembled those of a butterfly or bird, which are both universal motifs of the soul and its transcendent quality. Psyche's descent and return from the underworld symbolized crossing the barriers of consciousness, a journey Freud attempted psychologically, resulting in transformation. During the period of his descent into the unconscious, he isolated himself and underwent a serious course of self-analysis and meticulously recorded images from his dreams and their repressed memories, as he believed that unconscious content revealed itself in symbolic metaphors and analogies.

Freud emerged from this ordeal transformed and he was inspired to publish *The Interpretation of Dreams* in 1899. In this seminal work, Freud illustrates how similar unconscious content and underlying themes also manifested in the dreams of his patients. He acknowledges that some of this material is not strictly personal, but appears to symbolize remnants from the history of humanity, accessed through "an unsuspected source of stimulation."[5]

Freud theorized the unconscious was a reservoir that stored repressed childhood memories and accompanying emotions, together with primordial drives and instincts. He also felt that one of the greatest challenges for the human being was to incorporate the death drive and the life force. Finding a balance between these two opposing energies could, according to Freud, result in an existence that enabled Eros, the life force, to keep our destructive forces in check. He also maintained that denial of death led to unconscious psychological consequences:

> In our civilized attitude towards death we are once more living psychologically beyond our means . . . .Would it not be better to give death that place in actuality and in our thoughts which properly belong to it, and to yield a little more prominence to that unconscious attitude toward death which we have hitherto so carefully suppressed?[6]

Carl Gustav Jung started out working at the Burgholzil Hospital in Zurich, where many of his patients had been diagnosed with severe psychotic disorders, including schizophrenia. During this period, Jung noticed the frequency of universal associations and images. He was fascinated by the parallels found in the fantasies of his patients and how they related to mythic patterns. He writes that these images "live in a world quite different from the world outside . . . . No wonder their nature is strange, so strange that their irruption into consciousness often amounts to a psychosis.

They undoubtedly belong to the material that comes to light in schizophrenia."[7] This intriguing insight led Jung to concur that there was a further dimension to the unconscious, beyond that of personal repressed memories and representations that formed the basis of Freud's theories, which he expanded upon.

In his private practice, Jung began to analyze the dreams of his patients that also presented images associated with ancient rites and myths. As a result, he suggested the existence of a 'collective' unconscious that contained primordial patterns of human behavior and experience. To help his patients in moving beyond the 'personal' material of their dreams, Jung amplified the mythic dimensions of such contents. He described the tendencies to form images from these recurring motifs and patterns as being *primordial* images, but he later named them as *archetypes.* He also acknowledged that the Biblical philosopher, Philo had already proposed the concept of the *Imago Dei,* translated to mean the God-image found within all human beings. The term *archetype* was also used in the *Corpus Hermeticum* in which God is depicted as the "archetypal light."[8]

Such archetypal energies, according to Jung, reside deep within the unconscious aspects of the psyche, seeking to bring images from a distant past that contain the inherited experiences of humanity to light, as they become actualized and take form to be perceived as living realities in conscious awareness. The archetype can thus be regarded as having the potential to form a pattern that reveals itself in images. This vast storehouse of the psychic history of humanity is 'neutral' in that there is no differentiation between good and evil, or beauty and ugliness. However, these contents *acquire* their relative value as they emerge into consciousness.

Rediscovering the concept of eternal and transpersonal dimensions can occur through reconnecting with the energy patterns depicted in ancient myths, as archetypal content has an invisible quality that still influences both the behavior and attitudes of the human being. William Doty writes, "There is a certain numinosity about archetypal images, recognized by the effect experienced when personal feelings are particularly engaged by a dream or mythic image."[9] When archetypes appear, they often herald changes taking place within the individual, who is searching to discover a new and more meaningful personal myth.

Today, we often find ancient ***symbolic*** forms that express archetypal energy unfamiliar and hard to translate, but they still profoundly affect psychic life, as not only do they provide an outer objective meaning, but they also awaken consciousness to a hidden profound interpretation.

For the early Greeks, symbols represented the two halves of a coin or object that signified a pledge, and they were later used to prove the identity of the holder. The concept of something missing that is then restored can psychologically be interpreted to mean retrieving the missing or split-off part of the individual, in order to create a totality or sense of wholeness.

A symbol appears to facilitate the transformation of psychic energy, suggesting the symbol is *alive* and can convey meaning to an unknown unconscious content that is not consciously apparent, or visible to the observer. In order for a symbol to have such an effect, it adopts a form and produces a pattern that creates an expanded state of awareness, but the individual must be able to recognize a prevailing pattern within the image. Energy and form are the central characteristics of a symbol, and what is separated by an objective state of consciousness is united through a profound symbolic consciousness, which is beyond the grasp of rationality. Understanding symbolic representation necessitates bypassing the intellect and opening to the mystery the symbol may reveal. To be considered a *living* symbol, an intense emotional response must be generated, as a symbol is constantly evolving, and energy is in perpetual motion. D. Stephenson Bond writes:

> The symbol of the cross. A chalice. An altar. A mosque. The Star of David. A prayer wheel. A Tibetan mandala. A totem pole. A crystal you want to buy in the New Age store. Does it have intensity? Does it stir the imagination from sleep? Does it grip your fascination? If so, then it is living. If not, then it has died. If so, then it has become symbolic. If not, then it has become simply historical. [10]

Altered states of mystical consciousness are, by their very nature, symbolic. Evelyn Underhill describes symbolism as providing the key to the mystical experience. She writes:

> A good symbolism, therefore, will be more than a mere diagram or mere allegory; it will use to the utmost the resources of beauty and of passion, will bring with it hints of mystery and wonder . . . . Its appeal will not be to the clever mind, but to the desirous heart, the intuitive sense, of man.[11]

Ancient civilizations were rich in symbolic motifs and metaphors and early Egyptian religious rites and rituals for both the living and dead were preserved in the hieroglyphics discovered in tombs and temple sites that revealed potent images of the posthumous journey of the soul.

Through interpreting and comparing the parallels found in the analogies of ancient myths to the symbolic content of modern dreams, Jung theorizes that the capacity to form symbols, expressed by early people in rituals and beliefs, continues to reside within the collective unconscious. Symbols, therefore, are guardians of primordial knowledge and affirmations that remain constant throughout eternity and are unaffected by cultural and religious changes evolving throughout society. Most importantly, symbols are *mnemonic*—they prompt us to remember ancient sacred truths.

Jung had many mystical epiphanies throughout his lifetime

and he formulated his own method to delve deep into the unconscious. Every morning, he translated archetypal imagery from his dreams by writing and drawing everything that came into his conscious awareness. During this intense reflection, Jung encountered the archetypes that manifested more clearly, both in human and animal forms. Like Dante, who in *The Divine Comedy*, was guided through the realms of hell and greater part of purgatory by the poet, Virgil, Jung also had a guide in this great undertaking named Philemon, who led and instructed him in this journey of descent.

Jung encountered biblical figures, including an old man with a long beard called Elijah, and a young blind woman, Salome. Elijah said the couple had been together throughout eternity. A black serpent accompanied them that showed a fondness for Jung, who described these meetings as events and experiences, rather than giving them an intellectual definition. However, he later recognized Elijah as symbolizing knowledge and wisdom and Salome as representing the *anima,* and viewed the figures to be embodiments of Eros and Logos. The black snake was of great interest to Jung, for it seemed to display parallels to the hero-myth and he pondered over the many similarities. "For example, the hero has eyes like a snake, or after his death he is changed into a snake and revered as such, or the snake is his mother, etc. In my fantasy, therefore, the presence of the snake was an indication of a hero-myth."[12]

Jung's encounters with Salome and Elijah continued for a period of time and then the figures disappeared. He was astounded when they returned as though nothing had changed in his life. Jung believed the images had receded back into the unconscious and, therefore, into a timeless quality that was out of contact with changes taking place in the ego. Jung experienced feeling 'separate' when Salome and Elijah reemerged, signifying the primary discrimination made by an ego consciousness that creates a barrier and divides subjects and objects. The notion of space and a divide only came into being when the Egyptian god, Shu, separated the earth from the sky by standing between them. Erich Neumann writes, "Only then, as a result of his light-creating intervention, was there heaven above and earth below . . . only then was space recognized with reference to an ego."[13]

Jung realized that the underworld realms threatened to submerge him and were full of potential danger, even though this descent would ultimately prove to be an initiation into an alternate dimension of reality. He grounded himself with mundane aspects of daily life, such as chopping wood and spending time with his family. As a result, he was able to overcome the perils of his hazardous undertaking, and emerge from this odyssey having discovered a new image of 'God' in his psyche.

During this voluntary period of surrender to the unconscious, Jung experienced a spectacular archetypal vision depicting the ancient solar myth of death and renewal, which was symbolized by the motif of the Egyptian scarab. The solar-hero myth represents the psyche's natural translation of the sun's journey and this archetypal content enables the ability to translate physical manifestations into psychic representations.

In his latter years, Jung was to comment to a friend in a letter that his most important task was to awaken human beings into remembering that they had a soul.[14] He describes an instance when he felt his soul fly away from him to the "land of the dead," which he deemed to be a paramount experience, because it signified the soul forming a relationship with the unconscious and the mythic realms of the ancestors:

> This was a significant event: the soul, the anima, establishes the relationship to the unconscious. In a certain sense this is also a relationship to the collectivity of the dead: for the unconscious corresponds to the mythic land of the dead, the

> land of the ancestors. If, therefore, one has a fantasy of the soul vanishing, this means that it has withdrawn into the unconscious or into the land of the dead. There it produces a mysterious animation and gives visible form to the ancestral traces, the collective contents.[15]

Following his underworld descent, Jung believed that images of the dead voiced the mystery of life and death and explained the unanswerable. The conversations he had with entities, such as Philemon, who appeared to be real and acted as a guide or guru, instilled Jung with new knowledge; for Philemon symbolized a higher state of awareness and wisdom. These archetypal experiences led Jung to underscore the importance of the nature of images from the unconscious, as he realized they did not represent obsolete archaic forms, but rather continued to be of paramount importance in the world of the psyche.

As Jung emerged from this period of intense inner reflection, he made another important discovery—his underworld descent had resulted in a symbolic death and rebirth, which led him to experience a sense of 'wholeness' and the discovery of the Self. He named the assimilation of the unconscious into conscious awareness as being that of "individuation," which he believed, led to a harmonious relationship between the unconscious and the ego in a mystical marriage of the union of opposites, described as being the "transcendent function."[16] Through this consummation, fresh conscious attitudes emerge from within the individual, and Jung recorded over 1000 hand-written pages with accompanying illustrations meticulously detailing his *nekyia* or descent, which are preserved in the Red Book, posthumously published in 2009.

Jung encountered many archetypes and the ones he felt to be central and of universal value included: the *persona*, the *shadow*, the *anima/animus*, the *Self*, the *wise old man*, and the *mother*. The capacity to translate ancient symbols and archetypal images that manifest in dreams or states of psychic distress still resides in the unconscious to indicate possible, but previously unknown avenues of possibility. Unlike temporary human existence, archetypes are timeless and they can appear as spiritual guides. From the wealth of archetypes, this chapter focuses on the archetypal energies of the *shadow* and the *Self* that are most commonly said to manifest during the NDE and the numinous transpersonal quality of such encounters.

During his confrontation with the unconscious, Jung had a dream in which he was with a small "unknown brown-skinned savage."[17] Together, they shot and murdered the German hero, Siegfried. The small colored savage initiated the demise of Siegfried, and Jung believed he embodied the primitive shadow that personifies negative and split-off character traits. This dark shadow aspect can be transferred or projected onto another person; in some cases, the shadow can take over the complete personality of the individual, who is unaware of these negative patterns.

One of the most popular stories regarding the shadow is to be found in Robert Louis Stevenson's *Dr Jekyll and Mr Hyde*. Stevenson was greatly interested in 'sub-consciousness' and placed great importance on archetypal dream imagery. During a bout of serious illness, he was to have a dream from which the story of a divided self that was based on his own experience originated. Having been brought up as a strict Calvinists, Stevenson and his friend, Charles Baxter, would assume the identities of Johnson and Thomson, who roamed the streets of Edinburgh at night and challenged the values of their upbringing through bouts of heavy drinking.

In the tale, Hyde personifies the evil dark aspect of the benign and upstanding Jekyll, and Stevenson uses powerful symbolic images to conjure up the reality of Hyde's shadow embodiment, described as a "creature that cannot be denied."[18] The projection of the shadow was also depicted in the collective of mid to late eighteenth-century life in other literary works, including *The Double*, by Dostoevsky and Oscar Wilde's *The Picture of Dorian Gray*. These archetypal characterizations of a divided self provide examples of how the *shadow* can break away from the conscious personality to have a dark evil life of its own.

In ancient Western traditions and throughout Eastern mythology, the opposites contained in the archetypes remained united and full of inconsistencies, but over time a division took place. This is particularly noted in the Jewish deity, Yahweh, who contained both light and dark aspects, but following Christian reformation, was to become an all encompassing 'good' God, as these negative attributes were transferred to the devil. However, Eastern traditions incorporate intellectual intuition and, therefore, the gods and goddesses remain 'whole.' Kali manifests both light and dark forces and retains her paradoxical nature. Known as the Madonna in Western cultures, the archetype no longer contains shadow aspects, but the darkness still exists and cannot be denied and so is projected on to the psyche of the human being.

Aspects of the shadow can be encountered during 'hellish' NDEs. Rather than experiencing positive near-death journeys, some individuals describe disturbing visions that contain archetypal dark images, including the devil, hell, and suffering. Such negative experiences may reflect the shadow of the collective unconscious manifesting in destructive human behavior that Christopher M. Bache suggests "reaches into the very depths of our individual *and collective* existential confusion about what we are and our group failure to grasp the most fundamental spiritual truths about ourselves."[19]

Many near-death experiencers confront their personal shadow aspects during a life review. Judgment of the soul following death is commonly found in the mythologies of world religions, such as the deceased being ushered into the presence of the Egyptian god, Osiris, or the Day of Judgment associated with

Christianity.

According to Jung, the individual psyche contains the totality of both conscious and unconscious dimensions of experience and a unifying principle integrates all of this varying archetypal material. This principle is referred to as the archetype of *wholeness* that is referred to as the Self. The ego is the center of conscious experience, but is subordinate to the Self, which functions as an inner experiential sense of a higher power or deity. The Self contains symbolism representing unity, such as the *world navel* or the *axis* of the universe, and comprises of a union of opposites that makes order out of chaos. The Self encompasses both the personal and transpersonal and signifies a numinous encounter between the human being and 'God.'

The relationship between the ego and the Self is of paramount importance and reflects the individual's concept of a Creator, often symbolized in religious myths. Throughout history, humans have possessed an intuitive awareness that an inner center exists, and the Greeks referred to it as being the internal *daimon*. The Egyptians thought it manifested as the *Ba-soul,* and the Romans paid homage to the *genius* found within each individual. The characteristics and totality of the Self are symbolized by a circle or *mandala,* a universal motif that represents wholeness and appears in many religious mythologies.

Jung was reportedly told by a Tibetan monk that the most striking mandalas were created by the imagination during periods when psychological balance was disturbed, or when searching for an elusive truth. This striving, depicted in the mandala, represents the principle of restoring order through creating something new. Jung believes that he witnessed a living symbolic image of the mandala during his NDE, when he saw the outline of the entire global shape of the earth shining with a silvery gleam and bathed in blue light.[20]

The motif of the mandala has remained central in both ancient and modern-day burial rituals and is characterized by an offering of flowers, which are often shaped in the form of mandalas and so present symbolic representations of the Self. In Hindu mythology, the lotus flower is revered and its many synonyms from the Sanskrit translation represent divine attributes. The divinity, Vishnu, is often depicted holding a lotus or wearing a wreath of lotus-buds. Other deities, including Lakshmi, Ganesha, and Ganga are portrayed sitting on lotus flowers to represent the flowering of ignorance into an awareness of one's true nature. The placement of flowers on the graves of the deceased not only symbolizes feelings of empathy, but also an unconscious hope for resurrection into the realm of the gods.

During the initial stages of life, preceding the birth of the ego, the Self forms the primordial totality of the psyche, symbolized by the circular image of the tail-eating serpent, known as the *uroboros*, which can be traced back to early Egyptian, African, Mexican, and Indian mythologies. The serpent provides an image of self-sufficiency; for through digesting its own tail, self-fertilization takes place.

Undertaking the spiritual pilgrimage from the outer circle to the inner center is archetypally portrayed in the universal image of the labyrinth, often etched on ancient cavern walls or temples of worship, and associated with triumph over death. In the nineteenth century, remains of a huge ancient Egyptian labyrinth complex were discovered at Knossos. Tombs of Etruscan dignitaries also contained a labyrinth and the Romans portrayed this symbol in mosaic designs on temple floors. Labyrinths also emerged in India and throughout Native American cultures. Some of the most spectacular labyrinths are still to be found in the European gothic cathedrals of Chartres, Reims, and Amiens.

Throughout early life, emphasis is placed on separating from the Self and forming the ego's development. The latter part of life is when the ego and Self reunite to encompass the totality of the conscious and unconscious in a harmonious balance. The alternating cycles of union and separation between the ego and Self occur continually throughout the human life span and this individuation process is associated with immortality, as personified in the Egyptian myth of Osiris.

The Sacred Scriptures of Hinduism contained in the early Sanskrit texts of *The Upanishads*, which date back to 4000 or 5000 BCE, reflect the transcendent pure nature of the immortal Self:

> He (the Self) is all-encircling, resplendent, bodiless, spotless, without sinews, pure untouched by sin, all seeing, all-knowing, transcendent, self existent: He has disposed all things duly for eternal years.[21]

The task of self-realization varies among individuals, and is never totally complete. How much progress can be made is largely dependent on how willing the ego is to listen and take note of the messages from the Self, which emanate from unconscious images and symbolism. The belief in a higher power providing guidance in life is also contained in the archetype of the Self, which is structured around *a priori* knowledge of 'God' or deity that represents a primordial unconscious sense of perfection and unity. Human's sense of nostalgia over personal and cultural origins is believed to stem from the stirrings within the psyche of connection to this original knowledge and affirmation.

Near-death survivors often express realization of the Self archetype in feelings of profound bliss, peace, love, and cosmic unity. Symbolism and archetypal energies encountered during such mystical events appear to echo the contents of the mythological reservoir of the collective unconscious. Following such numinous experiences, the illuminating insights may imbue individuals with fresh perspectives on the nature of reality and foster the emergence of a new personal myth.

Rudolf Otto coined the word ***numinous*** to expand and give special meaning to the word *holy*, encompassing an aspect of

God that is part of the great mystery and so cannot be rationalized, but only experienced. Although it is impossible to determine how far back into the history of human consciousness the concept of the *numinosum* first emerged, C. S. Lewis writes:

> We do not know how far back in history this feeling goes. The earliest men certainly believed in things which would excite the feeling in us if *we* believed in them, and it seems therefore probable that numinous awe is as old as humanity itself. The important thing is that somehow or other it has come into existence, and is widespread, and does not disappear from the mind with the growth of knowledge and civilization.[22]

The nature of the numinous stirs and grips the human being in intense feelings, which then generate an earth-shattering emotional response from the mind that is propelled into an altered state of awareness. The archetypal content of such an experience is sacred and transpersonal; it can exist outside of traditional religious examples, and is also independent of cultural heritage. A numinous quality manifests in various forms that can include: dreams, waking visions, bodily sensations, synchronistic events, the creative arts, and encounters in nature. Benedictine monk and mystic, Bede Griffiths, related a mystical vision that occurred in 1924, when he was a seventeen-year-old schoolboy walking alone near his school playing fields:

> One day during my last term at school. I walked out alone in the evening and heard the birds singing in that full chorus of song, which can only be heard at that time of the year at dawn or at sunset. I remember now the shock of surprise with which the sound broke on my ears. It seemed to me that I had never heard the birds singing before and I wondered whether they sang like this all the year round and I had never noticed it. As I walked on I came upon some hawthorn trees in full bloom

> and again I thought I had never seen such a sight or experienced such sweetness before. If I had been brought suddenly among the trees of the Garden of Paradise and heard a choir of angels singing I could not have been more surprised. I came then to where the sun was setting over the playing fields. A lark rose suddenly from the ground beside the tree, and then sank back still singing to rest. Everything then grew still as the sunset faded and the veil of dusk began to cover the earth. I remember now the feeling of awe that came over me. I felt inclined to kneel on the ground, as though I had been standing in the presence of an angel; and I hardly dared to look on the face of the sky, because it seemed as though it was but a veil before the face of God.[23]

The Hindu mystic, Ramakrishna, writes of a vision in which "houses, doors, temples and everything else vanished altogether; as if there was nothing elsewhere! And what I saw was an intimate shoreless sea of light; a sea that was consciousness. However far and in whatever direction I looked, I saw shining waves, one after another, coming towards me."[24]

The *numinosum* is universally portrayed through the archetypal image of light. Icons of religious figures, such as Christ or the saints, are often adorned with a halo or circle of bright light to signify an outer symbolic manifestation of numinous wisdom. The Bible describes the reward for gaining wisdom, which is likened to shining like the stars for eternity. "Those who are wise shall shine like the brightness of the sky, and those who lead many to righteousness, like the stars for ever and ever" (Daniel 12: 3).

Circle imagery, depicted in the mandala, represents a perfect form. Ancient art denoting the numinous quality of a deity is also preserved and illustrated in depictions of halos of light surrounding the Hindu god, Krishna; the Greek god, Apollo; and the Buddha. The climax of the Isis mystery rites celebrated in ancient Egypt culminated in deification, as an initiate became identified with the sun god, was anointed, and received the crown of life

Cultural heritage from around the world contains myths that depict the emergence of light, symbolizing the dawning of the ego and the spark of consciousness emerging from the unconscious depths. In hero myths, the light is the core component of the reality of the hero, who triumphs to conquer darkness.

Light depicting a numinous conversion experience is noted in the New Testament, as St. Paul is on the road to Damascus and "suddenly a light from heaven flashed around him" (Acts: 9: 3). The conversion of Paul, through such a mystical vision provides a sacred realization; for although Paul persecuted Jesus and his followers, his true identity to become a disciple of the Lord was revealed through his numinous experience. Such a confrontation that includes an incarnation of God can psychologically be translated as the human being's encounter with diametric opposites, resulting in an awareness and emergence of the higher Self.

Jung underwent a profound experience as he travelled through Africa. Watching the day break from his campsite, he noticed extreme variables between the light and the darkness. He writes, "At such moments I felt as if I were inside a temple. It was the most sacred hour of the day. I drank in this glory with insatiable delight, or rather, in a timeless ecstasy."[25]

Many world religions revere the ineffable quality of the light representing God or the Creator. An example is found in the *Upanishads*, the ancient Hindu scriptures that encompass the teachings of the *Vedanta*:

> The sun doesn't shine there
> nor does the moon, nor the stars,
> nor the lightning,
> not to mention this earthly fire.
> Only because This shines,

> all else shines through its effulgence.[26]

Homage to the transcendent power and realization of the eternal light, projected in the form of the gods, can also be found in the world's greatest literature and poetry. D. H. Lawrence writes:

> O, if a flame is in you, be it so!
>
> When your flame flickers up, and you flicker through in sheer purity for a moment pure of all conceit of yourself, and all afterthought you are for that moment one of the gods, Jesus or Fafnir or Priapus or Siva.[27]

In the contemporary world often blind to the numinous entering life, it is still possible to see an archetypal image of light known as a *scintilla,* derived from the Latin to mean a flash or spark of many lights, in the Christmas tree. Although the tree has little association with Christmas and can be better referenced as a midwinter tree, the image is one that personifies a mythological tree that is ablaze with light particles. The legend of such a tree was related to Martin Luther, the German reformist of the Protestant religious tradition. While walking through a forest one winter's day, Luther saw an evergreen tree illuminated by the light of shining stars; he was overcome by this vision and was said to have taken the tree home and decorated it with candles. The continuing ritual of trimming the midwinter tree and emblazing it with light has become an act of devotion common to many people from varying religious cultures and keeps an archetypal pattern alive, through living symbolism.

For many ancient civilizations, including that of the Egyptians and Romans, the midwinter solstice festivals and accompanying rites were a time of celebration that marked the rebirth of the sun, which symbolized the light and energy of the divine and the triumph of life over death. The modern-day celebration of Christmas and the image of the tree sparkling with light is also a mythological commemoration of the birth of Christ, whom Christians believe to be the shining savior and bearer of light. Such a reenactment creates psychic energy that manifests from the ancient archetypal symbolism of the light. On a psychological level, the motif of the tree reflects the mysterious relationship between life, death, and renewal.

Experiencing the *numinosum* manifests in novel ways that may not be fully recognized in the Judaeo-Christian format that Western cultures have been conditioned by. The fourth core state of the contemporary near-death journey contains one single feature—the appearance of a bright light, often described as having a golden hue. Although of brilliant intensity, this light does not damage the eyesight of the experiencer and is described as being comforting, restful, and of great beauty. This light appears to signify emerging from darkness, and thus symbolizes a threshold to a new phase of experience. Many participants in Kenneth Ring's research into the NDE spoke of being enveloped by the light and drawn to it. One lady says, "I just seemed to be surrounded by a velvet blackness . . . . And then, sort of at the periphery of the velvet blackness, there was a brilliant golden light. And I don't remember feeling frightened at all, just perfectly at peace and perfectly comfortable, as if this is where I should be."[28] The appearance of the light during the NDE thus bears much resemblance to that described in numinous religious experiences and visions.

The roots of ***alchemical*** motifs are also associated with immortality and can be traced back to ancient Babylonia, Greece, Arabia, Egypt, China, and India. One of the earliest alchemical texts is accredited to Olympiodorus of Thebes, a historical writer from the fifth century. The Arabs translated many of the texts from the original Greek, and from 644 AD, Islamic communities cultivated alchemical traditions into a religious context, because they recognized the symbolism as being more spiritual than chemical.

Ancient Egypt was imbued with alchemical practices and was referred to as "The Land of Khem," translated as "black earth." The word *alchemy* was thought to have derived from *khem* or *chemia* meaning 'black' and the origins of alchemy were bound to death and immortality. Early Egyptian texts describe transformation of dead matter (the body) into the rebirth of the soul and they were associated with the myth of Osiris and burial rites, as the practice of embalming the corpse of the dead pharaoh ensured an alchemical transformation and becoming one with the eternal Osiris.

According to the myth, which will be expanded upon in a later chapter, the sealed chest that contained the bodily parts of Osiris was covered with black lead, before being thrown into the sea. He asphyxiated in a coffin sealed with lead and this represented the death of *prima materia*—or the physical body.

The lead coffin represented the grave of Osiris in which not only does the god mysteriously prepare for rebirth, but this magical resurrection also symbolizes the renewal of the world. The apparent death-like state culminated in only a temporary disappearance of consciousness, for Osiris is immortal and within the divine god, the form of the divine spirit is assumed in death. What was of supreme importance to the alchemists was that bodily remains contained the possibility for new life.

Early Egyptian alchemists viewed the body of the deceased as symbolizing buried treasure and believed the perfect human being was a corpse, because the infinite nature of the individual was buried within the body and resembled the mummy buried in the tomb. Ancient Egyptian art depicts the resurrected Osiris in the form of a ladder. This image symbolizes the pure spirit that when freed from the corrupted earthly body may climb the ladder to the celestial realms.

Psychologically, alchemical funerary symbolism represents an experience of psychic reality; for the psyche cannot manifest as a detached entity until the demise of the physical body. The realms of the collective unconscious resemble the underworld and a descent into this terrain is often referred to as a *nekyia*. The term originated from the ancient Greek cult practice of summoning the souls of the dead for divination purposes, and likewise, a meeting with the autonomous psyche is often described as the death of a certain kind of reality. Symbolism representing eternity was also thought to originate from early Egypt, where the deceased were believed to be transformed into stars that surrounded and accompanied the sun.

Resurrection following death and burial is imbued with alchemical beliefs in the regenerative cycles of the natural world, and with the germination and planting of seeds. Such symbolism represents a psychic reality that extends beyond life and death in a mysterious process that survives the temporary cycles of the flowering and decay of visible life. Ancient Egyptian artwork depicts sprouting stalks of grain emerging from the deceased body of Osiris, representing the emergence of an eternal Self that arises from decay. The symbolism of ancient Egyptian alchemical symbolism expressed a reconciliation of opposites, which became unified at the moment of death. Marie-Louise von Franz writes:

> This is the reason that, in the Egyptian Book of Gates, at the end of resurrection, the deceased appears as a god with two faces (the heads of Seth and Horus) and accompanies the sun god during his transformation in the underworld . . . .This figure is called "His Two Faces." It embodies the nature of the opposites which have become one in the deified dead person.[29]

During medieval times, many alchemists were also physicians engaged in preparing a cadaver for the afterlife. They not only preserved their work in ancient texts, but also illustrated the symbolic analogy in surreal art forms that were often imagined through representations of the darker aspects of Nature. An example is Holbein's *The Dance of Death* painted in 1538, depicting a man contemplating a skull. The skull is evocative of human mortality and alchemical change. Edward Edinger writes, "To reflect on death can lead one to view life under the aspect of eternity, and thus the black head can turn to gold."[30] In much of the art work, the forces of good and evil collided to generate archetypal images, such as the devil and angelic beings, dueling for the soul of the dying individual. This struggle of opposites proved to be an illusion, as beneath the conflict, was to be found the Self in the unification of opposites. The notion that the moment of death represents the resistance of conflicting forces appears to be archetypal. In ancient Rome, duels between gladiators were held in commemoration of the dead and may have represented the symbolic battle between good and evil.

For the alchemists, discovering the secret matter was a search for God and was thought to be found in the *philosopher's stone*. However, some alchemists from the Middle Ages realized the elusive stone symbolized something that could only be located within the human psyche and represented an eternal quality that could not be dissolved or misplaced, but was likened to experiencing an inner mystical vision of God.

During the Renaissance, many alchemists translated the metaphor of the transformation of lead into gold, as symbolizing the emergence of divinity within the human being. The base matter in alchemy corresponded to the immaturity of the ego, which would be transformed into divine essence by the *philosopher's stone*, resulting in the transmutation of the corruptible human corpse into an incorruptible light-filled body. *Remembering* that a divine essence existed within humans represented the underlying goal of the alchemists—a quest in which, through corruption and decay, the imagination would be stimulated to reconnecting with such divine origins and primordial affirmations.

The invisible figure of Hermes was connected to alchemy and

he embodied the spirit or archetype of the unconscious. He was associated with the metal mercury, because it retained the ability to remain fluid in temperatures that make other metals hard. Described as a *psychopomp* or leader of the soul, Hermes Mercurius crossed boundaries and was of great importance in medieval alchemy and the pursuit for personal transformation, because it was he who accompanied and directed the *opus* or central goal of the alchemists and guided initiates through the various stages of the process. Seeking a deeper meaning, portrayed through alchemical metaphors of transformation involved hearing both the voice of the philosopher, and the stone, embodied by Hermes.

Although alchemical texts are confusing and chaotic, it is the archetypal symbolism that relates to chemical change and transformation that is of prime importance. In the alchemical Latin writings of the Middle Ages, the procedures of reducing solid matter through chemical means to a pure state were associated with the myth of death heralding new life. These alchemical experiments mimicked the processes of the natural world, which the alchemists believed mirrored the cycles of death and new life of human beings.

One of the principal themes of the alchemical *opus* was that of redemption and the releasing of the divine soul incarcerated in matter. This metaphor of retrieving the hidden God from matter was underscored by the ancient Gnostics in the myth of Sophia, who personified divine wisdom and is often depicted with a crown of stars to symbolize her divinity. During creation, Sophia descended into matter and then lost her way and became captive to matter, and so personified the hidden God that is in search of liberation. Her redemption symbolizes the divine spark of creation that is unsullied by the chaos of matter. This early myth may later have become expanded within the Marian myth and the Assumption of the Blessed Mother from the earthly to heavenly realms.

The transcendent nature of alchemy alters perception and changes a lead-based everyday consciousness into a golden understanding. The most essential teaching of the *opus* was that it provided the individual with the psychological goal of a lifetime—that of individuation and the metaphor was understood by the ancient alchemists and philosophers engaged in these early practices.

Alchemical ideas have continued to be of great interest to many important thinkers. While reading through ancient alchemical texts, Jung found them to be provocative and stimulating and came to the realization that the alchemists wrote in the language of symbols. One night when immersed in this world, he had an archetypal dream and found himself in the seventeenth century. He interpreted the dream to mean that he needed to study alchemy in depth and gradually solve its principal hypothesis. The decade Jung spent reading through ancient texts led him to compare alchemy, and its Gnostic roots, to his work in the unconscious realms. In summing up the important dimensions that alchemy provided for his work, Jung writes:

> The experience of the alchemists were, in a sense my experiences, and their world was my world. This was of course a momentous discovery: I had stumbled across the historical counterpart of my psychology of the unconscious. The possibility of a comparison with alchemy, and the uninterrupted chain back to Gnosticism, gave substance to my psychology. When I poured over these old texts everything fell into place: the fantasy-images, the empirical material I had gathered in my practice, and the conclusions I had drawn from it.[31]

Isaac Newton was recognized as being one of the most influential figures in history and revered as the founder of modern science. However, when many of his private papers later came to light, it was discovered that Newton was also a practicing alchemist. Michael White writes, "Newton was motivated by a deep-rooted commitment to the notion that alchemical wisdom extended back to ancient times. The Hermetic tradition—the body of alchemical knowledge—was believed to have originated in the mists of times and to have been 'given' to humanity through supernatural agents."[32]

The alchemist's quest for the *philosopher's stone* symbolized human yearnings to transform the corruptible self into a sacred gold body of light that would merge with the divine. It appears that near-death survivors undergo a mystical transformation at the point of death that mirrors the alchemical process, in which the pure soul leaves the discarded matter of the physical body, and this stage of 'separation' is a central component of the NDE. The Egyptian myth of Osiris resulted in the deceased becoming transformed and 'one' with Osiris. The NDE echoes this ancient metaphor of alchemical transformation, through symbolizing that consciousness exists beyond the dead body and the perception of encountering 'God.'

Notes

1 Jolande Jacobi, *Complex/Archetype/Ego* (Princeton: Princeton University Press, 1959), 32.

2 Heraclitus, *Fragments* (New York, 2003), xix.

3 Irwin Edman, ed. *The Works of Plato* (New York: Random House, 1956), xii.

4 Bruno Bettelheim, *Freud and Man's Soul* (New York: Vintage, 1984), 12.

5 Sigmund Freud, *The Interpretation of Dreams* (New York: Avon, 1965), 75.

6 Sigmund Freud, "Thoughts for the Time on War and Death" (1915) in *Civilization, Society and Religion*, trans. Albert Dickson (New York: Basic Books, 1985), 88-89.

7 C. G. Jung, *The Archetypes and the Collective Unconscious, CW*

Vol. 9:1, trans. R. F. C. Hull (Princeton: Princeton University Press, 1980), 287.

8 As discussed in C. G. Jung, "The Archetypes of the Collective Unconscious." CW Vol. 9:1, trans. R. F. C. Hull (Princeton: Princeton University Press, 1980), 4.

9 William G. Doty, *Mythography: The Study of Myth and Rituals* (Tuscaloosa: Alabama University Press, 2000), 200.

10 D. Stephenson Bond, *Living Myth: Personal Meaning as a Way of Life* (Boston: Shambhala, 1993), 82.

11 Evelyn Underhill, *Mysticism: A Study in the Nature and Development of Human Consciousness* (Stilwell: 2005), 90.

12 C. G. Jung, *Memories,* 182.

13 Erich Neumann, *The Origins and History of Consciousness* (Princeton: Princeton University Press, 1970), 108.

14 Quoted by Dr. Gerhard Adler in *Dynamics of the Self* (London, 1979), 92.

15 C. G. Jung, *Memories,* 191.

16 C. G. Jung, "The Archetypes of the Collective Unconscious." CW 9:1, trans. R. F. C Hull (Princeton: Princeton University Press, 1980), 288-89.

17 C. G. Jung, *Memories,* 180.

18 Robert Louis Stevenson, *Dr. Jekyll and Mr Hyde,* ed. Emma Letley (New York: Oxford University Press, 1987), 75.

19 Christopher M. Bache, *Dark Night,* 113.

20 C. G. Jung, *Memories,* 289.

21 Swami Paramananda, *The Upanishads* (www.fullbooks.com /The-Upanishads.html).

22 C. S. Lewis, *The Problem of Pain* (San Francisco: HarperCollins, 2001), 8.

23 Bede Griffiths, *Essential Writings (Modern Spiritual Masters Series),* int. Thomas Matus (Maryknoll: Orbis, 2004), 27.

24 Christopher Isherwood, *Ramakrishna and His Disciples* (New York, 1965), 65.

25 C. G. Jung, *Memories,* 268.

26 Pandit Rajmani Tiqunait, trans, *The Pursuit of Power and Freedom: Katha Upanishad* (Honesdale: Himalayan Institute Press, 2008), 5: 15.

27 D. H. Lawrence, "Be It So," *The Complete Poems* (Middlesex: Penguin, 1967), 674.

28 Kenneth Ring, *Life at Death* (New York: Coward, McCann & Geoghegan, 1980), 57.

29 Marie-Louise von Franz, *On Dreams and Death: A Jungian Interpretation,* trans. Emmanuel Xipolitas (Boston: Shambhala, 1987), 22.

30 Edward F. Edinger, *Anatomy of the Psyche* (Chicago: Open Court, 1991), 168.

31 C. G. Jung, *Memories,* 205.

32 Michael White, *Isaac Newton: The Last Sorcerer* (New York: Basic Books, 1999), 109.

Chapter 2

Resurrection Myths and Otherworldly Journeys

Eternity forbids thee to forget
Lord Byron, *Lara*

The word *mythology* refers to a body or collection of myths from any given tradition and derives from the Greek *muthos* (story) and *logos* (speech.) For some, *myths* conjure up vague recollections of fanciful stories or epic tales and legends, which originated in early Greek civilization. However, at a deeper level, many of these ancient stories preserve a history of how humans have struggled to come to terms with the pilgrimage and mystery of life and death.

Although the most widely recognized mythologies tend to be those of the Greeks, Romans, and Egyptians, all world cultures have an important mythological heritage. While there is no specific universal myth, research has unearthed how widespread are the many symbols and archetypal motifs and primordial affirmations that recur throughout various societies and eras.

Many cultures include creation myths that tell of 'beginnings' and how the world came into being, as a certain kind of reality was born; these range from illustrating how supreme supernatural deities fashioned the earth out of abstract chaos, and mythic representations of recurring destruction and renewal that are allegories to seasonal death and rebirth.

The rise and fall of a *Golden Age* of primordial peace, harmony, and tranquility, is another common theme weaved into diverse mythologies, including that of the Greeks, Romans, Scandinavians, and Hindus. The motif of the 'flood' is also universal and plays a key role in myths that tell of the annihilation and recreation of the world, or a particular society. Nature myths describe the origins of the elements and the gods who governed them. They illustrate how ancient cultures discovered and revered a sacred magical power in the natural world around them, and why they believed that death related to the cycles of the sun, the moon, and the tides. The continuing relationship between the living and the dead also plays an important role in the mythologies of many religious traditions.

These sacred stories were frequently endorsed by rulers and priests and retold to preserve a secret esoteric *knowledge* that revealed *why* we are mortal, the origins of death, and spiritual rebirth. Through accompanying rituals, early people had genuine religious experiences in which the divine origins of human beings were made known and so life assumed a far deeper sense of purpose and meaning. For the particular culture in which certain myths evolved, they were regarded as true narratives from a distant past—a primordial age when the world was still evolving. Myths opened a portal of communication between the profane and the sacred, an open dialogue with divine deities and their transcendent values. They provided *living* and tangible examples through the poetic, yet powerful language of metaphors and symbolism that often related to the natural world.

Although human consciousness has evolved over time, the mystery of death remains beyond our rational perception. However, we can explore the possibility of death being a transition by looking back into the universal language of myth that contains repeating archetypal patterns, manifesting in both ancient and contemporary near-death journeys and suggesting the *same* primordial patterns continue to exist in the collective unconscious. Myths that seek to shed light on the mystery of death have been a constant source of fascination and have resulted in an enormous effect on consciousness, as they portray the collective quest to continually seek for imaginative ways to explain how life and death are inextricably linked.

The motif of the 'otherworldly' journey is universal, whether it is a journey of ascent and meeting with heavenly deities or through a descent to the underworld realms of the dead, accounts of such experiences exist throughout diverse world cultures and religious traditions. These directives for transcendence over death provide value for human life, because the insights are gleaned through sacred encounters with mythological ancestors or Divine Beings.

The wealth of resurrection myths, spiritual texts, and otherworldly journeys is vast and it is only possible to explore several from each category, but in all the following examples, the affirmation of death and spiritual rebirth is a recurrent one.

Although the epic of ***Gilgamesh*** is not a resurrection myth in the strictest sense, it provides a valuable foundation to illustrate how preoccupation with anxiety over death and a mission to discover immortality has been inherent in humans since time immemorial. Rainer Maria Rilke, whose *Duino Elegies* and *Sonnets to Orpheus* preserved a symbolic reminder of how the darkness of death could provide a torch of illumination for the living was captivated by the epic, which he believed, preserved the collective curiosity to penetrate the mysterious fathoms surrounding death.

It was from the ancient world of Mesopotamia where Gilgamesh reigned as historical king of Uruk, in the region between the Euphrates and the Tigris around 2750 BCE that the text originated. All reference to the epic disappeared for over two thousand years, but in 1850, parts of the clay tablets that bore the story were discovered and later translated. This geographical area heralded the dawning of Western civilization and despite modern-day scientific and medical advancements, the story remains inspirational in the quest to penetrate hidden layers of fascination and fear of death.

Gilgamesh is described as being two parts divine and one

part human. However, in spite of his divine qualities, Gilgamesh is a tyrant and servant of his ego. He has a mirror image in his close companion, Enkidu, who although more human than divine, retains more of a sense of connection to the rhythms of the natural world. The pair journey into the forest and slay the monster, Humbaba, for Gilgamesh believes that if he wishes to live eternally, this status will only be achieved by attracting fame in his earthly life.

After killing the monster, Enkidu has two prophetic dreams forewarning death in which images of an envisioned gloomy Mesopotamian afterlife are revealed. In one dream, Enkidu sees his journey of descent into the land of the dead, where he is transformed into a bird by a bird-man figure, who accompanies him to the underworld. Feathers cover his arms and bind them behind him, and Enkidu says:

> I saw proud kings who had ruled the land.
> Who had set out roast meat before the gods
> and offered cool water and cakes for the dead.[1]

In ancient Mesopotamia, the deceased were envisaged as taking the form of a bird and they conceptualized the idea of a "bird-soul." From the reference made in the dream to an afterlife state where Enkidu viewed the miserable fate of the dead, it would appear that this early culture did not believe that death was the end, but rather that following death, the soul separated from the body and while the earthly remains were buried in the earth, the soul continued its journey. It may well be that from such ancient myths, the eventual development of an immortal soul finds its way into consciousness, and becomes referenced in the New Testament. The Letter of Paul to the Romans states that "to those who by patiently doing good seek for glory and honor and immortality, he will give eternal life" (Romans 2. 5-7). Rivkah Scharf Kluger writes of how the mythological epic mirrors eventual advances in consciousness:

> Myths are like reflections or mirrorings of certain cultural situations of mankind, and like great, archetypal dreams, they contain deep intuitions and anticipation of further developments, and thus they can be considered as *milestones in the development of human consciousness.*[2]

Following the dreams, Enkidu then falls ill and does eventually die, leaving Gilgamesh distraught with grief and in fear of his own mortality. The death of Enkidu symbolizes the death of the pure part of Gilgamesh that must be reborn in order for him to achieve a union of opposites, and realize his eternal Self. He has an ancestor, Utnapishtim, who has been granted eternal life, and sets out to find him. Gilgamesh encounters many trials on this journey to seek immortality. The images he encounters while running through the dark tunnel to eventually reemerge into the light on his way to find Utnapishtim symbolize death and spiritual rebirth and these same images manifest in many mythic otherworldly journeys, including contemporary NDEs. However, Gilgamesh is not yet conscious enough to experience such a transformation.

Gilgamesh eventually finds Utnapishtim, who tells him that he must stay awake for seven days and six nights in order to discover the secret of immortality. The number seven symbolizes 'wholeness' and Dante describes seven heavens in *The Divine Comedy*. The Old Testament also tells of Elisha sneezing seven times and a child comes back to life (2 Kings 4: 35). But Gilgamesh is so tired that he immediately falls asleep and fails in his quest; he is then told of a plant that acts as an antidote to the fear of death. He retrieves the plant and places it on the ground, but a passing innocent snake carries it away and simply eats the plant and sheds a skin to renew itself.

Gilgamesh has a violent past and is a self-destructive

individual lost in his ego. He loses his gift and is unsuccessful in discovering the secret of eternal life. However, the snake symbolizes rebirth in Nature and is a universal motif of regeneration, depicted in many ancient myths. In the nocturnal journey of the Egyptian sun god, it is the serpent that gives birth to the renewed sun at dawn. The archetypal image of the serpent still manifests in the dreaming state to symbolize the healing and regenerative abilities that rise from the unconscious.

Gilgamesh does eventually find redemption, as his inner quest may have been to explore and integrate the humanness of his divinity that encompasses physical death. He subsequently returns to his city transformed and continues to rule, but as a more benevolent leader that shares the wisdom of his mythic journey with his people. One could suggest that Gilgamesh does discover a sense of immortality, not in the projection of an envisaged eternal life, but through accessing the eternal archetype of the Self. A process that Jung suggests represents a spiritual wholeness, which is part of a timeless eternity.[3]

The historical epic of *Gilgamesh* depicts the inner journey necessary to come to terms with the anxiety surrounding death through symbolizing the struggle to integrate a union of opposites—life and death. The story also hints at a sacred marriage of earthly humanity and eternal divinity that is preserved in the myth.

The Descent of Inanna, a moon goddess, often referred to as "Queen of Heaven," dates back to about 1750 BCE and it was through contemplating the continual symbolic lunar phases of death and rebirth that ancient Sumerians likened their own destinies and possibilities for survival. Mircea Eliade writes, "It was lunar symbolism that enabled man to relate and connect such heterogeneous things as: birth, becoming, death, and resurrection."[4]

Inanna is queen of the celestial realms and the earth, but she has no knowledge of the underworld and the part of her own identity that is concealed within its darkness in the form of her sister, Ereshkigal, queen of the underworld. However, Inanna hears the desolate cries of her sister and in order to achieve true wisdom and understanding, she must descend from the Great Above to the Great Below. This journey of descent into death, followed by rebirth and ascension back into the light, will enable Inanna to experience a sense of wholeness and spiritual rebirth through an encounter with the terrifying shadow aspects of Ereshkigal—her other 'self.' These central motifs of personification and transfiguration continue to appear in contemporary stories of similar otherworldly journeys and in the mythological teachings of world religions, indicating that they are still fully alive in human consciousness. Evans Lansing Smith writes:

> Inanna's descent and return also has an astronomical corollary which survived in the hermetic and Gnostic traditions: the naked soul descends from its celestial home in the empyrean by passing through each of the seven planetary spheres, to assume its appropriate material element before becoming fully incarnate on earth. When it returns at the moment of death, the soul sheds each material element at each of the seven planetary spheres until the body is transfigured into pure spirit.[5]

In order to enter the realms of the underworld, Inanna must be prepared to abandon her powers and adornments. This sacrifice and willingness to experience rebirth is the common denominator to be found in the many myths of resurrected deities. Through this descent, Inanna will gain necessary wisdom on both life and death that will enable her to become a revered and honored guide to the land.

Inanna gathers the seven *me* or attributes that define her royal status and makes her way to the fate of the underworld, known as the *kur* or Land of No Return. As she passes through each of the seven gates, she is required to relinquish articles of clothing and accessories, for these outer elements are worthless in the realms of the underworld. Inanna enters the throne room of her miserable sister, Ereshkigal, and is confronted by the seven judges of the underworld who detect her split-off hidden shadow aspects and condemn her to death:

> The Annuna, the judges of the underworld, surround her.
> They passed judgment against her.
> Inanna was turned into a corpse,
> A piece of rotting meat,
> And was hung from a hook on the wall.[6]

Ereshkigal's existence is bleak in the underworld, and she symbolizes the archetype of the "wicked witch," who is filled with rage and rejection. Inanna's death, however, causes her suffering as she moans in agony for both her "inside" and her "outside" while her sister dies; for Inanna represents the discarded light part of Erishkigal's 'self' that also wishes to be reborn, enabling her to become complete. The dark goddess receives comfort through the compassionate mirroring of her discomfort from small creatures that the God of Wisdom has sent to save Inanna. Such kindness has a transformative effect and opens Ereshkigal's heart to a more generous state and eventually, she agrees to release her sister. The tiny creatures then sprinkle the food and water of life on the rotting corpse. As with heroes and heroines in similar myths symbolizing resurrection—the goddess is reborn, for these stories reflect the ancient archetypal affirmation of death and rebirth, often portrayed in allegories of the continual regeneration of the natural world.

Inanna prepares to leave the underworld for she has transcended death, and her rebirth creates a passageway between the conscious in the Great Above and the unconscious in the Great Below. This portal must now remain open, but nobody has ever been allowed to leave before. New conditions must be set and Inanna is told that she must provide a substitute to take her place. She offers her husband, Damuzi, in exchange for her freedom. However, she later regrets this action and it is agreed that Damuzi will divide his time in the underworld to spend six months of the year with Inanna, who thus grants him both death and everlasting life. Through this loving action, Inanna alters cosmic order and guarantees renewal.

Damuzi portrays the image of the mythological shepherd king, who through death becomes immortal, and he symbolizes a future representation of Abel and Christ. He is also depicted as a vegetation god that dies following the long hot summers, and then comes back to life in the spring to renew the seasons and cycles of the crops. The rites and rituals that took place annually in Sumeria to commemorate Inanna and Damuzi acknowledged and reenacted the duality of life merging into death, and death heralding new life. These ancient people were also inclined to believe that the drama and life cycles of these divinities provided a metaphorical reality to explain the mystery of existence and paralleled the destiny of the human being.

Ancient resurrection myths, such as that of Inanna, suggest that these stories of descent to the underworld and death, followed by rebirth and transformation, had a purpose. They served to penetrate the uncharted layers of the psyche, which was mirrored in the seasonal cycles of vegetation. Jung writes: "This motif of the Nekyia is found everywhere in antiquity and practically all over the world. It expresses the psychological mechanism of introversion of the conscious mind into the deeper layers of the unconscious psyche."[7]

The story of Inanna recorded thousands of years ago continues to fascinate human beings, because it contains a universal message of hope for resurrection. Inanna made a descent to the underworld from which there was thought to be no return. She died and then achieved the seemingly impossible—she experienced rebirth. In psychological terms, rebirth symbolizes Jung's concept of individuation, which resulted in Inanna's ascent back into the heavenly realms as a complete individual. Survivors of an NDE, which may also contain a descent into the dark realms, also expand understanding of the essential mystery of death and rebirth through reinforcing ancient sacred wisdom, as they return to everyday life with a new perception of the reality of consciousness.

Inanna also opened a doorway between the Great Above and the Great Below, and this channel of communication must remain open. She hands this responsibility over to Damuzi and his sister, Geshtinanna, signaling that the task must be maintained by more mortal participators. Efforts to continue the dialogue between the conscious and unconscious realms through the medium of mystical states of consciousness will be further enumerated in the following chapter.

Homer's epic, ***The Odyssey***, is a mythological journey of symbolic rebirth in which the hero, Odysseus, leaves his homeland, faces many challenges, and eventually returns back to his city triumphant, having reached spiritual maturity. Brief mention of an afterlife is mentioned when he sets out to consult the blind seer, Tiresias. During his underworld descent, Odysseus sees many familiar deceased people, including his mother. A further reference to the destiny of the dead is made when, Hermes, known as a psychopomp or transition guide, summons the souls of the murdered suitors:

> And Hermes of Cyllene summoned for the souls
> Of the suitors, and he held in his hand the lovely gold wand
> With which he enchants the eyes of those men he wishes,
> And others he awakens even when they are asleep
> He stirred them with it and drove them. They followed squeaking,
> As when bats in the corner of prodigious cave

Squeak as they fly.[8]

In the above passage, the souls of the deceased are described as bats. The belief that the soul assumes a bird-like appearance as it leaves the physical body is also mentioned in the Mesopotamian epic of *Gilgamesh* and appears in many spiritual texts, including *The Egyptian Book of the Dead* that describes spells enabling the deceased to fly in the form of a falcon, hawk, swallow, or phoenix. For the ancient Egyptians, the falcon symbolized ascension and was associated with the sun god, Ra. Horus, the son of Osiris and Isis, was also known as the falcon-king. Such bird-like imagery also features in the mythologies of Indonesia, Siberia, and Central Asia. Ancient spiritual commemorations of the *Tree of Life*, found in Europe and Asia, also depict the symbolism of death and rebirth, as birds sitting in the branches represent souls of human beings.

As human consciousness expanded, the idea of flight like a bird became more widespread in religious mythologies, including Christianity. St. Joseph of Cupertino was famed for his mystical levitations. Often, while celebrating mass, he would enter a trance-like state and soar into the air above the altar. On occasions, he described how these levitations were accompanied by hearing a holy kind of music.

The notion that the souls Odysseus encounters are mere shades of their former selves is borne out by the belief that in order to achieve consciousness, they must drink the blood of sacrificial beasts. However, it is the psyche or soul that may survive without the constraints of the mortal body, in an unknown psychic underworld. James Hillman writes:

> When we use the word *underworld*, we are referring to a wholly psychic perspective . . . .The underworld Ba of Egypt and the underworld *psyche* of Homeric Greece was the whole person as in life but devoid of life. This means that the under-

> world perspective radically alters our experience of life. It no longer matters on its own terms but only in terms of the psyche.[9]

Perhaps, as Hillman suggests, the metaphorical description of Hades and the interpreted destiny of the soul require abandoning hope and expectation of an afterlife realm set in accordance with the guidelines of everyday life, and instead, suggests the exploration of underworld images and primordial affirmations that symbolize the soul existing beyond the boundaries of human existence.

A lesser known and simpler resurrection myth is that of ***Hyacinthus***, the youngest son of Amyclas, one of the ancient kings of Sparta. He was a handsome youth and drew the attention of the god, Apollo, who fell in love with him. One day, Apollo hurled a discus up into the air and Hyancinthus, wishing to impress the god, ran to retrieve it, but it struck him on the head and he immediately died. Apollo was overcome with grief at the death of his companion and a hyacinth, similar to a purple iris, sprang out of the blood of his lifeless body. The mortal remains of Hyacinthus were buried at Amyclae, beneath a statue of Apollo, and the inscription on his tomb describes how he ascended into heaven, accompanied by a celestial choir.

The myth of Hyacinthus was primarily a vegetation myth associated with the natural cycle of decay and renewal, symbolized by the hyacinth or lily that reemerged each spring. The death and resurrection of Hyacinthus was commemorated during the Hyacinthia, an important Spartan festival held during early summer at Amyclae, which lasted for three days. The sacred rites involved mourning the death of Hyacinthus, and then rejoicing in his rebirth. Through reenacting this mysterious dramatic myth of transformation from death to rebirth, the continual process of life, and the possibility of immortality, was revealed to the participants or initiates.

Ovid, who recounted a version of the myth, writes:

> Yet, in your way, you are eternal now:
> whenever spring has banished winter and
> the rainy Fish gives way before the Ram,
> it's then you rise and flower once again
> where earth is green.[10]

There are parallels to the Christian festival of Easter, when both the death and mystical resurrection of Christ are annually observed. According to Bede's early writings, *Easter* had its roots in the spring festival that honored the Anglo-Saxon Goddess, Eastre, and the festival venerated the newly born sun rising in the east that would regenerate the crops and fertility. Many other universal names for this archetypal goddess include, Inanna, Isis, Demeter, and Freya. However, some speculate that Easter had an ancient German root that symbolized *dawn* or the emergence of *light*. Either way, the celebration of resurrection was named Easter, symbolizing an image of light and new life that emanated from the rising sun. The archetype of the trinity appears in both interpretations to symbolize the human stages of *being, annihilation,* and *transformation*. Edward Edinger writes that this archetype "gives structure and meaning to the dynamic, temporal events of human life."[11] An early reference to the archetypal trinity was also referenced in Egyptian mythology, as the image of the sun god incorporated the trinity of Atum-Ra-Khepri.

Plato's early concept of *forms* and how contemplating eternal beauty enabled humanity to imagine the mystical nature of the divine is also depicted in a more recent rendering of the Hyacinthus myth in the novella, *Death in Venice,* written by Thomas Mann, in 1911. In the story that contains many references to Greek mythology, an ageing author, Aschenbach, falls in love with a beautiful youth. It is through this intense passion that he discovers the repressed Dionysian dimension of his psyche that links him to the divine. The handsome young man, Tadzio, becomes an effigy and mirrors spiritual beauty and perfection. As Aschenbach watches him, he feels a rush of ecstasy sweep through him and "he believed that his eyes gazed upon beauty itself, form as divine thought, the soul and pure perfection that dwells in the mind and whose human likeness and representation, lithe and lovely, was here displayed for veneration."[12]

The story illustrates how beauty represents a divine image that can be readily accessed through the five senses. As Aschenbach watches Tadzio, he imagines the archetypal form of Hyacinthus and the flower that appeared from the blood of his lifeless body. Aschenbach eventually dies, still rapturously watching Tadzio and, at the moment of his death, it appears that Eros and Thanatos are reconciled in a rapturous spiritual fulfillment, reflecting the Platonic concept that the ideal of the eternal form of beauty is that which enables the soul to sprout wings and dissolve into pure form.

Outer beauty enables a perception of a transcendent eternal *Beauty*. John O'Donohue, writes, "When beauty touches us, we remember who we are. We realize that we have come from the homeland of beauty."[13] The numinous state of the NDE surrounds the experiencer with an ineffable sense of beauty. Margot Grey writes that such individuals have "experienced a love and a beauty that surpasses anything known on this earth."[14]

The ancient myth of the dismemberment and rebirth of ***Osiris*** originated in Egypt over three thousand years ago. Plutarch of Chaeronea, the Greek writer, preserved the story that richly portrays and provides a foundation for understanding Egyptian religious mythological beliefs, symbolizing a possible afterlife state. Napoleon's discovery of the Rosetta Stone in 1779, gave both the Greek and Egyptian hieroglyphic versions of the myth. By matching these two versions, it appears that Plutarch gave a fairly accurate rendering, preserving the authenticity of essential Egyptian customs, which were then interpreted through the voice of Greek philosophical perception.

Osiris was pharaoh of Egypt and renowned for civilizing the country. The land suffered drought and the withering of crops after Osiris disappeared. He was lured by his brother, Seth, to enter a lead-lined chest, which Seth then cast into the river. Isis was broken-hearted as she searched for her husband. Eventually, she discovered the chest that was washed ashore near Byblos, and a beautiful fragrant tamarisk tree had sprouted and concealed the chest within its trunk. The archetypal motif of the *Tree of Life* symbolizes immortality, and Jung writes that the tree represents the ongoing "growth and development of psychic life."[15]

After overcoming many trials, Isis retrieved and hid the chest, but Seth found it while hunting one night and he hacked the body of Osiris into fourteen pieces and scattered them in different areas. Isis managed to locate all the body parts, except for the phallus, which she recreated. The motif of the phallus symbolized the thrust upwards toward the spirit world and may also represent the *axis mundi,* which connects the earthly realms to the divine transpersonal realms of existence. Isis was known as the Great Mother—embodying the archetype of the universal divine feminine that is also symbolized in: the Greek Gaia and Demeter, the Hindu Kali, the Buddhist Kwan Yin, and the Christian Virgin Mary. In *The Golden Ass,* Apuleius writes of a rapturous vision of Isis that manifested while Lucius was still in his asinine form:

> In this awesome shape the goddess, wafted over me all the blessed perfumes of Arabia, deigned to answer me in her own voice. "I come, Lucius, moved by your entreaties: I, mother of the universe, mistress of all the elements, first-born of the ages, highest of the gods, queen of the shades, first of those

who dwell in heaven, representing in one shape all gods and goddesses."[16]

Isis was imagined as a winged goddess, who carried the power of the wind. She was deemed to grant eternal life and was often portrayed as carrying or wearing an Ankh—the ancient symbol for everlasting life. She was associated with rebirth, resurrection, and transcendence over death and also depicted as a transition guide escorting the deceased on their journeys to the afterlife. An early bronze statue portrays the goddess suckling her son, Horus, and many believe this representation inspired later Christian depictions and icons of the Madonna and Child. In the Greco-Roman period, the popularity of Isis spread and the remains of her temples, altars, and statues have been unearthed in the Mediterranean Islands, Syria, Asia Minor, and Britain. With Christianization, the temples of Isis began to close, but she still commanded a following well into the sixth century AD.

Isis understood the secret of immortality and so refashioned her husband's dead body and through a magic ritual, she brought him back to life. From this mysterious ritual of resurrection, the child, Horus, was also conceived and born during the winter solstice. He came to symbolize the newly born sun that arose from the darkness of winter. The archetype of the trinity thus features in the myth. Mojsov writes that "the worship of Osiris explicitly encompassed the doctrine of One in Three: the Resurrected Redeemer, the Holy Mother, and the Savior-Child."[17] Osiris then ruled the underworld as Lord of the Dead. Dismemberment and eventual assimilation of the divided parts symbolized Osiris as being an immortal vegetation deity, who fertilized the land and incorporated the rites of death and rebirth.

For these ancient people, the corpse of the deceased symbolized something mysterious that was part of the resurrection process. They believed in the cycles of decay and renewal in a timeless eternity and so attempted to preserve bodily remains forever. Mojsov writes:

> The crown of all the earthly provisions was the mummified body. The word for mummy, *sah*, also meant "nobility, dignity." It was the name of the constellation of Orion—the spirit of Osiris—and also meant "spirit, soul." It denoted the elevated sphere of existence to which the deceased was initiated in the process of embalming. The rejoining of the limbs of Osiris furnished the mythical precedent and became the model for overcoming death. Mummification was more than the mere preservation of the corpse; by substituting perishable substances with everlasting ones, the body was transformed and "filled with magic." It became "an Osiris." [18]

Ancient Egyptian agricultural society was governed by the rhythms of the natural world, such as the flooding of the Nile, and these early people believed that the gods represented forces of Nature. The scattering of the bodily parts of Osiris over the land was associated with fertilization, and as his blood miraculously changed into water to saturate the earth, it gave birth to new life and crops. Oxide sediments that give the Nile a reddish hue are to this day compared with blood. The continual rising and setting of the sun each day also instilled the belief that the universe was founded upon a myth of an *eternal return* that incorporated the complex duality of life and death. For the Egyptians, the dismemberment and resurrection of Osiris in a transformed body, revealed an archetypal model to understand the mystery of death and what may lie beyond. Osiris was described as being barley or wheat, and all the deceased were referred to in the same manner. He was also known as the Lord of Decay and Lord of the Abundant Green, symbolizing the corruption of the physical body and reunification with Osiris at death.

The Egyptians believed a portion of the soul separated from the body at death. The *ka*, described as being the 'shadow,' referred to the vital life essence of both earthly and afterlife incarnations. The *ba* alluded to the breath of life that flew from the body following death, and the *akh* referred to radiance or light, described as the transcendent state of the shining purified soul. Egyptians believed it was the *ba* in bird-like form that followed the sun god Osiris/Ra on his nocturnal journey across the sky, while the *ka* remained with the corpse in the underworld. This separation suggests that rather than defining the free soul as a higher state of consciousness and the earth-bound element as the unconscious, both these portions represent a desire for unity and wholeness. Marie-Louise von Franz describes how, "The Chinese *hun* soul, the Egyptian *ba,* the Indian *jivan* etc., seem to correspond to a striving toward becoming conscious, toward awakening, toward detachment from the 'world,' to a longing for a nearness to God."[19]

An ensuing battle between Horus, who wished to avenge his father's death and the perpetrator, Seth, metaphorically symbolized the continual cosmic conflict between the forces of light and darkness, or good and evil, as the resurrected Osiris guided his son's eventual victory from the realms beyond death. Horus is depicted on the tomb of the Pharaoh Tutankhamen offering animal sacrifices to the deities Geb and Nut. These gifts represented Seth, and in this symbolic act, the life force that Horus had inherited transferred back from son to father. Psychologically, this offering symbolizes transformation through the union of ego and Self. Erich Neumann suggests this part of the myth reveals how the latent divinity of the individual is realized through the union "of the ego (Horus) with the self (Osiris)."[20]

During the Middle Kingdom period, the mystical initiations of ancient Egypt were widely documented by Greek writers, including Plutarch. He described how these rites took place in dark underground chambers of sacred temples, symbolizing a journey to the netherworld and the resurrection of Osiris.

Public rituals of bringing the god back to life were commemorated annually at the end of November in Abydos, the site of Osiris's tomb. Pilgrims flocked to the area, taking part in ritual prayer and chanting for the resurrection of the deity, as a chest symbolizing Osiris was placed to rest at his tomb. A three-day period of mourning gave way to jubilation, celebrating the deity's resurrection. For the participants, this was a festival of miracles and epiphanies that continued for thousands of years, and the rites were translated to mean the appearance of "God."

Complex funerary customs and rites were observed faithfully in order to ensure reinstatement of the deceased, who was identified with Osiris and shared his resurrection power, into the eternal continuum of life. The Egyptians believed death resulted in transcending the divide between mortals and the gods, and the ancient hymn that pays homage to Osiris illustrates their reverence for the god and the belief in his supernatural abilities as a resurrection deity that they would unite with following death:

> his mystery is thy mystery;
> his things are thy things
> his knowledge is thy knowledge;
> his magical powers are thy magical powers;
> he died not and thou shalt not die.[21]

A life review or judgment is also associated with Osiris, as the deceased were ushered by the transition guide, Anubis, into his presence in the Hall of the Two Truths on the first stage of the mythic eternal journey. At one end of the hall, Osiris was seated with forty-two divine Egyptian gods, who acted as judges. A set of scales held the heart of the deceased on one side and the feather of Ma'at, the goddess of truth and justice, on the other. The deceased solemnly decreed that they had upheld the moral laws; an important part of the life review was that individuals judged themselves through searching their own conscience, as Osiris merely presided over the events. The scales were checked to see if they balanced—if they did not, the deceased would be excluded from a joyous afterlife state. If the scales were evenly set, the reward would be gaining admittance into the realms of the god, as Osiris directed the way to immortality with a shepherd's crook.

The life review, followed by a coming forth into the light, symbolized how living a just life on earth resulted in becoming 'one' with Osiris. This concept of merging with the divine following death was later expanded in Christian mythology. Jung suggests that the development of the Osiris myth "culminated in the Christian idea that everyone has an immortal soul and shares directly in the Godhead."[22] The parallel of coming forth into the light contained in the myth of Osiris is an integral part of both contemporary and ancient near-death journeys, and this symbolism heralds dying into new life.

The myth of Osiris was not just associated with the moment of death, but also served as a preparation for dying. Stanislav Grof writes, "The sacred temple mysteries of Isis and Osiris temple rituals gave neophytes the opportunity to confront death long before age or disease made it mandatory, and to conquer it and discover their own mortality. In initiatory procedures of this kind, neophytes not only lost the fear of death, but also profoundly changed their way of being in the world."[23] Similar changes take place after confronting the threshold of death during an NDE, as survivors return having lost their fear of death, because they have glimpsed a future landscape and existence and know what to expect during this transition. The Osiris myth was later incorporated into the Hermetic tradition to symbolize both the 'god' that lived within the human being and the eternal soul that would meet the supreme deity in death.

The Egyptian Book of the Dead, known as *pert em hru*, ("a coming forth into the light,") originated from the spoils of

Egyptian robbers, who ransacked tombs and found papyrus scrolls containing funerary text belonging to the deceased, alongside their mummified remains. The texts confirmed the Egyptian unshakable belief in the myth of the everlasting life of the soul and a preserved papyrus in the British Museum states: "Thy soul liveth, she rejuvenatheth herself, she knoweth in eternity, for ever. She goeth to the place where Osiris is; she goeth and cometh upon the earth for ever."

The funerary texts comprise of a vast collection of magical spells, prayers, litanies, hymns, and mythological reenactments, originating from many different dynasties over a five thousand-year period. They were carved on tombs and temple walls and acted as transition guides that protected and provided a safe passage for the deceased pharaohs on their transformational hazardous journeys from the *sleep* of death to an awakened consciousness. A central component of the texts was the judgment of the deceased in the presence of Osiris.

However, around 1700 BCE, these practices that had previously been designated to royalty began to be used more commonly throughout the general population, with the advent of coffin texts that could be engraved on the coffin or appeared in scroll form. Throughout the long span of the funerary texts, many changes evolved throughout Egypt and were incorporated into the book, thus making it far more complex. The sun god, Ra, featured in later traditions, but in the more ancient texts, Osiris was deemed Lord of the Underworld. The followers of Osiris thought they would join him in a blissful paradise known as the *Field of Rushes*. A papyrus from *The Egyptian Book of the Dead* depicts the Field as being one of eternal harmonious life and fertility, conjuring up an image of a paradisiacal Nile Valley state. Spells associated with transition to the Field describe how the entrance to this afterlife state is located on the eastern horizon, where the sun rises. The deceased traveled to the Field in a boat and had to answer the ferryman's questions, before gaining admission and enjoying a bountiful and harmonious eternal existence.

The followers of Ra believed the deceased would accompany the sun god and other divine deities in a solar barque on their symbolic nocturnal journey through the land of the dead. They would pass through Tuat, which was a miserable realm full of terrifying monsters and challenges to overcome. After navigating these obstacles, the sun god would return newly born to the sky at dawn and it was believed that the deceased, after completing the sacred voyage with Ra, would be similarly revitalized and gain insight to the secret of eternal life.

The *Amduat* that describes the mythological twelve-hour passage through the night world creatively combined the mythology of Osiris with that of Ra. Mojsov writes:

> The poetic reconciliation of the two opposing visions of the afterlife proved ingenious. During the nocturnal journey of the sun, the being of light and the lord of the depths met one another half way, blending into a single entity in the sixth hour of the night. The idea of resurrection through Osiris was thus identified with sunrise and the daily birth of the sun. The myth of Osiris had provided a metaphysics that perfectly complemented the celestial physics of Ra. As the solar agency of Ra helped to resurrect Osiris, so the netherworldly agency of Osiris helped the sun return to dawn after it passed through his body at nightfall.[24]

This nocturnal journey not only provided guidance for the deceased, but also for the living, as the Egyptians remained convinced that earthly life was preparation for the eternal posthumous journey. Psychologically, this symbolic descent followed by ascension can also be imagined by the living to be part of an inner process of renewal. Jung believed this transformation to represent the merging of the mortal and immortal aspects of the psyche. He writes, "It shakes of the mortal husk that I am and awakens to a life of its own; it mounts the sun-barge and may take me with it."[25]

The value of the vast body of funerary texts not only preserved ancient Egyptian myths symbolizing death and possible afterlife of the immortal soul, but they also provided a legacy for the validation of Jung's theory of a collective unconscious, through the many images added and revealed in the Pyramid texts of the New Kingdom. Abt and Hornung write, "What is new in the New Kingdom, is the overwhelming abundance of images in these books, adding to the mere textual description and showing a great affinity to the world of dreams and of the unconscious."[26]

The mythic teachings of ***The Tibetan Book of the Dead***, also known as the *Bardo Thodol*, originated from the ancient oral traditions of ancient Tibet, prior to the advent of Buddhism, and were first recorded in the written word during the eighth century AD, by the grand master, Padmasambhava, who introduced Buddhism into Tibet. Although little is known of pre-Buddhist practices, one of the main tenets seems to have been a preoccupation with death, and what may exist beyond. Rituals for the dead that included sacrifice and food offerings were made to ensure a safe transition for the deceased into an envisaged afterlife.

Padmasambhava later buried the sacred texts in central Tibet, in an area known as the Gampo Hills, and transmitted the power for their rediscovery to his dharma heirs. They were later unearthed by Karma-Lingpa, who was a direct descendent of one of these chief devotees. The *Bardo Thodol* is essentially a guidebook that seeks to ensure liberation for the deceased and the dying and comprises of a set of instructions on how to navigate the intermediary *bardo* (translated to mean gap) state between death and rebirth, with the aid of an enlightened teacher. This liberation is achieved through a set of directives of the six forms of liberation accessed through: hearing, wearing, seeing, remembering, tasting, and touching.

The symbolic teachings contained in the *Bardo Thodol* are specifically aimed at liberating the deceased from the confusion and sense of duality that arise from identification with the perceived ego sense of the meaning of existence. In a dangerous journey through the intermediary *bardo* stages between death and rebirth that involves encounters with both divine and dark deities; the deceased experiences the illusion of death and recognizes the impermanence of all things. The ensuing dissolution of the former false projections of Self can result in a transcendent state of enlightenment and illumination, in which a merging with the Light of Pure reality or Dharmakaya takes place. The Inspiration-Prayer for Deliverance recited during the transition between death and rebirth poetically describes the deceased's journey to enlightenment:

> When through confusion I wander in samsara
> on the luminous light-path of the dharmadhatu wisdom,
> may Blessed Vairocana go before me,
> his consort the Queen of Vajra Space behind me;
> help me to cross the bardo's dangerous pathway
> and bring me to the perfect buddha state.[27]

Although this sacred text is primarily focused on dying and the deceased, there is also a valuable message for the living—for the *bardo* states of death and becoming are fully present in everyday life, as humans struggle with uncertainty to discover their deeper identity. Chögyam Trungpa writes:

> There are all kinds of bardo experiences happening to us all the time, experiences of paranoia and uncertainty in everyday life; it is like not being sure of our ground, not knowing quite what we have asked for or what we are getting into. So this

> book is not only a message for those who are going to die and those who are already dead, but it is also a message for those who are already born; birth and death apply to everybody constantly, at this very moment.[28]

There are also similarities between the archetypal manifestations of the *bardo* states and the near-death journey, for the clear light is also a main component of the NDE and many mystical visions. Near-death survivors bring back the same message contained in the *bardo* and Buddhist teachings—that of realizing the essential qualities in life are love, wisdom, and compassion.

The ancient civilization of the ***Maya*** had a rich cultural history, although many ancient codices that recorded their way of life were destroyed by Spanish invaders, Maya funerary art discovered on coffins, precious stones, and ceramic vases, symbolized belief in an afterlife. At the moment of death, the Maya believed that the soul would leave the body and enter the underworld, known as Xibalba. The challenges of this voyage through the underworld were known, and precautions for a safe transition were made through the funeral art depicted on the coffin and offerings made to accompany the deceased. Images of the imagined journey were richly preserved on funerary vases and depicted the soul encountering archetypal entities that included serpents and dragons. After successfully navigating this dangerous terrain, the soul would be reborn in a glorious resurrection.

Much of the journey of rebirth was based upon an important section of the *Popul Vuh*, a historical epic of the Quiche Maya that was written by an anonymous Guatemalan Indian sometime after the Spanish conquest. The epic tells of the victory of the Hero Twins, who entered the underworld to avenge their father's death. After overcoming the deities of the netherworld through trials of death and rebirth, which included dying into the flames of a huge fire and being reborn five days later, the twins subsequently hacked themselves to pieces in a rite of dismemberment and returned to life. Appearing rejuvenated, they eventually gained immortality, ascended into the heavens, and entered the eternal realm of the sun and the moon. Excavation at ancient Maya archeological sites provided relics of ancient funerary vases that appeared as codices and when placed in consecutive order, they represented the equivalent of a Maya Book of the Dead. The motif of the twins is embedded in many cultural mythologies to symbolize the duality of the physical and spiritual essence of all beings, and the heroic quest to slay the monster and transition from darkness to light, requires a sacrifice of self to be reborn and emerge victorious

The ancient Maya were fascinated in myths of an afterlife and it appears that they imagined the harshness of earthly life was reenacted during trials the soul encountered in the underworld, before being reborn into the heavenly realms. The miraculous death and resurrection of the Hero Twins mythologically symbolized an affirmation of celestial ascension and rebirth.

The ancient Maya cult of the dead was strongly linked to vegetation cycles and the Hero Twins were often represented by two maize stalks symbolizing the maize god, who contained the vital life force. Marie-Louise von Franz pieces together a few common Maya customs for the dead also strongly suggesting that the living accompany the deceased on the afterlife journey. She writes, "The Maya seems to have practiced a ritual in which they accompanied the soul of the departed into the Beyond, from the moment of his death until his rebirth. The souls of the dead had a close relation to the life of plants, especially the corn."[29] Vegetation imagery and metaphors represented belief in alchemical transformation, as plant life regenerates from dead matter and the elements of water, earth, light, and air to provide a fitting symbol that illustrated the body decomposing and being reborn in a similar manner.

The ***Ars Moriendi*** (The Art of Dying) was the first Western transition guide and comprises of a vast body of texts compiled in medieval Europe during the Middle Ages that reflect Christian myths of death and provides instruction on how to die well. The subject was of great interest to Europeans living in this era, as scenes of mass burials, the burning of corpses from the Black Death, and the execution of witches and heretics were part of daily life. Through constant exposure to death, coupled with the corruption of the establishment, religious scholars of the day were prompted to compile such a body of work. As with the 'Books of the Dead' from other cultures, the symbolic message contained in the *Ars Moriendi* was not just for the terminally sick or those close to death, but also addressed how the living could cope with the impermanence of earthly life.

An original long version of the text was replaced with a shorter one containing eleven woodcut illustrations and images that could easily be explained and memorized. Coming to terms and preparing for death was revealed in the literature in the first part of the work, which instructed the living on how to understand death through symbolism, metaphors, and parables. These analogies were often based on rich and well-known church and state dignitaries and illustrated the folly of accruing material possessions that in the face of death were worthless. Instead, the texts symbolized how wisdom was gained through realizing that death was the master of life and reinforced the concept that earthly life was to be lived in accordance with divine principles, which would prepare individuals to face death, whenever it may appear. The second body of the text aided those in the process of transition. Monks from the Dominican and Franciscan orders compiled a manual to instruct priests on how to support the dying and prepare them for the transcendent journey of the soul following physical death.

The myth of an afterlife remained a central theme of the *Ars Moriendi* and preparation for making a good death, through living a worthy life, enabled the soul of the deceased to enjoy everlasting bliss. The texts also included stern warnings as to the fate of those who died in sin. The Books of the Dead from various cultures all illustrated how myths of an afterlife state remained constant in symbolic content from the time of the ancient Egyptians to the medieval era.

Visions and archetypal journeys to an afterlife have been imagined in a myriad of ways, reflecting collective inherent immortal yearnings. Many diverse religious mythologies envisage an afterlife state that also provides a powerful reminder on how to live a more authentic earthly life. The ancient Egyptians believed that following death and judgment, the soul of the deceased would be reunited with the sun god Osiris/Ra. The sun changed its position in the sky throughout the day and then 'died' each night and so these different stages and locations were translated as being the afterlife destinies for the soul. The dark underworld was linked to night and the disappearance of the sun and was where the soul was judged. If this judgment received the approval of the gods, the soul would leave the underworld never to return and would come forth into the Field of Rushes where the sun rises, and enjoy a blissful eternal existence. This metaphor of the dying and reborn sun symbolized a destiny to prepare for and look forward to.

The Aztecs envisaged a paradise known as Tlalocan, which was an eternal realm of abundance and permanent summer. However, this heavenly bliss was reserved for those who perished in the storms sent by the rain god, Tlaloc, and so most mortals ended up in the underworld known as Mictlan, which was ruled by the lord of the underworld, Mictlantecuhtli, and his female consort, Mictlancihuatl. Although this netherworld was considered one of darkness, the Aztecs worshipped the sun, and so it could be that these ancient people believed the souls of the dead could experience the light, as the sun voyaged through Mictlan to the eastern hemisphere, where it would rise again.

For the ancient Celts, there existed the concept that the dead remained in their burial tombs with their belongings. These burial mounds were also thought to be the home of ancient gods that were banished to the underworld following Christian intervention. This underworld was considered to be a kind of *Valhalla*; a place where the souls of those killed in battle would spend eternity and continue to duel. The Isle of Avalon is famously associated with the legendary King Arthur, and although it has never been clear where this enchanted site was actually located, claims were made by the monks of Glastonbury that Avalon was the old name for Glastonbury. The ancient Britons were of Celtic origin and Avalon was the place where souls would gather to commence a new life. In Celtic mythology, Avalon was a hallowed place bathed in eternal summer and joy that was abundant with flowers and fruit.

The early Greek poets, including Hesiod, wrote of a lost mythical *Golden Age* when 'Golden Men' were created by the gods and lived a harmonious existence. They did eventually die, but this was a gentle transition and following death, they transformed into divine spirits that could watch over ordinary mortals. This idyllic state, however, came to an end as humans fell from grace and forfeited experiencing a paradisiacal afterlife and would instead be confined to the underworld. Pindar, however, introduced the idea of judgment for the deceased in the underworld where the good are rewarded and the unjust are condemned. The worthy souls traveled to the Elysian Fields and chose a new earthly carnation. Following three earthly lives, each of which was judged in a similar manner, the soul was liberated to enjoy eternal paradise in the Fortunate Isles, which was very similar to descriptions of the Elysian Fields, but located in a different area. Due to the gloomy outlook of an afterlife state spent in the underworld, many Greeks looked to the teachings of the Mystery Cults and the promise of an eternal paradise.

In Hinduism, the spark or *atman* of the divine Ultimate or Absolute, known as *Brahman*, lives within every human being.

Following death, the eternal *atman* or soul is judged according to good or bad *karma* that has been accumulated over a lifetime. Hindu mythology is very complex and describes multiple heavens and hells. But existence in these realms is not permanent, as there is a cycle of death and rebirth, until *right action* and eliminating all desire culminates in a realization of the divine, which can manifest in many Hindu deities, including Vishnu, Shiva, and Krishna. The Hindu heavens are to be found north of the Himalayas and are paradisiacal realms where those who are awaiting their next reincarnation enjoy a stay of pleasure and luxury.

The original teachings of Buddhism promoted the belief that it was possible to become liberated from the endless cycles of death and rebirth through shedding the shackles of desire and attachment and attaining the state of *Nirvana,* which is often described as a state of bliss and results from letting go of all sense of self; but it is not death or an afterlife state. These teachings that were primarily directives for the abstemious monks did not permit any desire, even those for a blissful eternal hereafter. However, in Mahayana Buddhism that originated in India in the first century BCE and spread its way throughout Asia, a new train of thought emerged that placed less emphasis on reaching the state of *Nirvana* and focused on the concept of many pleasant rebirths in more blissful and heavenly realms. The ultimate goal was still achieving *Nirvana,* but for those who found this a difficult ideal to envisage, the concept of rebirths into easier and pleasurable next worlds made the quest seem more realistic.

In ancient Jewish myths, the dead slept in the shadowy world of Sheol, described as a place of dust and continual darkness that can be likened to the Greek description of Hades. Jewish mysticism (Kabbalah) recognizes seven heavens presided over by angels, and although Judaism concentrates on the importance of earthly life, the Second Book of Enoch refers to both paradise and hell as being located in the third heavenly sphere, known as

Shehaqim.

For Native Americans, the natural world symbolizes a manifestation of the sacred. Life after death signifies reunification with the ancestors and the beginning of the individual's deeper spiritual connection to all of creation. The Proverbial *Garden of Eden* was mirrored in these people's imaginings of transition to the land of the *Happy Hunting Ground*.

In Book VII of the *Republic*, Plato refers to an ascendant journey as providing the way to true wisdom, saying, "If you interpret the upward journey and the study of things above as the upward journey of the soul to the intelligible realm, you'll grasp what I hope to convey."[30] Plato then amplifies the philosophical value of such a symbolic journey of ascension through recounting a journey of return from the portal of death. In this narrative, a warrior named Er, who is said to be the son of Armenius of Pamphylia, is killed on the battle-field. However, when the dead are collected ten days later, Er's body shows no sign of decomposition even though it displays no vital signs of life. His lifeless body is returned to his family for burial and two days later, he had been laid out on the funeral pyre, but much to the astonishment of his comrades, Er comes back to life. He subsequently relates a near-death journey that includes: a description of consciousness leaving the physical body, encountering archetypal divinities, and witnessing Divine Light. All of these characteristics continue to be central motifs in contemporary narratives of near-death journeys, which are still occurring thousands of years later.

Plato then describes Er's near-death journey:

> He said that, after his soul had left him, it traveled together with many others until they came to a marvelous place, where there were two adjacent openings in the earth, and opposite and above them two others in the heavens, and between them judges sat. These, having rendered their judgment, ordered

> the just to go upwards into the heavens . . . and the unjust to travel downward . . . with signs of all their deeds on their backs. When Er himself came forward, they told him that he was to be a messenger to human beings about the things that were there, and that he was to listen and look at everything in the place.[31]

Er then recounts how the souls reaped rewards for just behavior in life and punishment for ill deeds. Plato has probably drawn on similar analogies from ancient Greek or Egyptian myths to illustrate these ancient beliefs.

Er is later taken on a journey with other souls:

> On the fourth day of that journey, they came to a place where they could look down from above on a straight column of light that stretched over the whole of heaven and earth, more like a rainbow than anything else, but brighter and more pure. After another day, they came to the light itself, and there, in the middle of the light, they saw the extremities of its bonds stretching from the heavens, for the light binds the heavens like the cables girding a trireme and holds its entire revolution together.[32]

The whole cosmos was bound together and held in place by the Spindle of Necessity, presided over by the goddesses, Clotho, Lachesis, and Antropos, who governed fate and destiny. Lots were cast for future destinies and scattered between the souls for a further life on earth. The souls were then required to drink water from the River of Forgetfulness and have no lasting memory of what had transpired, and then return to earth in the form of a shooting star. However, Er was forbidden to drink and was to remember all he had witnessed.

Er's descent into the heavenly realms contains a similar sequence and much of the same symbolism found in otherworldly journeys spanning over thousands of years, which appear in a certain recurring sequence. Kenneth Ring suggests they unfold in accordance with "a *single pattern*, almost as though the prospect of death serves to release a stored, *common* 'program' of feelings, perceptions, and experiences."[33] Although symbolic and archetypal contents of such experiences are reinterpreted according to cultural mythologies and beliefs—the messages imparted from near-death journeys remain constant, and convey an expanded awareness of the mysterious cosmos. Plato's mythological account provided a metaphor for gaining philosophical wisdom. He believed this knowledge could be acquired by taking care of the immortal soul while on earth through virtuous behavior, and thus prepare for death and the journey beyond.

One of the earliest written narratives of a near-death journey was recorded by the Venerable Bede, an English monk and eighth-century historian. He describes how Drycthelm, who lived a seemingly devout life, became seriously ill one night and died. The following morning, however, he came back to life and described what he had witnessed when entering the threshold of death.

Drycthelm was met by a good-looking man, dressed in a luminous robe that acted as a guide through various realms of the afterlife. The first appeared as a vision of hell full of tormented souls, and suddenly, the guide vanished, leaving Drycthelm alone in the dark with hideous spirits threatening to seize him. However, a bright light appeared and the evil spirits vanished, as he then realized that the light *was* the guide in the glowing robe. Drycthelm then entered the clear light that formed a meadow full of spring flowers, where he witnessed many happy people dressed in similar robes, but he was told, "No, this is not the Kingdom of Heaven as you imagine."[34] Finally, he was led to an even more beautiful place suffused in an even brighter light, making the meadow seem pale in comparison. He hoped to enter the paradise, but his guide abruptly turned around and took him back along the road that they had travelled. Drycthelm was then told that he had witnessed the fate of the soul following death, comprising of: hell for those who had committed evil deeds, a pleasant place for those awaiting the final Judgment Day to enter heaven, and the destiny of those who had led exemplary lives—admittance to the celestial realms and the glorious light that he had glimpsed on his journey. Drycthelm was then instructed to return to his body and told that through living a more pious life, he too, would reap the rewards of entry into heaven.

Drycthelm was reluctant to leave the beauty and light that he had witnessed. Dr. Elisabeth Kübler-Ross, found this same unwillingness to return to the physical body featured in many similar contemporary near-death narratives related by her patients.[35] Having miraculously came back to life, Drycthelm realized that he must live differently following his numinous experience. He then prayed at the village church, divided up his property, and became a monk, spending his time in contemplation and counseling those who wanted to live in preparation for eternal life and heavenly bliss. Kübler-Ross also describes how modern-day NDEs have a profound effect on the future lives of survivor's, resulting in new insight and knowledge about how to live more consciously.[36]

This eighth-century narrative of a near-death journey contains similar mythic images to those found in ancient Egyptian descriptions of the afterlife state. Mojsov writes, "Within this veritable web of charms and incantations we can glimpse the netherworld of the common man. It was divided into three parts: a sphere of light where the justified lived in a divine community centered around Osiris, a region of chaotic darkness where the damned suffered eternal punishment: and an area of 'filtering' where the evil were caught in a net of doom."[37] This depiction also foreshadows images and symbolism of realms of hell, purgatory, and the reward of heaven for the just, which are detailed in accounts of similar otherworldly journeys from medieval times, such as that of the Knight Owen, in which the central theme experienced, is that of a conversion. The dialogues of Gregory the Great, a sixth-century Pope and writer, also made reference to deathbed visions and glimpses of an alternate reality. Bede suggests the purpose of Drycthelm's experience was to instruct others and raise them from a state of spiritual dormancy. He writes, "In order to arouse the living from spiritual death, a man already dead returned to bodily life and related many notable things that he had seen."[38]

Contemporary near-death experiences also present similar archetypal images and symbolism described in Bede's narration and can include: the splendor of the light, the beauty of the paradisiacal vision of an afterlife, a life review, and occasional hellish aspects. The more disturbing visions or difficult challenges to overcome are also depicted in resurrection myths, including Inanna's descent. Desolation and gloom are imaginings experienced by the deceased in the Tibetan *bardo* realms of becoming, but ultimately, these negative perceptions result in a positive transformation and rebirth.

The central message that a modern-day survivor of a near-death journey conveys to humanity is still the same as that of Drycthelm—that of entering an altered state of consciousness, waking up, and becoming aware of the spiritual dimensions of existence. Bede's early account is translated from the perspective and consciousness of an early Anglo-Saxon era, but contemporary NDEs carry the same powerful teachings, even though they sometimes manifest in new images and forms that reflect the mythologies of many diverse religious traditions and cultural anomalies.

Dante's poetic masterpiece, *The Divine Comedy*, is recognized to be one of the world's greatest literary works, and seeks to convey a universal message. The narrative reflects and preserves

Christian mythological beliefs of the thirteenth-century Church on the life of the soul after death, and may have been influenced by both the mystical heavenly vision of the Prophet Muhammad, and Dante's deep appreciation for the works of the early Greek poets. However, the epic is not solely concerned with a mythic afterlife, but also seeks to convey a new imagined vision of the world and the way life should be lived. This medieval masterpiece describes the pilgrim, led by his guide, Virgil, as moving through the realms of *Inferno* and *Purgatorio* to then enter *Paradiso*, and parallels can be drawn from Bede's earlier narration. The work is vast, but of prime importance is the beatific vision described in *Paradiso* 1.

In this Canto, Dante emerges from his descent into the underworld, as his journey through the realms of hell and purgatory has resulted in initiation and purification. He is now ready to transcend the limitations of the profane aspects of earthly consciousness to become reunited with the light of a divine source. His transcendent ascent to the celestial realms and higher state of consciousness is made possible by merging with the divine feminine, in the form of Beatrice. For Dante, Beatrice is the incarnation of beatific love and beauty. Joseph Campbell describes a similar stage in the hero's journey as being a meeting with the goddess. He writes, "The ultimate adventure, when all the barriers and ogres have been overcome, is commonly represented as a mystical marriage . . . of the triumphant hero-soul with the Queen Goddess of the World."[39]

In this initial ascension, Dante reconnects with the imagined destiny of the soul. He remembers "things that he who from that height descends, forgets or cannot speak (*Paradiso* 1. 5-7). He is so overwhelmed in trying to articulate his vision that he asks Apollo to help him "show the shadow of the blessed realm inscribed within my mind" (1.23-24). A person having a near-death experience also finds it hard to articulate the ineffable magnitude of such a revelation.

The pilgrim deconstructs the myth of earthly existence as representing ultimate meaning and realizes that "our intellect sinks into an abyss so deep that memory fails to follow it" (1.8-9). Dante's perception in this mystical state of enlightenment penetrates the veil of illusion to merge with his divine essence that descends to encompass him. He believes that he has been permitted to glimpse "that place, made for mankind as its true home" (1.17). He watches Beatrice look into the sun and follows her gaze and stares into the sun and sees it "sparkling . . . like molten rock emerging from the fire" (1.19-20). In this moment, his poetic imagination takes a giant leap into an expanded form of consciousness, for the molten iron appears to symbolize the alchemical life force that emerges from the fire of creation.

The pilgrim then turns to watch Beatrice with rapt attention. She has become more beautiful and, as her beauty increases, he finds himself forever changed. This mystical transformation comes about through his ecstatic love for Beatrice, who looks into the light of the eternal presence and represents divine love. He is anxious to understand the source of "the great light" (1.82). Beatrice dispels the illusion of darkness and makes Dante aware of the limitations of "false imagining" (1.89). She tells him that he is living within the constraints of a delusion, and says, "You are not on the earth as you believe; but lightning, flying from its own abode, is less swift than you are returning home" (1.91-93). She gently admonishes Dante, as would a mother with an ignorant child, and tells him of the natural order of the universe that is formed in the image of God. Beatrice then describes how earthly distractions cause the human being to stray from the light and seek gratification in "false pleasures" (1.97). The pilgrim is reminded that the journey of the soul transcends its earthly existence, as Beatrice explains the true cause for wonder would be "if no longer hindered, you remained below, as if, on earth, a living flame stood still (1.139-141).

Through the transcendent power of love, Dante begins to

imagine the connectedness of all forms to the Light that makes the rhythms of the continuum of consciousness flow through the universe. In this merging of the poet and pilgrim, ineffable bliss is experienced that is beyond the articulation of speech and results in a state that Jung described as being that of "absolute knowledge."

There is no concrete proof that Dante's poetic imagination transcended an ordinary state of consciousness and enabled his journey of mythic archetypal visions, but Helen M. Luke writes, "I find it unbelievable that he could have written the opening words of the *Paradiso* . . . still less the final canto itself, unless he had, however briefly, past consciously beyond all images to that inexpressible realization."[40]

The Divine Comedy was written by Dante in Italian, the common language of the people. The epic appealed to the masses and has retained a timeless quality, because through the symbolism of his mystical journey, Dante carried his audience into an understanding of mythic motifs and affirmations and an interconnectedness that never changes. He also wrote simply, as a mortal man, who, nevertheless, experienced the nature of the divine. Similarly, the contemporary near-death journey seeks to convey the same teaching—that of gaining awareness of the greater spiritual dimensions of the cosmic drama of life and death.

One of the more contemporary stories of a near-death journey is that of Black Elk, a revered medicine man of the Oglala Sioux, recounted by the Canadian poet and writer, John Neihardt. This poetic account portrays the natural world of an ancient culture and also contains many of the core characteristics of near-death experiences that have been recorded over the centuries.

Black Elk was born in the Moon of the Popping Trees in 1863. As a young boy, he became seriously ill and lost consciousness. His body appeared lifeless, but it was at this moment that his spirit left his physical body and undertook a near-death journey to the spiritual world and portal of connection with the sacred. Black Elk encountered two guides carrying long spears that had lightning flashing from their tips. In Greek mythology, lightning is associated with Zeus and symbolizes spiritual wisdom. The guides tell Black Elk to hurry because his grandfathers are calling him. He is carried up into the heavens by a fast-moving cloud and finds himself amongst snow-capped mountains and hills, symbolic of ascent. The two guides call out to the boy to look at a bay horse that has appeared. The horse begins to talk: "'Behold me! He says. 'My history you shall see'. Then he wheels about to where the sun goes down, and says: 'Behold them! Their history you shall know.'"[41] This part of Black Elk's experience contains a life review that denotes transcendence of time and the bipolar nature of the archetypes, for he senses visions of both the past and the future.

Near-death experiences incorporate the personal cultural symbols of the experiencer and also collective images, which form the language of the sacred. The familiar horses reveal the mystery of creation to Black Elk in the symbolic imagery of his culture and people. They personify the spiritual transcendent power that is present in the natural world. Some are adorned with necklaces made of elk's teeth and bison hoofs, while others have horns on their heads. These items are sacred to the tribes and symbolize the motif of death and renewal. For the Sioux, the mythological divine presence, known as *Wakan Tanka*, manifests unceasingly in all of creation and reflects a timeless mythology that is alive in the mysterious powers of images from Nature.

Black Elk is led by the horses to a tepee and enters the open doorway framed by a rainbow, which not only symbolizes the bridge that links the heavens to the earth, but is also a motif of rebirth. Through the door, Black Elk can see six ancient men sitting side by side. He describes these archetypes as resembling "old hills, like stars."[42] He is told that these ancestors have called him to learn something. Black Elk becomes afraid, for he believes that he is in the presence of the Powers of the World.

Each of these ancestral grandfathers endows Black Elk with special powers and as the sixth grandfather gives the boy the ability to see beyond linear space and time and witness the connectedness of all beings, Black Elk recedes "backwards into youth."[43] He recognizes that this last grandfather represents the Spirit of the Earth and, as the grandfather changes into a boy, Black Elk realizes that he is looking at an image of himself. The gifts that Black Elk receives include the power to grow and transform and the ability to heal others. This capacity to transcend the constraints of time, both forwards and backwards is also characterized in modern-day NDEs.

The insight that Black Elk receives when he sees himself in the sixth grandfather is similar to that of many survivors of such a near-death journey. These experiencers also describe being in the presence of a higher form of consciousness, often said to manifest as a Being of Light, and then come to realize that they are part of that Light. When Jung writes of his own mystical near-death experience, he also comments that he was "about to enter an illuminated room and would meet there all those people to whom I belong in reality."[44]

Black Elk eventually passes through a village full of the dead and dying. However, when he glances behind him, the people are all reviving. He then hears a voice saying, "Behold they have given you the center of the nation's hoop to make it live."[45] Many indigenous nomadic tribes of North America placed stones to form circles, wheels or hoops, representing sacred images of the mandala of wholeness in the form of a 'magic' circle. Some are at least 4,500 years old and are often aligned with astronomical paths of the planets. They represent primal shrines of worship where rituals of divination and vision quests took place. Many of these structures are extremely large and can be found throughout the Northern United States, Canada, and Mexico. One of the most noted is the Big Horn Medicine Wheel, in Wyoming.

Black Elk takes the bright red stick shown to him by the fourth grandfather and pushes it firmly into the earth, where it miraculously grows into a huge tree; under the branches, he can see people living happily. The blossoming of this sacred stick symbolizes an archaic motif of regeneration, symbolized in vegetation that was also depicted in biblical and pagan myths, including that of the Egyptian god, Osiris, and the later image of Christ represented on a cross with leaves sprouting from the wood, dating back to about 1220.

The climax of Black Elk's vision takes place as he glimpses the totality of the universe and finds himself sensing the connectedness of all beings. The grandfathers then tell Black Elk that it is now time to return to earthly existence endowed with his special powers. Suddenly, he finds himself back on the reservation and makes his way back home, where he sees his parents tending the body of an unconscious boy. He knows that he is that boy and as he reenters his body, he is sad to think that mother and father have no idea of where he has been or what he has seen.

Black Elk's near-death journey is said to have opened up his ability to channel new psychic and healing gifts that appeared to emanate from his otherworldly encounter with archetypal energies. He was acknowledged by many to be a healing prophet, following his illuminating boyhood transcendent experience.

The myths, out-of-body narratives, and spiritual texts highlighted in this chapter contain many similar archetypal motifs and reoccurring primordial patterns that include: death, the underworld, judgment, celestial realms of paradise, and rebirth. Myths of death and renewal also reflect the dynamic symbolism of the continual cycles of regeneration found in the natural world. The mystical teachings that are handed down from ancient oral traditions, spiritual texts, and narratives of otherworldly journeys all reiterate a similar theme—that of using the symbolism of death as a motivating force to live life consciously and well, and thus gain wisdom and spiritual maturity. Preparation for death in most cultures also includes an imagined construct of what might come after.

Notes

1. Stephen Mitchell, *Gilgamesh: A New English Translation* (New York: Free Press, 2004), Book V11, 143.
2. Rikvah Scharf Kluger, *The Archetypal Significance of Gilgamesh* (Switzerland: Daimon Verlag, 1991), 17.
3. C. G. Jung, *Jung on Death and Immortality*, 131.
4. Mircea Eliade, *The Sacred and the Profane: The Nature of Religion*, trans. Willard R. Trask (New York: Harvest, 1959), 156.
5. Evans Lansing Smith, "Doorways, Divestiture, and the Eye of Wrath: Tracking an Archetype" (Janus Head Journal, July 1999), 1-2.
6. Diane Wolkstein and Samuel Noah Kramer, *Inanna: Queen of Heaven and Earth* (New York: Harper Row, 1983), 60.
7. C. G. Jung, *Analytical Psychology: It's Theory and Practice. The Tavistock Lectures* (New York: Pantheon, l968), 41.
8. Homer, *The Odyssey*, ed. and tr. Brooks Haxton (New York: Penguin, 2003), XX1V 1-7.
9. James Hillman, *The Dream and the Underworld* (New York: HarperRow, 1979), 46.
10. Ovid with Allen Mandelbaum, trans. *The Metamorphoses of Ovid*, (Orlando: Harcourt, 1993), Book X: 335-339.
11. Edward Edinger, *Ego and Archetype* (Boston,: Shambhala. 1992), 185.
12. Thomas Mann, *Death in Venice*, trans. Michael Henry Heim (New York: Echo, 2004), 82.
13. John O"Donohue, *The Invisible Embrace of Beauty: Rediscovering the True Sources of Compassion, Serenity and Hope*

(New York: HarperPerennial, 2005), 210.

14. Margot Grey, *Return from Death,* (London: Arcana, 1985), 49.
15. C. G. Jung, "Approaching the Unconscious," *Man and His Symbols,* eds. C. G. Jung and M. L. von Franz (New York: Dell, 1968), 152).
16. Apuleius, *The Golden Ass,* trans. E. J. Kenney (London: Penguin 1999), 197.
17. Bojana Mojsov, *Osiris Death and Afterlife of a God* (Malden: Wiley-Blackwell, 2005), p. 91.
18. Ibid., 18.
19. Marie-Louise von-Franz, *On Dreams and Death,* 4.
20. Erich Neumann, *The Origins and History of Consciousness* (Princeton: Princeton University Press, 1970), 252.
21. E. A. Wallis Budge, *The Gods of the Egyptians: Studies in Egyptian Mythology, Vol. 1* (New York: Dover, 1969), 150.
22. C. G. Jung, *Jung on Death and Immortality,* 49.
23. Stanislav Grof, *Books of the Dead: Manuals for Living and Dying* (New York: Thames and Hudson, 1994), 11.
24. Mojana Mojsov, *Osiris Death and Afterlife of a God,* 86.
25. C. G Jung, *Jung on Death and Immortality,* 55.
26. Theodor Abt and Erik Hornung, *Knowledge of the Afterlife: The Egyptian Amduat – A Quest for Immortality* (Zurich: Living Human Heritage, 2003), 144.
27. Francesca Freemantle and Chögyam Trungpa, trans, and commentary, *The Tibetan Book of the Dead* (Boston: Shambhala, 2000), 100.
28. Ibid., 1-2.
29. Marie-Louise von-Franz, *On Dreams and Death,* 37.
30. Plato, *Republic,* V11: 517b.
31. Ibid., X: 614 b, c, d.
32. Ibid., X: 616 b.
33. Kenneth Ring, *Life at Death,* 15.
34. Bede, *A History of the English Church and People,* trans. Leo Sherley-Price (New York, Dorset Press, 1968), 292.

35. See Elisabeth Kübler-Ross, *The Wheel of Life: A Memoir of Living and Dying* (New York: Touchstone, 1998), 188.
36. Ibid., 191).
37. Bojana Mojsov, *Osiris Death and Afterlife of a God*, 88.
38. Bede, *A History of the English Church and People*, 289.
39. Joseph Campbell, *The Hero with a Thousand Faces* (New York: Princeton/Bollingen, 1968), 109.
40. Helen M. Luke, *Dark Wood to White Rose* (Pecos: Dove, 1972), 91.
41. John Neihardt, *Black Elk Speaks* (Nebraska: University of Nebraska Press, 1968), 19.
42. Ibid., 21.
43. Ibid., 25.
44. C. G. Jung, *Memories, Dreams*, 291.
45. John Neihardt, *Black Elk Speaks*, 28.

Chapter 3

Altered States of Consciousness

The urge to transcend self-conscious selfhood is, as I have said, a principal appetite of the soul.

Aldous Huxley, *The Doors of Perception*

The authentic mystical experience is one in which the experiencer senses an encounter with an invisible, transcendent, reality. Descriptions of near-death journeys include feelings of the soul or essence appearing to detach from the physical body, resulting in a *disembodied* state of consciousness. Archetypal images and symbolism manifesting in this state would, therefore, supposedly be free from bodily sensations and emanate from some 'alternate' source of consciousness.

Such altered states that can be accessed in: dreams, visions, meditation, rituals, the use of hallucinogens, the creative imagination, and sudden trauma to the body, as in a near-death experience, appear to trigger what can be defined as an 'enlightenment,' which radically changes the experiencer's perception of the meaning of existence. These heightened states result in a merging of two interdependent, but separate areas of consciousness—that of the immortal illumined Self and that of ego. Mystical insights are not subject to any particular religious orientation, but originate from the realms of the eternal Self. However, integrating an illumined experience into everyday consciousness is dependent on interpretation and often translated in relation to a particular religious mythological background and so in Western cultures, a mystical experience is likely to be colored with Christian symbolism and images.

Discovering a deeper meaning of life and death appears

unfathomable in everyday consciousness, but mystical states can result in profound insights into both individual consciousness and that of an expanded universe. Charles Tart writes:

> My research with altered states suggests this very strongly: ultimate questions about the meaning of life and death cannot be adequately answered in ordinary consciousness. If a person has been totally blind from birth, he may reason about visions, but he will never really understand the beauty of a sunset. Until we have at least flashes of objective consciousness, we will never fully understand the nature of life.[1]

There is an inherent desire within the human psyche to discover and manifest ways of gaining access to these transcendent states. This goal is fuelled by an inner longing to merge with an expanded state of being and gain wisdom drawn from archetypal patterns and rich symbolic imagery that reveal the mystery, complexity, and wonder of the natural world and the source of life. For ancient Greeks, the goddess, Mnemosyne, preserved the memory of oral stories that told of the dynamic energies of the cosmos and the cycles of life and death, reminding humans of the soul's divinity. She was also known as the mother of the Muses, who inspired poets, artists, and musicians from the eternal font of creativity.

The possibility to deeply reflect on the nature of reality exists in every moment. William James suggests everyday events, such as hearing beautiful music or poetic musings can trigger vague recollections that transcendent insights exist in the collective unconscious, even though they never completely consciously manifest. James believed that we all experience mystical epiphanies that "bring a sense of mystery…of the metaphysical duality of things, and the feeling of an enlargement of perception which seems imminent but which never completes itself."[2] These hints from the unconscious indicate a realm of the psyche that is not subject to constraints of linear time and space, and instill the imagining that human concepts of world order may conceal another timeless dimension.

For ancient Greeks and Egyptians, the timeless language of myth preserved a divine legacy and inspired rituals of communication with their gods. Through yearly festivals comprising of secret rites and initiations commemorating the eternal realm of the deities, these early people reactualized the narration of original primordial events, and so entered the realms of *sacred* time. This repetition of mythological symbolism instilled hope that the eternal life of the gods provided a divine model for humans to determine their place in the cosmos.

The personality of ***Dionysos*** included the absorption of two distinct non-Hellenic deities: a god from Thrace, who was associated with the vine, altered states of ecstasy, and orgy, and the characteristics of Zagreus, a Cretan mystery deity, linked to the Egyptian Osiris, god of immortality. Dionysos was a Nature god associated with fertility. His dismemberment, *second* birth, and renewal came about when Athena preserved the last remaining part of his body, the heart, from which he was born again. The 'magical' resurrection of Dionysos symbolized wholeness and provided the theme of initiation into the rites of death and rebirth.

Dionysos is further connected to the mysteries of death and rebirth, as he descended to the underworld realm of Hades and brought Semele back from the dead. However, he paid a high penalty to release his mother—his masculinity, symbolized by a phallus formed from fig-wood that he instituted as a cult symbol. Having entered and returned from the underworld, the god was believed to communicate with the dead and the ancient religious cult of Dionysos celebrated life and the eternal source from which that life emanated.

The image of Dionysos conjured up an altered state of consciousness, induced by initiates drinking fortified wine, mixed with plant or herb derivatives, believed to contain hallucinogenic properties that provided the prime stimulant to transport neophytes out of the limitations of the 'sober' self. James writes, "The drunken consciousness is one bit of the mystic consciousness, and our total opinion of it must find its place in our opinion of that larger whole."[3]

The Mystery rites of Dionysian worship were based on finding the god *within,* through festivals commemorating the deity. The myth of Dionysos was not simply an analogy depicting the symbolic cycles of a vegetation deity. Instead, it was a *living* myth in which the continual death and rebirth of the divinity was experienced as a reality by the initiates, who were mainly women, for the world of Dionysos was the world of the *feminine,* which personified a sacred wisdom and laid the foundation for understanding the unknown secrets of death. The primal wildness and abandonment these women displayed symbolized the inner essence of the god, who churned up the diametric opposites of the ecstasy of life that was fuelled by the turmoil of death. For initiates, holding the tension of these two opposing forces and confronting both the death and rebirth of Dionysos, revealed the mystery of experiencing *oneness* and non-duality.

The presence of Dionysos was invoked by a large mask depicting his penetrating energy of confrontation, and communion with the god was accomplished by drinking the wine mixture. The resulting intoxication, trance-like state, and orgasmic sexual activity resulted in accessing an altered state of consciousness, whereby the shackles of conformity and the ego were abandoned, as the mask was lifted on all that was civilized within individuals and plunged them into an intense frenzy, in which the exuberance of life was fired by death and the past, present, and future all existed in the moment. Goldberg writes:

> Almost all wore masks representing satyrs, fauns, nymphs and Bacchae, all sorts of real or phantastic creatures. Everyone

> was scantily dressed; parts commonly covered were left bare and parts uncovered by custom were hidden in clothes. Their hair was disheveled, their eyes dilated with drink. They were pushing and jostling and falling upon each other. Here they sang the *phallicoe*, love songs of unusual frankness. There they swore and cursed in a fashion incredible to themselves on any other occasion. Behind them came the symbol of their songs, the *phalos*, carried by the *phalopitares*.[4]

In this feral state, perception was altered and participants were initiated into the mysterious secrets of Nature and felt the presence of Dionysos within their own being. He existed in the flesh of the wild beasts they consumed, in the wine they drank, and in the effigies of the phallus they displayed—no duality existed—and life and death subsisted simultaneously in every moment. Through repeated reenactments of such rituals, both men and women could continually imagine a merging with Dionysos, and live their lives interwoven with that of the god. Walter F. Otto describes how initiates had "been flung into the primeval cosmic turmoil in which life, surrounded and intoxicated with death, undergoes eternal changes and renewal."[5] Through the projection of the god, the paradox of life revealed itself. Breaking down the barrier between the gods and mortals to experience a spiritual transfiguration was the primal objective of the ancient Mystery cults.

The *Homeric Hymns* dedicated to Dionysos describes how the untamed androgynous qualities of the god stimulated poetic imagination into remembering the sacrosanct mythic aspects of existence, for Dionysos transformed human life into the ecstatic and he was symbolized by the world tree, the mystic marriage, and the goat-god:

> Be good to us, you crazy goat—
> we, the poets,

begin
and end our singing
through you—
and it's impossible without you,
without remembering you
we can't remember our sacred song.[6]

The myth of Dionysos celebrated the continual process of death and rebirth. Jung suggests *rebirth* to be an archetypal energy that repeats a primordial affirmation, which manifests psychically in rituals that transcend everyday consciousness to reveal the continuum of life through renewal and transformation. The sensation of immortality experienced by the initiates was, according to Jung, connected to the unconscious. He writes, "The feeling of immortality, it seems to me, has its origin in a peculiar feeling of extension in space and time, and I am inclined to regard the deification rites in the mysteries as a projection of this same psychic phenomenon."[7]

Dionysos personifies the divine archetype of the raw and indestructible force of the natural world. Through rituals that evoked altered states of consciousness, disciples manifested the same qualities within themselves in intense emotional experiences that affirmed the eternal cycle of death and renewal.

During contemporary near-death experiences, the perceived barriers of time and space also dissolve and primordial images, which are unavailable in everyday consciousness, emerge into a more expansive present to symbolize similar visions of eternity to those experienced in ancient Mystery rites and rituals.

Orpheus, known as the founder of the Orphic Mysteries, was recognized as the son of the muse, Calliope, and the Thracian river god, Oeagros. The Greek poet, Pindar, refers to him as being the offspring of both Oeagros and Apollo and he acknowledged Orpheus as the "father of song."

Several writers, including Pausanias and Ovid, gave various

versions of the myth of Orpheus, who is best known for his journey to the underworld to rescue his wife, Eurydice. Similar accounts of such a descent also exist in the mythologies of diverse cultures, including that of the Maori hero, Hutu, who descends to the nether realms to rescue the soul of the Princess Pare, and succeeds in bringing her back to life. Orpheus, however, fails in his quest by disobeying the gods, and his backward glance toward the realm of the dead may symbolize his attempt to unravel the mystery of death. But, through this heroic descent and return from Hades, which was initiated by the soothing melodies of his lyre, Orpheus was considered to be an intermediary between the living and the dead.

Orpheus symbolizes the hope of transcending death through the magical quality of his music and words. He is eventually stoned to death by a group of crazed Maenads and in the *Sonnets to Orpheus*, Rilke writes of how the music of Orpheus even soothed the rocks that killed him:

> No one to call when they raged and wrestled
> but the jagged stones they hurled
> turned gentle when reaching you,
> as if able to hear you.[8]

The decapitated head of Orpheus was still heard to be singing as it floated down the river Hebrus, signifying survival of bodily death. The narration of Er's near-death journey describes Orpheus as choosing a future incarnation of a swan, which through its whiteness and grace, symbolizes pure Light, imbued with a mysterious holiness. The swan also depicts the image of the poet and the inspirational power of poetry.

Orpheus was not acknowledged as a god, but he was believed to possess supernatural powers and so was recognized as a seer and emissary, who founded a religious cult that was a reformed modification of the Dionysian Mysteries. Life after death was a central Orphic belief, as Orpheus had already demonstrated the power to calm those in the underworld, and he might manifest these abilities on his disciple's behalf at death, if they lived their lives directed by his teachings.

Dismemberment, such as that of Orpheus is featured in myths of many world spiritual traditions. Anita Barrows and Joanna Macy write:

> In varied ways they all suggest that it is essential to the ongoing nature of life. The breaking to pieces of the Egyptian god Osiris was necessary for his resurrection and the fertility of the land, as was also the case for Tammuz in Babylonian culture. To the primordial Hindu mind, the creation of the world originated in the sacrificial self-dismemberment of the first being, the Mahapurusha. Such ritual self-offering holds an important place in Tibetan Buddhism . . . . Ancient stories about the bodhisattvas, the heroes of the Mahayana tradition, recount the same kind of self-mortification . . . . For many Christians, the Last Supper of Jesus, with the breaking of the bread, embodies a similarly redemptive self-offering, ritually reenacted in the ceremony of the Eucharist.[9]

While initiates in Dionysian rites and rituals transcended consciousness through wild ecstatic states, the followers of Orphism sought to access a profound mystical enlightenment through purification, resulting in psychic transformation and expectations about death and its aftermath. Symbolic death and rebirth were part of Orphic initiation rites practiced in ancient Greece, and Orpheus continued to be revered for at least a thousand years.

Orpheus was considered to be initiated into the magical arts through the divine essence of his music and poetry. The poet has the ability to enable the imagination to step outside of time and space, and so becomes a visionary. Orpheus facilitated altered states of consciousness amongst initiates, animals, and even the forces of Nature through playing his lyre. On the expedition of Jason and the Argonauts, he charmed the sirens, calmed a turbulent sea, and soothed the clashing rocks. An ancient vase painting depicts a tranquil scene of people mesmerized and contented, as they listened to his songs.

The Greeks thought Orpheus had knowledge of the mysterious divine world of the gods, as his language surpassed that of normal speech, thus entrancing and captivating his followers. He conveyed otherworldly wisdom through stories, which provided the central theme of cult practices, and initiation was reliant on the supernatural quality of the poet and priest's words and melodies.

Orphism was closely aligned with Nature and the religion was founded on the sacred Mysteries of the gods. All religions encompass portrayals of archetypal figures, and Joseph Henderson comments that both the Dionysian and Orphic Cults "brought forth symbols associated with a god-man of androgynous character who was supposed to have an intimate understanding of the animal or plant world and to be the master of initiation into their secrets."[10] The religion was one that incorporated beauty and its eternal essence. Hermann Broch writes:

> Certainly many instances of earthly beauty—a song, the twilit sea, the tone of the lyre, the voice of a boy, a verse, a statue, a column, a garden, a single flower—all possess the divine faculty of making man hearken unto the innermost and outermost boundaries of his existence, and therefore it is not to be wondered at the lofty art of Orpheus was esteemed to have the power of diverting the streams from their beds and changing their courses, or luring the wild beats of the forest with tender dominance, or arresting the cattle a-browse upon the meadows and moving them to listen, caught in the dream and enchanted, the dream-wish of all art: the world

> compelled to listen, ready to receive the song and its salvation.[11]

The Orphics believed that the human being comprised of a Dionysian eternal soul, incarcerated within the confines of a flesh covered Titanic body. The ancient Titan gods, who preceded the Olympian pantheon, dismembered, cooked, and ate the young god, Dionysos, and Zeus annihilated them for committing this treacherous act with a thunderbolt. According to Orphism, the human being was formed from the ashes of the defeated Titans and so contained the duality of both Titan wickedness and goodness of Dionysos that the Titans had consumed before their own destruction. Through living a pure and pious life, the soul could be liberated from the tainted body that held the evil Titanic dimension and actualize its immortal destiny. Initiates also believed that through following the teachings of Orpheus, they would be living their last mortal incarnation and achieving the status and final destiny of the deified soul. This flight of the soul from the body is also described in contemporary near-death journeys. Michael Grosso writes, "One thinks of the ancient Orphic formula *soma sema* (the body is a tomb); true life must be then to exit from the body."[12]

There is some reference to the fact that ritual sacrifice did not include animal offerings, as Orpheus taught humans to refrain from killing. However, ritual offerings were made, followed by prayer and sacred chanting. Part of the rites also included stepping in and out of a circle or enclosure, symbolizing the Wheel of Life, and then climbing a ladder, a motif of gradual ascension that connected earth to the heavens and signified communication between the two spheres. In ancient Egypt, a great many artifacts bearing images of ladders or steps were discovered in tombs of the Old and Middle Kingdoms. *The Egyptian Book of the Dead* also refers to a ladder, which enables entrance into the realm of the gods.

Orphic initiation rites and the history of Orphism were recorded on small gold bars that were buried with the dead. The inscriptions that were repeated on several of the tablets detailed instructions for the deceased upon their arrival in Hades, and initiates were reminded to drink from the *Lake of Memory* rather than from the *Spring of Forgetfulness*. Tablet 2 that originated from Petelia in *Magna Grecia*, states:

> You will find in the house of Hades, on the right side, a spring
> and standing by it a white cypress.
> Do not approach this spring!
> Ahead you will find, from the Lake of memory,
> cold water pouring forth: there are guards before it.
> They will ask you by what necessity you have come.
> You tell them the whole entire truth.
> Say, "I am a child of Earth and starry sky.
> My name is "Starry," I am parched with thirst. But grant me
> to drink from the spring.[13]

Having drunk from the Lake of Memory, the soul of the deceased is rewarded for a pious earthly life and along with other joyful initiates, enjoys eternal life.

The legacy of Orpheus still lingers in psychic consciousness, for Orpheus confronted the threshold of death and returned to validate an ancient myth of resurrection and renewal.

Rilke reveres and illuminates the timeless and archetypal eternal quality of the intermediary priest and poet:

> Is Orpheus of this world? No. The vastness of his nature
> is born of both realms.
> If you know how the willow is shaped underground,
> you can see it more clearly above.
>
> We are told not to leave food

on the table overnight: it draws the dead.
But Orpheus, the conjuring one,
mixes death into all our seeing.[14]

The beautiful transcendent melodies of Orpheus can still be heard in the collective archetypal realms and are accessible in altered states of consciousness manifesting in NDEs. Ring relates a survivor describing how she heard the most beautiful "spiritual" music in a very pretty valley.[15] Moody writes of a similar case, "A young woman who nearly died from internal bleeding associated with a blood clotting disorder says that at the moment she collapsed, 'I began to hear music of some sort, a majestic really beautiful sort of music.'"[16] These ancient musical echoes herald a glorious homecoming and glimpse of eternity.

The *Homeric Hymns* comprise of epic poetry that records the long span and development of Greek mythology. They are credited to Homer, but continued to be revised over hundreds of years. One of the oldest of these compositions is the *Hymn to Demeter* that recounts the myth of **Demeter** and **Persephone**, which was primarily associated with the vegetation cycles.

Persephone's descent and return from the underworld resulted in her being linked to the seasons. Her time spent with Hades represented the fall and winter, when the earth would remain fallow and barren. Persephone's return symbolized spring, regeneration, and renewal of the crops. Her mother, Demeter, revealed the sacred mysteries of the corn. Both mother and daughter were personified in corn symbolism. The old crops, represented by Demeter, gave way to new growth, embodied in the figure of Persephone. Ancient monuments and art portray the goddesses wearing crowns of corn and holding stalks of corn in their hands.

Persephone was also one of the few mythological figures that visited the realm of the dead and was allowed to leave, thus symbolizing transformation and renewal. The central motif of death and rebirth, was, therefore, not just confined to the crops, but was also an allegory for the destiny of the human being. Worship of the two goddesses took place during the **Eleusinian Mystery** rites that also prepared the initiates for death and possible immortality, and consisted of a ritual using a dead-looking barley stalk. This metaphor of the grain symbolizing immortality was also repeated by St. Paul. When speaking of how the dead came back to life, he states, "What you sow does not come to life until it dies. And as for what you sow, you do not sow the body that is to be, but a bare seed perhaps of wheat or some other grain (1 Corinthians 15:36-37).

The significant religious aspect of the Eleusinian Mysteries was that participants believed an encounter between the Persephone, queen of the underworld, and the living would take place, symbolizing the continual cycles of regeneration and the notion of an eternal life-force. The rites instructed the living on how to prepare for death in order to undertake the necessary transition and such an initiation determined the individual's fate in the afterlife, promising a joyous existence in Elysium or the *Islands of* the *Blessed*, rather than the miserable outlook in Hades.

The rites were shrouded in secrecy, but commemorated annually for over a thousand years during the Greek month of Boedromion, which would fall around September/October. Neophytes would purify themselves by bathing in the sea and then sacrifice a young pig, which symbolized the Great Mother and otherworldly projection, to Demeter and Persephone. Initiation at Eleusis comprised of two levels. The first involved eating small cakes and drinking the *kykeon* in a holy communion. The second involved candidates preparing for as long as a year in order to be part of the Grand Mysteries that concluded with a sexual union between the High Priest and Priestess, celebrating the mysteries of love and regeneration. Funerary vases found at an ancient burial site depict the final stages of initiation and portray symbolic scenes of the *heiros gamos* or sacred marriage.

Homer describes how the initiated are those lucky enough to be prepared for death and what may lie beyond:

> Happy
> is that man
> among the men
> on earth,
> who witnesses
> these things.
> And whoever
> is not initiated
> in the rites,
> whoever
> has no part in them
> he does not share
> the same fate,
> when he dies
> and is down in
> the squalid darkness.[17]

A prerequisite for initiation required entering an altered state of awareness and becoming still and receptive to experiencing psychic visions. In order to manifest such apparitions, participants would prepare through fasting, intense spiritual practice, and imbibing the *kykeon*, which was fermented into alcohol from roasted barley groats mixed with water, but may also have contained a third ingredient of a mind-altering substance.

Research indicates that the barley was infected by a fungus or mushroom contaminated with ergot that in the late 1930s was discovered by the Swiss chemist, Albert Hoffman, to contain similar chemical alkaloids to LSD. These properties were soluble and when added to the barley potion, they could produce hallucinogenic visions. Insects attracted to the mushrooms symbolized souls of the deceased, as the psychoactive honeydew caused them to appear dead, but they then later revived. Fungal fermentation produced bread from Demeter and wine from Dionysos and also enabled ancient cultures to triumph over death through the use of the mushroom properties. Great amounts of infected barley were harvested to prepare the *kykeon* and the high priests cultivated the fungus through the use of honeydew specifically reserved for this process. Drinking the *kykeon* resulted in an altered state of perception. Carl A. Ruck writes:

> The ancient testimony about Eleusis is unanimous. Eleusis was the supreme experience in an initiate's life. It was both physical and mystical: trembling, vertigo, cold sweat, and then a sight that all previous seeing seems like blindness.[18]

Exactly what took place during the Mysteries remains a closely guarded secret, but the rites that were celebrated for hundreds of years, appeared to open a portal for initiates to experience direct divine communication, as a psychic reality. The use of mind-altering substances may have provided the foundation for religious mythologies. Huston Smith writes, "More interesting than the fact that consciousness-changing devices have been linked with religion is the possibility that they may have initiated many of the religious perspectives which, taking root in history, continues long after their entheogenic origins were forgotten."[19] Certainly for Christians, the holy celebration of the mass and sacrament of communion symbolically recreates a union with Christ, as the bread and wine miraculously transform into his body and blood, enabling believers to 'eat' and 'drink,' and become 'one' with him. Bread symbolizes eternal life and The New Testament records the words of Christ, "I am the bread of life. He who comes to me will never go hungry and he who believes in me will never be thirsty" (John 6:35).

Initiates of the ancient Mystery rites were not required to learn theoretical knowledge, but experience and witness a direct *epiphany,* which originates from the Greek *epiphaneia* and signifies the apparition or manifestation of a divine being. Kerényi writes, "The *mystai,* 'initiates,' came in ritual procession to this festival of 'vision,' at which *epopteia,* the state of 'having seen' was attained."[20] The word *mystery* derives its etymology from the Greek *myein,* meaning to close and not divulge secrets. The Egyptian word *seshta* also carried a similar connotation of something that was withheld from general knowledge and inaccessible. For these ancient people, there was a mystery hidden in the depths of the underworld that enabled divine life to arise from death.

Evidence gathered from writers, such as Homer and Pausanias, together with depictions on ancient funerary vases, strongly suggest initiates received experiential revelations and underwent a spiritual awakening that led to losing the fear of death through communing directly with higher realms of consciousness, personified by the archetypal energies of the mother goddess, Demeter, and the goddess of rebirth, Persephone.

The NDE mirrors these ancient initiation rites and altered states of consciousness, resulting in a similar state of spiritual enlightenment. Kenneth Ring writes:

> Specifically, it seems to serve as a catalyst to promote the *spiritual awakening and growth* of the individual because of its power to thrust one into a transcendental state of consciousness whose impact is to trigger a release of a universal "inner programming" of higher human potentials. There may be in each of us a latent spiritual core that is set to manifest in a particular form if only it can be activated by a powerful enough stimulus.[21]

Initiates of the Eleusinian Mysteries may only have participated in the rites once during their lifetimes. However, these powerful rituals manifested visions of archetypal images, personifying 'God,' to enter the human psyche. A painted fifth-century plaque, dedicated to Demeter depicts how a blind man, Eukrates, had also 'seen' the goddess rising up before him, surrounded by a red aura.

Similarly, an NDE is usually experienced only once. However, even those that are blind describe 'seeing' mystical visions. The research of Elisabeth Kübler-Ross records how during near-death experiences, people perceive a sense of wholeness, which includes the restoration of sight in those who are blind in everyday consciousness.[22] The grain of Demeter provided symbolic seeds of enlightenment and the NDE may also be viewed as a germ promoting spiritual growth and bearing the fruit of divine wisdom.

It is over four thousand years since the ancient Greeks made use of psychotropic drugs to expand consciousness and escape from Plato's 'dark cave' back into the 'light' of an expanded awareness. However, they were not alone in this endeavor. Early Aztec civilizations incorporated mind-altering sacred mushrooms in their rites and rituals, and Native Americans have used peyote for hundreds of years and thought it personified divine communication. The Zoroastrians used hemp to facilitate altered states and gain enlightenment, and the Hindus cultivated the *soma* plant, which they believed when ingested, could confer immortality. Huston Smith suggests the holy texts of the *Vedanta* and spiritual teachings contained in the *Vedas* derive from use of the *soma* more than from any other source.[23] In all these practices, entering an altered state of consciousness was associated with archetypal images that initiated religious or spiritual wisdom and affirmed primordial affirmations.

Humans have continued to experiment with similar substances to expand and identify with cosmic consciousness and the archetypal energies of a parallel universe. Stanislav Grof writes, "In its farthest reaches, individual consciousness can identify with cosmic consciousness or the Universal Mind known under many different names—Brahman, Buddha, the Cosmic Christ, Keter, Allah, the Tao, the Great Spirit, Anima Mundi and many others."[24] The belief that mind-altering substances can result in mystical experiences is not readily accepted by some theologians, who believe that such epiphanies are gifts from God, reserved for saints and prophets of a holy nature. However, similar triggers, including fasting, meditation, and sleep deprivation have been part of religious rites for centuries. Walter Pahnke and William Richards write:

> The medieval monk in his darkened cell and the hermit in the deep recesses of his cave, for example, used not psychedelic substances, but the tools of sensory deprivation, sleep deprivation, meditative disciplines, and fasting to elicit biochemical changes and unlock the door to unconscious levels of the mind. The Hindu yogin uses similar methods in addition to autohypnosis and breath control, the latter increasing the amount of carbon dioxide in the blood and triggering unconscious levels of the mind . . . . It would appear logical to suggest that whenever altered forms of consciousness occur, whether they are anticipated or come as a complete surprise, underlying biochemical activity may be involved. Thus the Hindu yogin practicing breath control or the Christian monk spending long hours in solitary prayer may be seen to be influencing body chemistry in the same direction as the modern man who ingests a psychedelic drug.[25]

Such mind-altering practices raise consciousness to indicate the illumination of mystical epiphanies, as they manifest beyond human control and limitations, to reveal sacred and previously unknown wisdom.

William James experimented with nitrous oxide combined with oxygen. He writes:

> One conclusion was forced upon my mind at that time, and my impression of its truth has ever since remained unshaken. It is that our normal waking consciousness, rational consciousness as we call it, is but one special type of consciousness, while all about it, parted from it by the flimsiest of screens, there lie potential forms of consciousness entirely different. We may go through life without suspecting their existence, but apply the requisite stimulus, and at a touch they are there in all their completeness which probably have their field of application and adaptation.[26]

The reconciliation of opposites was the keynote of his experience, and James described appreciating the interconnection of all things, as all that appeared to be the 'other' merged into 'one.'[27]

The significance of modern-day mind-altering chemicals, such as mescaline and LSD, is that these drugs, like their earlier counterparts, can facilitate unconscious material becoming conscious. Huston Smith's experiment with mescaline revealed the vast, unconscious layers of the psyche that are normally unavailable. The famous philosophical allegory of Plato's story of the cave came to mind, as Smith articulated how archetypal images struck him "with the force of the sun, in comparison with which everyday experience reveals only flickering shadow in a dim cavern."[28] Such altered states are, according to Smith, similar and indistinguishable from mystical experiences that take place spontaneously and can lead to a psychological realization of the Self. He writes, "The fully realized human being is one whose doors of perception have been cleansed—I have myself referred to these doors as windows and envisioned them as successive layers of our unconscious minds."[29]

Grof's research into altered states, induced by psychedelics, documents that it is still possible to have experiences that closely resemble those described in the Mysteries, and that archetypal deities continue to manifest to individuals who have no previous intellectual awareness of the mythological realms they are experiencing.[30] In "The Miracle of March Chapel," which took place during a Good Friday Service in 1962, Dr. Walter Pahnke experimented with a group of theological students, who had never taken psychedelic drugs, and each were given either a placebo or dose of psilocybin in order to evaluate the possibility that the drug enabled archetypal religious epiphanies to manifest. Individual reactions were analyzed and many volunteers that had ingested the drug rather than the placebo, consequently reported similar or identical images to those revealed in mystical states of consciousness. Having taken part in this experiment, Smith described what he believed to be a personal meeting with God.[31]

It appears that contemporary use of psychedelics validates the possibility of spontaneous manifestations emanating from the archetypal realms, rather than dismissing such apparitions as being the product of primitive wishful thinking and magic. The recurring powerful motif resulting from LSD experimentation is the sensation of ego-death or annihilation followed by a spiritual rebirth, similar to that recorded in the ancient Mystery rites. Grof writes:

> The sense of ultimate disaster usually referred to as the ego death, is typically followed by visions of blinding white or golden light, intricate rainbow halos and peacock designs, or glorious celestial beings. There is a sense of spiritual liberation, divine epiphany, redemption and salvation. The universe seems indescribably beautiful and radiant, and evil appears ephemeral and unimportant.[32]

Insights from expanded mystical states of awareness continue to be of vital importance to human consciousness. Since the Cartesian era, the gods, their myths, and the numinous memory of what they represented are dying in Western cultures, resulting in the painful loss of mythological ways of imagining, which has disastrous effects on the capacity to engage with deeper aspects of the mind that can provide answers to fundamental existential questions. Aldous Huxley writes, "To be shaken out of the ruts of ordinary perception, to be shown for a few timeless hours the outer and inner world . . . as they are apprehended, directly and unconditionally, by Mind at large—this is an experience of inestimable value to everyone."[33]

Actor, Larry Hagman, describes how a period of deep depression led his therapist to suggest that he experiment with LSD. His ensuing altered state of consciousness manifested in archetypal dimensions of a near-death journey:

> I headed for the cave. As soon as I got to the doorway, BOOM, I was sucked inside and down a tunnel at incredible speed. At the end, I saw a light. As I came out of the tunnel, I was in a place where I was surrounded by bright and diffused light. I saw a person who called out to me. I didn't know if it was a he or a she. That person didn't talk, but without speaking somehow let me know, "This is a glimpse of where you've been, where you are going, where you are all the time."[34]

Hagman describes how he prepared himself for this venture through the ancient practices of fasting and meditation; he also took precautionary measures and was supervised by those well-acquainted with the use of psychedelics. The experience contained and confirmed the mythic teaching of *The Tibetan Book of the Dead* that Hagman was familiar with. Symbolic imagery he encountered also included strange animal forms and a gate that he had to pass through, in order to access this otherworldly state.

In early Egyptian mythology on the afterlife of the soul, gates symbolized the passage of transition, and they were an important part of temple architecture. Mojsov writes, "Four gates led to the holy of holies. Twelve gates protected the nocturnal regions of the hours of the night. Seven gates preceded the throne of Osiris. In tombs, auspicious images were placed above the doorways. Passing through gates invoked the soul's voyage through successive stages of spiritual initiation."[35]

Hagman's sensation of passing through a dark tunnel and coming forth into the light is not only associated with the envisaged stages to the afterlife of the ancient Egyptians, but also forms an integral part of a core NDE. Following his use of the mind-expanding stimulus, he had the following profound insight, "I was part of everything, and everything was part of me. Everything was living, dying and being reborn."[36] He did not repeat the experience, but stated that LSD removed his fear of death, which he now believes is just a transition to another familiar level of consciousness—a place that he had been to before.

Although experiences, such as Hagman's, may seem improbable to some, Huxley writes, "Nevertheless they exist, they are facts of observation, and as such, they cannot be ignored by anyone who is honestly trying to understand the world in which he lives."[37]

The shared archetypal characteristics of both psychedelic states and NDEs are widely recognized and relate to beliefs found in the doctrines on death of early civilizations. Research suggests that below our conscious awareness, mythic imprints and affirmations of an alternate reality are still retained within the collective unconscious. Those who are propelled into a state of mystical consciousness through either the use of psychedelics, or triggers, including the NDE, appear to discover revelations that are more powerful than anything they have previously experienced.

Mystical visions and apparitions, such as those manifesting in the Mystery Cults, were more prevalent in ancient times and are embedded in universal Holy Scriptures that describe ecstatic visions and epiphanies of saints and sages. However, religious historians often recorded these profound awakenings in a dry unimaginative way and failed to grasp their transcendent qualities. Kerényi writes, "We find little explicit testimony concerning what lies between the two extremes, although without such intermediate phenomena—the light, hovering visions of persons of moderate visionary endowment—a religion possessed of a living mythology would be unthinkable."[38]

The Buddha gained enlightenment while meditating under the Bodhi tree around 528 BCE. He did not consider himself to be a yogi or a saint, but rather one who was *awake*, and this distinction was reflected in the name 'Buddha' that originated from ancient Sanskrit and meant *to awaken and to know* the enlightened state of *Nirvana*. The literal meaning of *Nirvana* is to *extinguish* the false sense of ego-self, which is the source of craving and misery. In Buddhist philosophy, rich metaphoric teachings reinforce the impermanence of all things and symbolize how relinquishing ego attachment results in liberation from the cycles of life and death and the flowering of the human spirit. The Buddha says:

> Waves rise and fall, but the water remains. Without water, there could be no waves. The waves return to water. Waves are water, water is waves. Though the waves may rise and pass away, if they understand that they themselves are the water, they will transcend notions of birth and death. They will not worry, fear, or suffer because of birth and death.[39]

In Zen Buddhism, the term *satori* means individual enlightenment or a flash of sudden awakening that gives rise to the sensation of infinite space and an awakening to the *Absolute*.

The sixth-century Chinese philosopher, Lao Tzu, often referred to as the "ancient child," was said to have written the *Tao Te Ching* in three days, before vanishing into the mountains of Tibet. This classic work reflects the mystical philosophy of Taoism that incorporates: the *Way of Final Reality,* the transcendent nurturing essence from which all things are born, nourished, and return to at death; the *Way of the Universe,* the creative life force of Nature that governs the principles of life, and the *Way of Authentic Human Life,* which reveals how life should be lived simply and harmoniously within the balance of a peaceful mystery. Mystical awareness dissolves ego consciousness and through becoming 'empty,' one becomes infused with the translucent nature of reality to become everything. The Tao states:

Touch ultimate emptiness,
Hold steady and still.

Of all the world religions, perhaps Taoism stands out as the one that honors the unifying power of the sacred feminine to the highest degree, and thus offers a sense of mysterious liberation.

In Hinduism, *Brahman,* which has a dual Sanskrit meaning of both to "breathe" and "be great" is the name given to the formless ultimate reality that comprises of pure consciousness, pure bliss, and pure being that is ever present. The vast pantheons of various gods all represent aspects of this divine reality and its unifying core and Hindus believe that each human being is one with *Brahman* in their *Atman* or soul. The *Isha-Upanishad* states:

The Self is everywhere,
without a body, without a shape,
whole, pure, wise, all knowing,
far shining, self-depending,
all transcending

Life is to be lived consciously incorporating this knowledge and achieving such a transcendent state is accomplished through the practice of four different paths of yoga (meaning union with God) that suit individual personality types. *Jhana* yoga is associated with knowledge; *bhakti* yoga is through devotion to one of the many gods; *raja yoga* involves deep meditation, and *karma yoga* is the path of dedicated selfless action.

The Indian mystic, Ramakrishna Paramahamsa, experienced mystical visions from an early age. He later became a priest at a temple on the River Ganges that was dedicated to the goddess, Kali. As a full-time devotee of the goddess, he spent much time meditating and seeking a glimpse of her presence that finally appeared to him in a rapturous vision:

> The buildings with their different parts, the temple and everything vanished from my sight, leaving no trace whatsoever, and in their stead I saw a limitless, infinite, effulgent Ocean of Consciousness. As far as the eye could see, the shining billows were madly rushing at me from all sides with a terrific noise, to swallow me up. I was caught in the rush and collapsed, unconscious . . . . Within me there was a steady flow of undiluted bliss, altogether new, and I felt the presence of the Divine Mother.[40]

The *Kabbalah* that originated over two thousand years ago originates from the Hebrew "to receive" and the teaching present a visionary and experiential aspect of Jewish faith, rich in symbolism and metaphors, which provide insights into a divine inner nature and the presence of the sacred feminine, within a masculine outer core. The Kabbalah provides a path of direct mystical communication between the individual and the divine.

Islamic spirituality began with the mystical revelations contained in the *Qur'an*. The founder of Islam, the Prophet Muhammad, was said to have received these metaphorical communications direct from God/Allah following a period of solitary meditation in a cave at Mount Hira. In total, the sacred text comprises of one hundred and fourteen chapters and each is referred to as a *surah* that gives guidance on how to live life in accordance with the will of Allah. Muhammad did not adorn himself with an elevated status, but simply referred to himself as "God's messenger" and he appeared to enter an altered state of consciousness when he received the transmissions that resulted in strange seizures the moment he began to hear the holy words.

It is through analogy from the natural world that the *Qur'an* enables followers to directly experience connection to higher realms of consciousness. Symbolism that relates to the stars, the ocean, the moon, the sun, and all forms of wild life, infuse disciples of Islam with the true meaning of the pilgrimage of life, which is to be reunited with the Divine Presence. Chapter six of the *Qur'an* states:

> He is the One who has placed the stars
> to guide you through darkness on land and sea.
> **We have spelled out signs for people who know.**
>
> It is He Who has reproduced you from a single soul.
> and (granted you) a settlement (on earth)
> and a resting place (after death)
> **We have spelled out signs for people who understand.** [41]

Muhammad was also reported to have undergone a nocturnal vision known as the *al-mi'raj,* which is translated to mean "Night of the Journey and Ascension." The Prophet ascended into the celestial realms on the back of a mythical horse, and Seyyed Hossein Nasr writes, "He was taken from Mecca to Jerusalem, and from there he experienced gradual ascension through the hierarchy of being to the outermost regions of the cosmos . . . and then on to the Divine Proximity as described in Sura XV11 of the Quran."[42] Muhammad then met with previous prophets, including Adam and Abraham. He also encountered angelic entities as he journeyed through the seven stages of heaven to witness images of both hell and paradise, and the suffering or joy of their respective residents. Muhammad describes his ecstatic vision:

> Now when I was brought on my Night Journey . . . a thing too stupendous for the tongue to tell of or imagine or picture. My sight was so dazzled by it that I feared blindness. Therefore, I shut my eyes, which was by Allah's good favor. When I thus veiled my sight, Allah shifted my sight (from my eyes) to my heart, so with my heart I began to look at what I had been at with my eyes. It was a light so bright in its scintillation that I despair of ever describing to you what I saw of His majesty.[43]

Through this ecstatic vision, Muhammad experienced the eternal nature of the divine. The mystical path of Islam manifested in Sufism that reflected an inner desire to reconnect with primordial origins. Ecstatic Sufi poets expressed the path of the sacred heart through direct experience and saw the presence of God in all things. Such imaginings gave rise to some of the most glorious and enduring world poetry. Rumi writes:

> Work in the invisible world
> at least as hard
> as you do in the visible.
>
> Be a companion with the prophets
> invisibly, so that no one knows.
>
> You can't imagine what profit will come!
> When one of those generous ones
> invites you into his fire.[44]

In psychological terms, both the mystical heart of Sufism and the *Qur'an* reveal a pilgrimage of exile and homecoming that dissolves ego identification and leads to the discovery of the Self. In order to enable the heart to open to these revelations, a mantra, known as the *dhkir*, is repeatedly recited. Through intense concentration, the Sufi turns attention towards God/Allah and is infused as a lover with the bliss of reconnecting with the Beloved.

Skeptics may define the Prophet's enlightenment as the delusion of a man in the throws of an epileptic seizure. However, rather than dismissing such mystical manifestations, we may all benefit through considering the possibility that such profound spiritual experiences may reveal the more authentic dimensions and affirmations of human nature.

Muhammad's mystical vision is of particular interest, as it shares many similarities with the narratives of contemporary near-death survivors: coming forth into the bright light, the meeting with a higher presence, a reluctance to return to the physical body, and gaining new insights and wisdom of a transcendent ultimate reality, which are revealed through symbols, images, and metaphors.

As illustrated, diverse spiritual literature constantly references mystical and psychic experiences, and the Judaeo-Christian Bible proves no exception. The Old Testament includes examples of visionary states, including that of Moses talking to Yahweh from the burning bush (Exodus 3:2), and Isaiah's vision of God (Revelations 6:1). At the very heart of Christianity lies the mythic life of the crucified Prophet Jesus, and the New Testament details such events, as Christ walking on the water (Matthew 14:25). One of the most noted mystical visions is that of St. Paul on the road to Damascus (Acts 9:3-9).

Ancient Greek and Egyptian mythology tells of dying and resurrected gods, and the ensuing Mystery Cults sought to invoke the archetypal energies of these deities. This same yearning to transcend consciousness and witness divine apparitions appears to be inherent within human beings and Christians looked to the insights of those including St. Gregory the Great and Augustine, who were endowed with mystical perception. Thomas Merton writes, "The mystic is led by a sure spiritual instinct to seek God wherever he may be found."[45]

There have been several Marian apparitions recorded over time, detailing supernatural appearances of the Virgin Mary to one or more people that are validated by the Papacy. Mary is not worshipped as a deity in Roman Catholicism; however, she is venerated as the Divine Mother, who embodies many of the archetypal qualities of the ancient Great Mother goddesses, including Persephone and Isis. Visions of Mary include: Our Lady of Guadalupe, Our Lady of Laus, Our Lady of the Miraculous Medal, Our Lady of Lourdes, and Our Lady of Fátima. Many basilicas and shrines were later built in these areas around the world to commemorate these sightings. Most recently, many were said to share apparitions of Our Lady of Assiut in Egypt, when, during mass, several icons of the Virgin started to radiate a light throughout the church, which was also seen to emanate from above the building. Millions of pilgrims continue to visit such shrines that echo reminders of the ancient annual processions and rites of the Mystery Cults. Every year on May 13 and October 13, commemorations of the Fatima apparitions take place and more than a million people gather at the Sanctuary of Our Lady of Fátima in Portugal.

Sightings of Christ following the Crucifixion are recorded in the New Testament, and they include, Mary's vision of Jesus at the empty tomb (John 20:11-18), and the appearance of Jesus to the disciples gathered in Jerusalem (Luke 24:36-43). Many Christian mystics have also had visions of Christ. In 1208, St. Juliana of Liege was told by Christ to institute a solemn commemoration for the Holy Eucharist as the Body of Christ. In 1624, upon hearing of these visions, Pope Urban IV granted this request and declared the feast day of *Corpus Christi*. Saint

Catherine of Sienna experienced similar visions in 1336 and again in 1370 when she was instructed to leave her life of solitude and work for the reformation of the clergy, which resulted in her becoming one of the few female Doctors of the Church.

Some mystics claim to experience physical manifestations. Most notably, St. Francis of Assisi and Saint Padre Pio, were both associated with the *stigmata,* translated to mean marks on the feet or hands that resemble the crucifixion wounds of Christ. Padre Pio's case was investigated for over fifty years, but there was no medical diagnosis that could explain the mystery of his bleeding wounds that remained free of infection.

The Spanish poet and monk of the Carmelite order, St. John of the Cross, was divinely guided during his deep mediation practice, and subsequently wrote a full treatise on mystic theology known as, *The Dark Night of the Soul,* which told of the transcendent path to finding God:

> In order to arrive at having pleasure in everything,
> Desire to have pleasure in nothing.
> In order to arrive at possessing everything,
> Desire to possess nothing.
> In order to arrive at being everything,
> Desire to be nothing.[46]

Following death, his relics were believed to bare mythological images, including that of Christ at the Crucifixion, the Blessed Mary, and certain other saints. For much of his lifetime, St. John of the Cross was closely associated with St. Teresa of Avila.

St. Teresa was a Carmelite nun, who suffered from ill health and repeatedly recited a prayer that provided guidance on achieving a state of recollection and union with God. She started to experience transcendent states of calmness, even though her symptoms steadily worsened. At one point, she lapsed into a coma and was so close to death that a grave was prepared, but she eventually recovered consciousness. Experiencing a near-death is common in the lives of Christian mystics. Elizabeth Petroff writes:

> A surprising number of biographies and autobiographies tell of an apparent dying, often when a teenager, of being taken for dead and perhaps even put in a coffin but then miraculously coming back to life, often with an explicit visionary message for the world. This happened to Christina Mirabilis, Catherine of Sienna, Madalena Beuthler, St. Teresa of Avila, and Julian of Norwich.[47]

The excruciating pain St. Teresa suffered continued over a twelve-year period and appeared to act as a pivotal trigger for her numerous visions.

As St. Teresa deepened her prayer practice, she started to receive 'favors' from God. In this deep state of contemplation, she experienced mystical unions with the Almighty and heard a voice giving her instructions on how to evolve her spirituality. During some of these visions, she described leaving her physical body and ascending to heaven and being given further revelations. St. Teresa, like many other mystics, found it difficult to describe the ineffable transcendent quality of theses states, but she detailed what took place in order to help her fellow nuns resolve their difficulties with prayer. She also began to have painful convulsive spasms that racked her entire body, but viewed this intense physical discomfort to be a sign of further purification, bringing her closer to God and enabling a 'peak' vision during which, she imagined a crystal castle with seven mansions, symbolizing the soul's journey to its final resting place. E. Allison Pears writes, "The figure is used to describe the whole course of the mystical life—the soul's progress from the First Mansion to the Seventh and its transformation from an imperfect and sinful creature in the Bride of the Spiritual

Marriage."[48] St. Teresa perceived the key to opening the castle door was obtained through prayer, devotion, and a pious life.

St. Teresa believed that fully merging with God required relinquishing all attachments to the outer world, and she conveyed her meaning in the metaphor of the life-cycle of a silkworm, saying, "When it is full-grown, then . . . it starts to spin its silk and to build the house in which it is to die. This house may be understood here to mean Christ."[49] She further writes, "Let the silkworm die—let it die, as in fact it does when it has completed the work which it was created to do. Then we shall see God and shall be ourselves completely hidden in His greatness as is this little worm in its cocoon."[50] The death of the silkworm results in the birth of the butterfly, which could fly to the seventh mansion, symbolizing complete union of the unfettered soul with God.

William James again reminds us that on an intellectual basis, it is possible to narrow such a mystical vision into a field of pathological states, but this does little to expand knowledge of altered states of consciousness purported to be experienced during an ecstatic divine union. He writes:

> This overcoming of all the usual barriers between the individual and the Absolute is the great mystic achievement. In mystic states we both become one with the Absolute and we become aware of our oneness. This is the everlasting and triumphant mystical tradition, hardly altered by difference of clime or creed. In Hinduism, in Neoplatonism, in Sufism, in Christian mysticism, in Whitmanism, we find the same recurring note, so that there is about mystical utterances an eternal unanimity . . . .[51]

St. Teresa's spasms and convulsions ceased after the revelation of the seventh mansion, indicating attainment of a higher state of awareness. Her mystical visions from the medieval Christian era, symbolizing otherworldly projection and unification with God, were shared by other well-known saints. They also contained similar characteristics to religious practices of both the ancient Egyptians, who sought to become 'one' with Osiris and the early Greeks Mystery rites that attempted to experience a total union with the divine realm of the gods.

Linked to both mystical visions and contemporary NDEs is the urge to expand a spiritual practice. Near-death survivors may also experience changes in values leading to a more contemplative life, similar to that of mystics and reflecting a heightened state of spiritual understanding and maturity. Ring's research into personality and value changes following an NDE reveals lessened emphasis on material values and "an increased appreciation of solitude."[52]

St. Teresa believed that earthly life is a preparation for the eternal life of the soul and that those who fully understood this concept lose all fear of death. She writes: "the two lighted candles join and become one; the falling rain becomes merged in the river. There is complete transformation, ineffable and perfect peace; no higher state is conceivable, save that of the Beatific Vision for the life to come."[53] Many near-death experiencers come to share divine her wisdom and insight.

Our mystical inheritance reflects teachings of world religious traditions and the common characteristic is the narration of stories and metaphors that are shaped by the mythic imagination. The intrinsic value of such mystical experiences, reach far beyond the personal and can be interpreted to reveal profound insights into the meaning of existence. Many near-death researchers discover a direct link between mystical visions and the NDE and Ring's *Omega* research led him to state:

> NDEs, in my view, represent a brief but powerful thrust into a higher state of consciousness . . . . In this respect, the NDE resembles a full-blown mystical experience and—this is the key—the *effects* of that experience *also resemble those that stem*

> *from a mystical experience.* A journey into higher consciousness, I am saying, has effects that are independent of the way it is attained.[54]

All religions contain mystical seeds for potential awakening, in which the central affirmation of death and rebirth results in liberation from the narcissistic false sense of Self. There are many examples and indications that humans are capable of accessing transcendent states that give rise to visionary epiphanies. For many indigenous cultures, coming-of-age rituals and initiations also involve fasting and staying out in Nature until such visions manifest.

The altered state of consciousness manifesting in the dreaming state is universal. In the nocturnal dream world, a bridge links the conscious to the unconscious realms, freeing the imagination from the limitations of everyday reality. With closed eyes, we can all experience *second* sight, revealing archetypal symbols and images that extend far beyond waking perceptions, based on rationality and logic. Dreams reunite us with our essential original nature that is buried in the collective unconscious, but manifests symbolically in the dreaming state to link modern-day consciousness to that of early ancestors.

In many ancient cultures, dreams facilitated an ongoing transcendent dialogue between mortal beings and the immortal gods, providing guidance and divination. Dream images were alive and brought direct healing that manifested spontaneously into consciousness, resulting in change or transformation. For early Egyptians, dreams played an important part in the Mystery Rites of Osiris. After initiates had spent three days in mourning, celebrating the resurrection of Osiris was preceded by "the night of sleeping." Mojsov writes, "During that night, the 'Sem Priest'—the son of Osiris—slept on a low couch in front of the god's statue in the Golden House—the temple sanctuary. He called upon the soul of his father, hovering in the night air. . . . In his dream, he encountered the soul, caught it like a bird, and instilled it into the statue. In the morning he announced that the buried god had come back to life."[55] Further dream gods and goddesses, including Isis and Thoth, also had such temples and those wishing to receive a cure or divine guidance would be plunged into holy water for purification and then sleep in the temple, described as being a type of 'sanatorium.' Malign forces were often perceived to cause illness and so it was common practice for the priests, interceding for various deities, to invoke the healing energies through spells and incantations.

Dreams were also an important aspect of early Babylonian religious practice. The goddess of dreams, Mamu, had a shrine in Balawat. In order to invoke the healing power of Mamu, the giver of life, supplicants would offer prayers and ask for favorable dream omens:

> Reveal thyself unto me and let me see a favorable dream,
> May the dream that I dream be favorable,
> May the dream that I dream be true,
> May Mamu, the goddess of dreams stand by my head;
> Let me enter E-Sagila, the temple of the Gods, the house of life.[56]

It was, however, in early Greek civilization that dream temples and the incubation of dreams flourished most profusely. Disciples of the Orphic cult and the Greek philosopher, Pythagoras, deemed dreams to signify communion with divine divinities and healing sanctuaries spread over Greece for at least a thousand years. In 600 BCE, the main sanctuary was at Epidaurus and dedicated to Asklepios, the god of medicine and divination. Later, an extended amphitheater was built that could hold up to fourteen thousand participants. After ritual purification, initiates waited in small sleeping chambers hoping to have dreams in which Asklepios would appear and indicate the cure for their particular malady.

Such healings took place spontaneously through invoking imagery of the god encountered in the dream, and this archetypal energy can still be accessed in the dreaming state of modern-day individuals. James Hillman writes, "The healing dream is an Askeplian ritual of cure through sleeping within the temple precinct . . . . The cure was God's presence in person, and healing did not require translation of images into concepts....These figures are imaginal statements....These persons continue to appear in our dreams."[57]

Not only do the image and healing properties of Asklepios linger in the collective unconscious, but the beliefs of the ancient cult that existed for over eight hundred years, still manifest in the consciousness of dedicated contemporary healers. Thomas E. Gaddis writes, "The modern doctor has a snake symbol of Esculapius bolted to the license plate of his car. His prescription pad carries at its top the eye of Horus. In ancient times and today, the doctor addresses himself to the problem of how to get the recuperative powers of the person into motion."[58]

The Greek god, Amphiaraus, was also a dream divinity. Associated with Asklepios, he was given healing powers by Zeus and was considered to be an expert in dream divination. Pausanias described a healing temple of Amphiaraus that bore a white marble statue of the god and writes that Amphiaraus was dedicated to dream enlightenment:

> My opinion is that Amphiaraus devoted himself most to the exposition of dreams. It is manifest that, when his divinity was established, it was a dream oracle that he set up. One who came to consult Amphiaraus is wont first to purify himself. The mode of purification is to sacrifice to the god, and they sacrifice not only to him but also to all those whose names are on the altar. And when all these things have first been done, they sacrifice a ram, and, spreading the skin under them, go to

sleep and await enlightenment in a dream.[59]

The altered state of dream consciousness was also documented and illustrated in Jacob's dream of a ladder that reached from the Earth to the Heavens from which angels ascended and descended (*Genesis* 28-12). The Buddha received his awakening after falling into a deep sleep and having series of dreams, which appeared to signify that he was soon to be enlightened. Such an awakening accessed through the dreaming state, results from mythological symbolism emanating from the unconscious.

The dawning of the Cartesian era, spearheaded by René Descartes, excluded numinous dream images of early civilizations. Instead, a form of sterile objectivity involved abandoning all unnecessary spiritual symbolism and the sense of interconnectedness with a wider cosmos. However, this new intellectual vision was clouded by Descartes' disturbing nightmares that were full of images invoking feelings of dread and anxiety. He translated these dreams to signify that a scientific mathematical approach would re-vision an understanding of Nature. Descartes was not suggesting a form of sacred geometry, as used by the ancient Egyptians to communicate with the gods, but rather an intellectual standpoint in which Nature was to become alienated from its divine sacred origins. The dreams Descartes experienced may have been prophetic, because the result of this 'new philosophy' gradually revealed the terrifying impoverishment of the soul, due to lack of imagination. However, through reconnecting with symbolic wisdom available in the dreaming state, this rift can be reconciled.

Jung had many prophetic dreams revealing images of death. One night, he dreamed of an entity that bore a resemblance to his wife. A woman, wearing a white robe interfaced with strange black symbols, was floating out of a deep pit. As he awoke, Jung realized that it was 3:00 a.m. He sensed the dream signified death and a few hours later, he received the news that his wife's cousin had died at exactly that time.[60] Shortly before his death, Jung was to recount a dream containing alchemical symbolism of immortality. Marie-Louise von Franz writes:

> He saw a great round stone in a high place, a barren square, and on it were engraved the words: "and this shall be a sign unto you of wholeness and oneness." Then he saw many vessels in the night in an open square and a quadrangle of trees whose roots reached around the earth and enveloped him and among the roots golden threads were glittering.[61]

Symbolic images of impending death can also often signify a journey, such as taking a train or boat. Dreams may also impart images on the possible evolution of the soul following transition. Jung had such a dream after the death of his wife, Emma. He awoke convinced that he had spent the day with her in Provence, where she was continuing her Grail legend studies. From this and other similar dreams, he considered the theory that humans tend to psychically imagine that the souls of departed loved ones continue to individuate, and this is beneficial to the living.[62]

Jung concludes that although there is no irrefutable proof of an afterlife, images and symbolism contained in universal dreams centered on death that reconcile the clash of opposites—life and death—set humans the metaphysical task of seeking enlightenment. He thought this task could only be accomplished through remythologizing symbolic motifs arising from unconscious archetypal realms, which appear to signify that the 'land of the dead' exists in the psychic realms. Jung also observed that Christian believers often lamented no longer 'hearing' the voice of God, as in previous eras. Even though the Catholic Church accepted *somnia a Deo missa* (dreams emanating from God), the faithful no longer remembered that the words of God are mainly heard in the unconscious realms of visions and dreams.[63]

In *The Miracle of Death*, Betty J. Kovacs describes a poignant journey through the realm of dreams and visions that led to her own awakening, following the death of her son, Pisti:

> The symbolic... dreams, precognitive experiences, synchronistic events, and waking visions, flooded our lives during a ten-year period from 1991 to 2001, from the death of our son to the completion of this book. However, during the two years prior to 1991, my husband, our son, and I experienced dreams and visions, we later realized, helped to prepare us for events to come. There were two earlier dreams—our son's dream of his death before he was twelve and my dreams of his death a few months before his birth—that also revealed their place in this living puzzle. Our son Pisti, the girl he loved, Jenny, my husband Istvan, and I were later to discover that we were all participants in a reality that was far larger and more inclusive than we could have imagined before we entered this most unusual journey.[64]

Such prophetic dreams are often regarded as 'rehearsals' of what can later transpire into reality. They are usually clothed in meaningful symbolism that gives voice to something that would otherwise be inexplicable—life and death.

Kovacs' dreams, visions, and synchronicities transcended the barriers of space and time and brought a mythological guide, the Egyptian jackal-headed Anubis, who had a central role in ancient death rituals. She describes a dream set in an Egyptian museum, where Anubis made his presence felt:

> As I turn towards my right and begin to look at some of the artifacts in cases. I suddenly become aware of the jackal figure standing to my right. He begins to explain the artifacts. He tells me that I can learn about Egyptology and the ancient world through books, but he can tell me everything. I don't need books. With this, I look at him and ask, "Who are you?"

> He then dissolves before my eyes. A panel of black wood appears in his place. Its very essence is a blackness that appears to be breathing. I realize this is a living force. A voice answers me, "The All, the Void." [65]

Anubis, known as "The Opener of the Way," guarded the underworld and acted as an intermediary between the cycles of life and death. He assisted Isis to bring Osiris back to life and so humans hoped he would restore their bodies in a similar way. Priests at ancient Egyptian funerary rituals would wear jackal masks to invoke the powers of Anubis as a transition guide. The image of Anubis was fully alive and made his presence felt, as he led Kovacs on a journey through the darkness of grief and the archetypal dimensions of the dream world, which ultimately resulted in a transformation. During this symbolic mythic pilgrimage, she realized that it was possible to imagine a unity that transcends sensory-intellectual consciousness.

Vegetation symbolism from ancient myths can also still emanate in modern-day dream consciousness. Marie-Louise von Franz narrates the dream of a man, who, shortly before he died, described being in a beautiful garden with an unusual kind of grass, and seeing a dancing green man formed of grass. She suggests the green man embodies a vegetation spirit. "Whatever this mythical figure means in itself, it has something to do with death and with life's further blossoming. The . . . dancing man must also represent such a May King, an image of life and death symbolized by vegetation."[66]

Transpersonal experience arising from the dreaming state can enable connection between the material and mythological realms, although this ability may well be dismissed by Western culture, as not being ontologically genuine. However, Kovacs earlier dream demonstrates how communication with mythic deities and experiences of alternate dimensions exist in the boundless world of dreams. Grof writes:

> These experiences involve deities and demons from various cultures, abodes from the Beyond such as heavens and paradises, and legendary or fairy-tale sequences. For example, we can experience communication with Jesus, Virgin Mary, or the Devil; have a shattering encounter with the Hindu goddess Kali; or identify with the dancing Shiva. We can also visit various mythological realms, such as the paradise of the Aztec rain god Thaloc . . . or one of the Buddhist hot hells. Even these episodes can impart accurate new information about religious symbolism and mythical motifs that were previously unknown to the person involved.[67]

Dreams, such as Jung's featuring his deceased wife, do not automatically result in a lessening of grief and anguish when someone dies. Rather, they give an inner understanding that extends beyond a limited outer conception of death. The imagery from the NDE also helps change perception of death as being more than the cessation of consciousness.

Near-death imagery can be accessed through deep meditation and contemplation. For the mystic, this type of practice acts as a gateway to transcend consciousness. The Buddhist Vispassana (meaning insight) meditation can include the sensation of an out-of-body state and an encounter with light, which are both characteristics of the NDE. Altered states that give rise to this type of imagery are also recorded in Zen Buddhism. In a Zen teaching on how to prepare for death, Rev. Master Joyu-Kennett describes sacred motifs and symbolism she encountered while in a deep state of meditation when she was seriously ill, and close to death. She passed through a tunnel and experienced several universal components of a near-death journey, including a life review and passing through a tunnel into divine light:

> Absolute blackness, the great darkness of this seeming tunnel

> is impenetrable. Directly ahead of me is the great iron pillar, penetrating the universe. From a great distance a bright light flashes, hitting the pillar. This is the road to heaven. I have said no to the abyss, cleansing my heart of its past wrongdoing; I can go into this bright, beautiful light.[68]

In all the examples of altered states of consciousness described in this chapter, a transcendent susceptibility appears to be activated and reveals mystical insights, resulting in fresh perspective of the deeper spiritual Self. Similar psychic realms and revelations are shared in a near-death journey, as the core NDE provides the experiencer with a new perception of this previously unconscious realm.

Notes

1. Charles Tart, *Waking Up* (Boston: Shambhala, 1987), 219.
2. William James, *Varieties of Religious Experience: A Study in Human Nature* (Charleston: Bibliobazaar, 2007), 336.
3. Ibid., 338-39.
4. Goldberg, B. Z. *A History of Sex in Ritual Religion and Human Behavior* (New York: Citadel, 1974), 180.
5. W. F. Otto, *Dionysus: Myth and Cult*, tr. Robert B. Palmer (Bloomington, Indiana University Press, 1965), 140.
6. *The Homeric Hymns*, trans. Charles Boer (Putnam: Spring, 1970), 17.
7. C. G. Jung, *The Archetypes and the Collective Unconscious*, para 249.
8. Rainer Maria Rilke, *In Praise of Mortality*, trans and ed. Anita Barrows and Joanna Macy (New York: Riverhead, 2005), XXV1, 105.
9. Ibid., 7.
10. Joseph Henderson, "Ancient Myths and Modern Man," *Man and His Symbols*, 134.

11. Hermann Broch, *The Death of Virgil*, trans. Jean Starr Untermeyer (London: Vintage, 1977), 135.
12. Michael Grosso, "The Archetype of Death and Enlightenment." *The Near-Death Experience A Reader*, ed. Lee W. Bailey and Jenny Yates (New York: Routledge, 1996) 141.
13. See Fritz Graf and Sarah Isles Johnston, *Ritual Texts for the Afterlife: Orpheus and the Bacchic Gold Tablets* (London: Routledge, 2007), Tablet 2, 98-99.
14. Rainer Maria Rilke, *In Praise of Mortality*, 77.
15. Kenneth Ring, *Life at Death*, 62.
16. Raymond Moody, *Life After Life* (New York: Bantam, 1988), 30.
17. *The Homeric Hymns*, iii.
18. Carl A. Ruck, *Sacred Mushrooms of the Goddess: Secrets of Eleusis* (Berkeley: Ronin, 2006), 14.
19. Huston Smith, *Cleansing the Doors of Perception: The Religious Significance of Etheogenic Plants and Chemicals* (Boulder: Sentient, 2003), 18.
20. Carl Kerényi, *Eleusis*, 47.
21. Kenneth Ring, "Implications for Human Evolution and Planetary Transformation," *The Near-Death Experience A Reader*, 190.
22. Discussed in Elisabeth Kübler-Ross, *The Wheel of Life*, 190.
23. Huston Smith, *Cleansing the Doors of Perception*, 46.
24. Stanislav Grof, *The Ultimate Journey: Consciousness and the Mystery of Death* (Ben Lomond: Multidisciplinary Association for Psychedelic Studies, 1976), 139.
25. Walter Pahnke and William Richards, "Implications of LSD and Experimental Mysticism." *Journal of Religious Health, Vol. 5* (1966), 175-208.
26. William James, *Varieties of Religious Experience*, 339.
27. Ibid., 340.
28. Huston Smith, *Cleansing the Doors of Perception*, 11.
29. Ibid., 74.

30. Stanislav Grof, *The Ultimate Journey*, 54.
31. Huston Smith, *Cleansing the Doors of Perception*, 100-101.
32. Stanislav Grof, *Books of the Dead*, 29.
33. Aldous Huxley, *The Doors of Perception & Heaven*, 73.
34. Larry Hagman, *Hello Darlin'* (New York: Simon & Schuster, 2001), 139-40).
35. Bojana Mojsov, *Osiris Death and Afterlife of a God*, 4.
36. Larry Hagman, *Hello Darlin,'* 140.
37. Aldous Huxley, *The Doors of Perception*, 84.
38. Carl Kerényi, *Dionysos: Archetypal Image of Indestructible Life*, trans. Ralph Manheim (Princeton: Princeton University Press, 1976), 15.
39. Thich Nhat Hanh, *Old Path White Clouds* (Berkeley, Parallax Press, 1991), 444.
40. *Gospel of Sri Ramakrishna*, trans. Swami Nikhilananda (New York: Ramakrishna-Vivekananda Center, 1985), 14.
41. "Livestock," *The Qur'an*, tr. T. B. Irving (San Francisco, 2004), 97-98.
42. Seyed Hossein Nasr, ed., *Islamic Spirituality* (New York: Crossroad, 1987), 78.
43. Ibid., 79.
44. Jalal Al-Din Rumi, Michael Green, Coleman Barks, *The Illuminated Rumi* (New York: Broadway Books, 1997), 23.
45. Thomas Merton, *The Ascent to Truth* (Orlando: Mariner, 2002) 149.
46. St. John of the Cross, *Ascent of Mount Carmel*, ed. Henry L. Carrigan Jr., (Brewster, MA, 2002), 38.
47. Elizabeth Alvilda Petroff, *Medieval Women's Literature* (New York: Oxford University Press, 1968), 40.
48. E. Allison Peers, "The Mansions," int. *Interior Castle*. By St. Teresa of Avila (New York: Dover, 1946), 4.
49. St. Teresa of Avila, *Interior Castle*, 71.
50. Ibid., 71-72.
51. William James, *Varieties of Religious Experience*, 367.

52. Kenneth Ring, *Life at Death*, 144.
53. St. Teresa of Avila, *Interior Castle*, 6.
54. Kenneth Ring, *Heading Toward Omega* (New York: William Morrow, 1984), 170.
55. Bojana Mojsov, *Osiris Death and Afterlife of a God*, 52.
56. See Walter Addison Jayne, *The Healing Gods of Ancient Civilizations* (New York: Yale University Press, 1962), 101-102.
57. James Hillman, *Re-Visioning Psychology* (New York: Harper Perennial, 1976), 34.
58. Thomas E. Gaddis, int. *The Healing Gods of Ancient Civilizations*, by Walter Addison Jayne, vi.
59. Pausanias, *Attica* 1: 34-35.
60. C. G. Jung, *Memories*, 302-03.
61. Marie-Louise von Franz, *Time, Rhythm and Repose* (London: Thames & Hudson, 1979), 287.
62. See C. G. Jung, *Memories*, 309.
63. See C. G. Jung, "Approaching the Unconscious." *Man and His Symbols*, eds. C. G. Jung and M-L von Franz (New York, 1968), 92.
64. Betty J. Kovacs, *The Miracle of Death* (Claremont: Kamlak Center, 2003), 8.
65. Ibid., 44.
66. Marie-Louise von Franz, *On Dreams and Death*, 25.
67. Stanislav Grof, *The Ultimate Journey*, 141.
68. Rev. Master Jiyu Kennet, *How to Grow a Lotus Blossom* (Mount Shasta: Shasta Abbey 1993), 21.

Chapter 4

Contemporary Near-Death Experiences

Let your mind start a journey thru a strange new world. Leave all thoughts of the world you knew before. Let your soul take you where you long to be.
Erich Fromm

Research into what could take place as an individual encounters the threshold of death was initially undertaken seriously by Albert Heim, a Swiss geologist. Heim became interested in the subjective dying process after having had an almost fatal climbing accident in the Alps. For many years, he collected stories from those who had been involved in similar life-threatening situations, and presented his findings in the paper, *Remarks on Fatal Falls,* published in 1892. This comprehensive investigation analyzed central archetypal components of the near-death journey that include: a life review, hearing glorious music, and sensing feelings of peace and tranquility that transcended pain and anxiety. Heim describes his experience:

> I saw my whole past life take place in many images, as though on a stage some distance from me. I saw myself as the chief character in the performance. Everything was transfigured as though by a heavenly light and everything was beautiful without grief, without anxiety, and without pain. The memory of tragic experiences I had was clear but not saddening. I felt no conflict or strife; conflict had been transmuted into love. Elevated and harmonious thoughts dominated and united the individual images, and like magnificent music a divine calm swept through my soul. I became even more surrounded by a

> blue Heaven with delicate roseate and violet cloudlets. I swept into it painlessly and softly and I saw that now I was falling freely through the air and that under me a snowfield lay waiting . . . then I heard a dull thud and my fall was over.[1]

An important similarity between Heim's narrative and medieval near-death stories exists, as both describe the life review as being involuntary and an external projection of inner contents such as, past actions, words, and thoughts. Heim's personal experience and other similar accounts suggested that those facing impending death often underwent a mystical transformation, which registered in the memory as a profound and euphoric transfiguration. Although interest was generated by Heim's research, the eternal archetypal qualities of NDEs would not be brought to the forefront of public attention until decades later.

Swiss psychiatrist, Elisabeth Kübler-Ross, a pioneer in the field of thanatology, became aware that many of her patients related similar stories of what they experienced when having been declared clinically dead. During the 1970s, she interviewed approximately 20,000 people from diverse cultures and religious traditions, including Native Americans, Muslims, Protestants, and Eskimos and detailed her findings that determined there were four distinct phases attached to the dying process. In the first, individuals left their physical bodies, regardless of the manner of death, and could clearly recollect what had taken place at the point of dying. In the second, an after-death state occurred, described as being one of energy or spirit. Phase three consisted of being met by a spirit guide and entering a tunnel or crossing some kind of a barrier, such as a body of water or gate, and seeing a bright light in the distance. An overwhelming sense of unconditional love was also experienced, accompanied by the feeling of returning 'home.' During the fourth phase, encounters with a Higher Power or heavenly deity took place, giving rise to ineffable feelings of unity and 'wholeness.' Following a life review, NDErs were then instructed to return to their physical bodies and expressed reluctance to leave the blissful state they found themselves in.[2]

Kübler-Ross concludes such narratives are authentic descriptions of what takes place at the moment of death, as consciousness appears to separate from the physical body:

> Not only were we told that the death experience was free from pain; people reported that they did not want to come back. After being met by loved ones, or guides, they traveled to a place that was so loving and comforting that they did not want to return. They had to be talked into it. "It's not time," was something practically everyone heard.[3]

Widespread interest in the phenomenon grew after the publication of *Life After Life* in which author, Dr. Raymond Moody, detailed numerous accounts of what he was to term as being the "near-death experience." Moody became interested in the phenomenon after hearing a talk given by a respected doctor and psychiatrist, George Ritchie, who made reference to his NDE. Over time, Moody collected at least 150 similar stories, some of which were referred to him by doctors, who had resuscitated patients claiming to have had a near-death experience. He subsequently established fifteen components that frequently occurred during the dying process: *Ineffability, Hearing the News, Feelings of Peace and Quiet, The Noise, The Dark Tunnel, Out of the Body, Meeting Others, The Being of Light, The Review, The Border or Limit, Coming Back, Telling Others, Effects on Lives, New Views of Death, and Corroboration.*[4] Moody then compiled a composite of the NDE that incorporated these core principles.

Dr. Kenneth Ring expanded Moody's work, using modern research techniques to ascertain the demographics of the NDE. In 1980, he published his findings in "The Connecticut Study." Using Moody's earlier blueprint, he interviewed over 100 NDErs, who described their personal experiences and then answered probing questions in order to corroborate that the same central characteristics took place. This study provided a more in-depth and exclusive assimilation of the core components and stages, which Ring noted as being; *peace and the sense of well-being, body separation, entering the darkness, seeing the light, and entering the light.* Ring's model of the NDE showed many parallels and similarities to that of Moody's. He stressed that his findings were not presented to consciously validate Moody's previous research, but stemmed *"from the (apparent) extraordinary similarity between his findings and mine."*[5]

Dr. Michael Sabom was also intrigued by Moody's findings, but was far more skeptical and viewed NDEs as being a collection of stories, rather than providing a scientific line of inquiry. However, he later writes:

> Perhaps the most startling discovery I made through my research was that, as many people come close to death, their essence, or spirit, actually seemed to leave their body . . . . These people . . . saw details of their resuscitation that they could not have otherwise seen . . . . In many cases I was able to confirm the patient's testimony with medical records and with hospital staff.[6]

One of the most influential cases that came to Sabom's attention, detailed in *Light and Death*, was that of Pam Reynolds, who according to a clinical definition of death recorded no vital signs in a brain operation that completely drained the blood from her head. This case is important, as it not only defines the state of death, but also because it measured so highly on the NDE scale.

As chief surgeon Dr. Spetzler exposed her brain to remove a potentially lethal aneurysm, deeply anaesthetized Reynolds described hearing the pneumatic cutting blade entering her skull. "As I listened to the sound, I felt it was pulling me out of the top of my head . . . . I remember seeing several things in the operating room when I was looking down. It was the most aware that I think that I have ever been in my life . . . . It was brighter and more focused and clearer than normal vision."[7] As the operation progressed, the surgeon realized that hypothermic cardiac arrest would be required, and as her brain waves began to flatten and extinguish in her dying heart, and her body temperature dropped to 60 degrees on the Fahrenheit register, Reynolds's body was tilted upwards and the blood completely drained from it. It was at this point that her near-death experience deepened and she describes being pulled into a tunnel:

> At some point very early in the tunnel vortex I became aware of my grandmother calling me. But I didn't hear her call me with my ears . . . . It was clearer hearing than with my ears . . . .The feeling was that she wanted me to come to her, so I continued with no fear down the shaft. It's a dark shaft that I went through, and at the end there was this very little tiny pinpoint of light that kept getting bigger and bigger and bigger. I noticed that as I began to discern different figures in the light—and they were all covered with light, that they *were* light, and had light permeating all around them—they began to form shapes I could recognize and understand.[8]

At this point, the operation had been successfully concluded and surgeons started to replace the blood and restart the heart. As her body began to come back to life, it could also have coincided with Reynolds experiencing images of deceased relatives feeding and nurturing her:

> They were not doing this through my mouth, like with food, but they were nourishing me with something. The only way I know how to put it is something sparkly. Sparkles is the image

> that I get. I definitely recall the sensation of being nurtured and fed and being made strong.[9]

A short while later, Reynolds's heart stopped again and two defibrillator paddles were placed on her chest to revive her failing heart. The second jolt was successful and the monitor registered a normal heartbeat. In speaking of reentry into her body, she describes being accompanied back through the tunnel by a deceased uncle, and upon seeing the state of her body, was afraid. As her uncle pushed, she felt, "The body was pulling and the tunnel was pushing."[10] This description that sounds like the birthing process, as the fetus is pushed along and through the narrow birth canal, led to Reynolds finding herself back in her body. This sensation of rebirthing features importantly in Grof's psychedelic research into altered states of consciousness.

The Pam Reynolds case that contains many classic elements of the NDE—the dark tunnel, coming into the light, meeting deceased relatives, and being told to return to the physical body—had a great impact on Sabom, who found the whole thing incredulous. On obtaining a copy of Spetzler's report of the operation from the Barrow Neurological Institute in Phoenix, Sabom was astounded to see the surgeon corroborated the story. By modern-day criteria death is said to take place with the loss of brain activity, which was certainly the case with Pam Reynolds, whose brain was ascertained to be 'dead' according to the three clinical tests that determine this state. On interviewing Reynolds, Sabom discovered that she had the deepest NDE compiled in his "Atlanta Study"—her experience scored a depth of 27.0. This total was based on a scale set up by fellow NDE researcher, Dr. Bruce Greyson, to measure how many core components were present in a near-death event—the average NDE scored around 13.3.

While controversy exists in determining if in fact Pam Reynolds was dead, as she subsequently revived, Dr. Spetzler writes, "If you would examine the patient from a clinical perspective during that hour, that patient by all definition would be dead. At this point there is no brain activity, no blood going through the brain. Nothing, nothing, nothing."[11]

Sabom's years of investigation led him to alter his previous conviction that the NDE was a near-death event, into believing that the phenomenon constituted of an after-death spiritual experience. He also concurred with Moody's suggestion that the NDE forms a definite pattern.

During the 1980s, following a transformational NDE, Psychologist, Margot Grey, subsequently carried out a cross-cultural investigation. Using Ring's five stages as a basis for her comparative study, Grey interviewed thirty-two British, and nine American near-death survivors. Although this was a relatively small sampling, her findings still concurred with those of Ring's earlier study. Grey further observed that both American and English subjects used very similar phrases to describe these vivid experiences, which seemed indelibly imprinted within the psyche. The words that most commonly expressed the transcendent mystical encounter, included: *peace, happiness, beauty, and love*. Grey writes, "The narratives all emphasize that the surroundings encountered are of supernal loveliness and surpass anything that can be imagined on this plane of existence. The implications are, therefore, that the journey is much the same for nearly everyone who undertakes it."[12]

In 1995, Dr. Peter Fenwick, a Fellow of the Royal College of Psychiatrists and leading near-death researcher in the United Kingdom, compiled his findings after interviewing over three hundred NDE survivors. He was greatly interested in the cross-cultural aspects, and so included the testimony of both Indian and Chinese participants in his study. Fenwick assessed the consistency, symbolic, and spiritual implications of the NDE and came to the following conclusions:

> Everywhere we find the concept that between life and death there is a symbolic divide, a border to be crossed which forms a point of no return. Some features (the tunnel, the feelings of peace and joy), seem to figure more often in Western experiences. Others (the life review) seem to be more predominant in America and China . . . .The common ground between cultures and between individuals is that the NDE seems to be an "awakening" experience, often arousing a sense of spirituality and a stimulus for personal development.[13]

Near-death researchers each have their own particular lens of viewing and translating data. For some, the phenomenon has strong mythic religious connotations, which are beyond scientific evaluation. Sabom writes, "Thousands of carefully documented testimonies speak to the near-death experience as being a spiritual experience perceived to be both 'real' and 'otherworldly.' Much of the content of the experience is spiritual."[14] Sabom parallels NDEs with biblical references, such as Job's description of the soul leaving the body swiftly at death (Job: 14-2). He also interprets religious imagery to personify a meeting with the projection of invisible God-like qualities, rather than an actual face-to-face encounter, although he concurs that it is impossible to determine the mystery of how these revelations occur.

NDE accounts are also consistent with myths of reincarnation, found in Eastern religions, including Hinduism. Although this diverse difference in beliefs suggests a dualism existing in beliefs of an afterlife state, in which traditional Western theories view the soul as returning to a spiritual realm and God, as opposed to a continuum of the matter bound life-death cycle of Eastern philosophy, *liberation*, and *reunification* still form the basis of these varying anomalies. Reconciliation was also symbolized in ancient myth when, following death, the earth-bound matter and freed spiritual essence become reunited, modeled in the Egyptian concept of the *ba* and the *ka* soul.

Mythologies of reincarnation suggest that beyond one's personal history, there exists a 'collective' identity, known to reincarnationists as an *oversoul*, which embodies an expanded form of consciousness integrating the experience of individual life. Research indicates that NDE survivors are more open to evaluating the concept of reincarnation.

The image of a living hell and punishment for living an unjust life are fear-provoking human imaginings. Several NDE researchers include testimonies describing such a negative event. Grey writes:

> A negative experience is usually characterized by feelings of extreme fear or panic. Other elements can include emotional and mental anguish, extending to states of the utmost desperation. People report being lost and helpless and there is often an intense feeling of loneliness, during this period coupled with a great sense of desolation. The environment is described as being dark and gloomy, or it can be barren and hostile. People sometimes report finding themselves on the brink of a pit or at the edge of an abyss, and state that they need to marshal all their inner resources to save themselves from plunging over the edge.[15]

Rare hellish NDEs contain frightening archetypal images, resulting in sensations of dread, loneliness, discomfort, alienation, and extremes in temperatures. Dr. Maurice Rawlings resuscitated a patient suffering a cardiac arrest, who informed him that he had experienced terrifying visions of hell. Rawlings, a non-believer in an afterlife, was so struck by the impact of this man's NDE that he started to collect his own data on the phenomenon. As a result, he believes, "More patients who recovered from a serious illness say there is a heaven and a hell."[16] Bruce Greyson and Nancy Evans Bush, both pioneers in near-death research, also interviewed fifty people reporting similar experiences, and they concluded that distressing experiences fell into three categories. The first comprises of a hostile experience that can resolve into a more peaceful one; the second leads the individual to sense feelings of 'nothingness' and despair, and the third contains terrifying imagery, often accompanied by sounds of acute distress. Both Greyson and Bush suggest parallels to the imagery manifesting in medieval near-death journeys investigated by Carol Zaleski in *Otherworld Journeys*.[17]

Although negative NDEs are the subject of much debate, there is a possible archetypal explanation that suggests entering the 'shadow' side of the collective unconscious. This theory will be expanded upon in a further chapter. However, the main point in relation to both positive and negative near-death events is the experience itself and that the 'deceased' experiences *another* realm of consciousness at death.

Moody's initial research opened the floodgates to further investigation and generated a huge tide of public interest, because NDEs address the subject of death that is a taboo in many areas of society, both psychologically and culturally. The two contrasting ideas on what death may mean—the total annihilation of consciousness or the widely held mythic belief in the transition of the soul to another dimension—are wildly debated topics that affect human behavior.

Fascination with NDEs emerged following the interest in altered states of consciousness, reported in psychedelic experiments of the 1960s and 1970s. The motif of death and rebirth was a central component of these transpersonal experiences, and parallels are found in the visions of the dying. Psychedelic experiments may be viewed as unorthodox or even 'new age' by the establishment. However, Grof writes, "In this context no distinction is made between a mystical or spiritual experience and psychotic experience."[18]

NDEs are still of vital interest, as the mysterious phenomenon continues to provide insight into the human condition and reconnects individuals with beliefs of ancient cultures, whereby myths of death and images of the gods were not avoided, but accepted as an integral part of spiritual life that inspired much architecture, art, and sacred rituals.

As contemporary Western society rejects the structure of myth and renounces primordial images that once instilled a sense of order prevailing in the cosmos, coping mechanisms to compensate for the lack of the authentic numinous experience and image of 'God' place the world in a hazardous position. In this perilous state of inner confusion and denial, humans veer between the polarities of secularism and religious fundamentalism, which reflect the inability of traditional religions to encompass the notion of modernity. As illustrated in the horrific events of 9/11, the loss of life from present day religious conflicts is alarming. For Fundamentalists, only one sacred belief exists, and alternative points of view are marginalized or considered to represent a rejected *other*. This way of thinking poses a critical challenge to world order and psychic structure. Malise Ruthven writes, "Fundamentalists repress or bleach out the multifaceted polysemic ways in which myth and religion appeal to all aspects of the human psyche."[19]

Religious symbolism expressed certain moral and mental attitudes, inherited from those depicted in ancient resurrection myths that were closely aligned with the natural world. However, as the myth of medieval Christianity died in Europe and became replaced by a form of sterile objectivity, religious dogmas excluded and disassociated from the voice of Nature. Such a separation fom natural order edged the *feminine* influence that bears the gift of mystical illumination and the image of 'God' out of human consciousness. This loss had dire consequences and led to a tension within humanity that Jung writes could be projected onto Wotan, the god of war in ancient Germanic mythology or "'State' or something else ending with –ism, even atheism, of which people, believe, hope and expect just as much as they formerly did of God."[20] In this state of fear and alienation, the psyche desperately seeks to reinvent an escape from the gulf of emptiness and reunite with some form of authentic structure. Many renowned philosophers, poets, and psychologists, including Rilke, Jung, Holderlin, and Heidegger, all described current existence as being spiritually impoverished without the archetypal image of God.

Such a profound loss results in inflation of the ego and the emergence of the *puer*, the archetype of the willful child that refuses to grow up and so remains immature and imprisoned within the ego. Greek mythology tells the story of Narcissus, an extremely attractive youth, who scorned the amorous advances of many, including the nymph, Echo. His lack of empathy to those around him angered the gods, who punished Narcissus by making him fall in love with his own reflection that was mirrored in a pool of water. In various renditions of the myth, Narcissus dies either through drowning, as he attempts to embrace and hold onto his own image, or through pining away by the edge of the pool. This myth symbolizes how our inner spiritual essence can wither and die without proper nourishment, and highlights the dire consequences of focusing attention inwards in self-absorption, rather than outward towards others.

The constructs and defenses that humans have manufactured to deal with separation from the image of God have resulted in spiritual dormancy, and the emergence of a false narcissistic self that teeters on the on the brink of total annihilation from a true sense of Self. Spiritual hunger manifests in neurotic symptoms, as illustrated in the case of Friedrich Nietzsche, the nineteenth-century German philosopher, who pronounced that God was dead and likened himself to a mystic who claimed "a *strange* voice was speaking here, the disciple of an as yet 'unknown god' who concealed himself beneath the cowl of a scholar."[21] His long-time friend and scholar, Lou Salome, described Nietzsche's motivating force was a compensation to rediscover a "mystical God-ideal outside of himself."[22] Nietzsche's last years lost to insanity indicate that his psyche was unable to function without an *inner* image of 'God,' and hence his raging battle between belief and his soul's yearning for salvation. This universal struggle highlights the severe psychological outcome emanating from the lack of numinous experiences and the God-image that could result in the twenty-first century becoming even more volatile than the last.

Jung's preoccupation with symbols, myths, and archetypes is paramount in his psychological theories. He refers to *amplification* as a way to rediscover sacred dimensions of God within the psyche and suggests that through translating and understanding mythological symbols, it is possible to reintegrate this vital image back into consciousness awareness. Jung's exploration into the unconscious realms included encounters with an entity known as Philemon, described as being a pagan that carried both Egyptian and Greek characteristics that were colored by Gnostic motifs. His interactions with Philemon gave an example of such amplification, as Philemon gave Jung the understanding that archetypal energies manifest independently in the psyche, imparting knowledge. Robert Romanyshyn writes, "Those subtle bodies, like Philemon, have less substance to them than things, but more substance than thought."[23]

The ability to access archetypal realms and revive symbolic meaning, which facilitate reconnection with an expanded awareness, can be discovered by each new generation. In emphasizing this point, Aldous Huxley, who was known for his interest in philosophical mysticism and parapsychology, writes:

> Visit the Louvre one night when the Greek and Egyptian antiquities are floodlit. You will meet with new gods, nymphs

> and Pharaohs, you will make the acquaintance, as one spotlight goes out and another, in a different quarter of space, is lit up, of a whole family of unfamiliar Victories of Samothrace. The past is not something fixed and unalterable. Its facts are rediscovered by every succeeding generation, its value reassessed, its meaning redefined in the context of present tastes and preoccupations.[24]

Although we may no longer hear the voice of God on a conscious level, the unconscious still hints at a sacred identity, which is demonstrated in the popularity of Eastern religions, such as Hinduism and Buddhism that more readily facilitate epiphanies manifesting from the collective unconscious. The resurgence and interest in archetypal near-death experiences that have been recorded since antiquity, also offer humanity the chance to reevaluate and amplify an imagined relationship with the Creator, as these narratives imply a meeting with the 'God' archetype and so reinstall beliefs that this image continues to live within the psyche. Jung writes that the image of God "already has a place in that part of our psyche which is pre-existent to consciousness. . . . He therefore cannot be considered an invention of consciousness. We neither make Him more remote or eliminate Him, but bring Him closer to the possibility of being experienced."[25]

Contemporary near-death personal testimonies imply a transcendent mystical encounter with 'God' in an ecstatic union that expands spiritual consciousness into an awareness of eternal life. Michael Sabom's "Atlanta Study" leads him to conclude "that the general revelation of God is occurring in the near-death experience."[26] Similar revelations have been shared by mystics throughout the ages, who have sensed the reality of a divine presence.

In discussing similar imagery, manifesting in the dream symbolism of his patients, Jung argues that although these dreams cannot not verify the existence of 'God,' they can prove that an archetypal image of the deity exists within the psyche and that it possesses a numinous quality, and so awareness of this image is, therefore, a religious experience.[27]

The near-death journey is prevalent in the collective at this present volatile period in world history, suggesting that powerful symbolic affirmations may occur more frequently during turbulent times. Certainly, hope is an integral part of human experience, and the NDE motif offers a narrative that generates hope, opening humans to infinite possibilities projected though the imagination.

Psychic phenomena, including the NDE are described as being 'paranormal' and this term originates from the Greek *para,* translated to mean beside or beyond, and *normal,* denoting something that can rationally be explained through scientific means and so *paranormal* is considered to be beyond the realms of human and animal capability, as understood by science. Such notable experiences, including: prophetic dreams, visions, ghostly apparitions, out-of-body experiences, deathbed visions, near-death journeys, and Psi (the human ability for extrasensory perception), have been studied extensively over the last century. Inspirational literature exploring whether consciousness may extend beyond physical death was referenced by both British and American early researchers in the field of psychical research. F. W. H. Myers wrote prolifically on the subject and states that resurrection following physical death was readily accepted by Western intellect during the popular era of Christianity, which was the guardian of this ancient archetypal structure. For over two thousand years, humans from many religious traditions had acknowledged an afterlife state.

As Christianity declined in popularity, however, interest in a spiritual and mythological world waned. But primordial images retained in the collective unconscious signifying transcendence over death still linger in the human psyche and they are constantly repeated through psychic, archetypal phenomena. Myers writes, "The laws of nature held their wonted way. As ever that which the years had once brought they brought again, and every here and there some marvel, likened to the old stories that anyone cared to assert, cropped up . . . as a precursor of the inevitable wider enquiry."[28] The value of Myer's work was in providing a model for the merging of transpersonal psychology and psychic research and was primarily concerned with breaking down barriers between superstition and science. This field of study was not primarily concerned with the dying person, but rather focused on the psychic, extrasensory, physical, and visionary manifestations that were reported to occur during the dying process.

Important research into a scientific evaluation of parapsychology was undertaken in the 1930s by J. B. Rhine from Duke University, who through his well-known experiments involving the use of cards, was able to substantiate the extra-sensory perception capabilities of human beings. These abilities enabled individuals to predict future events independently of the five senses, and seemed to originate from an independent channel of the mind. Rhine's work gave credence to parapsychological research and although his theories were not always readily accepted, Rhine believed that accounts of psychic phenomena gathered from seriously minded people warranted in-depth investigation. He writes, "Because we tend to think of our views of nature as complete, we think of any such apparent exception as almost a direct conflict. It becomes a conflict, then, in our system of beliefs. However, this does not mean necessarily a conflict in nature—a fact that is always hard to remember."[29]

Jung thought Rhine's research offered proof to illustrate that a portion of the psyche existed beyond the laws of time and space, and that it was necessary to incorporate this notion into human consciousness. Jung also detailed the manifestation of paranormal activity at his home one weekend, when his daughter reported seeing a ghost dressed in white, and he subsequently had the strangest feeling "that the air was filled with ghostly entities."[30] The following day, the doorbell continually rang and moved of its own accord, and the house suddenly felt as though it was again invaded by spirits.

Jung immediately detailed everything that had taken place, as the extraordinary images and events continued to make their presence felt over the next two evenings. The resulting *Septem Sermones* (The Seven Sermons to the Dead) were deeply ingrained in Gnostic beliefs and Jung appeared to channel the words of a great Gnostic teacher and poet, Basilides, who resided and taught in Alexandria during the second century AD. Although the *Sermons* are extremely complex and difficult to decipher, Jung believed communication from the dead enabled him to briefly glimpse the normally invisible archetypal realms. In the First Sermon, the term *Pleroma* describes a transcendent dimension that we are all part of. According to the Gnostics, death is a state that occurs through identification with the material world and loss of connection to alternate states of consciousness. Estrangement from an ultimate reality leads to feelings of alienation and sets the humans the task of individuation and the remembrance of a deeper identity within our true nature.

Deathbed visions that manifest when a dying person approaches death also suggest an alternate realm that exists beyond the one perceived through the five senses. The Buddha Amitabha, known as the *Buddha of Measureless Light* was not of this world, but presided from a separate universe in the west. He experienced countless rebirths and had been a monk in one lifetime that attained enlightenment and so had become a *Bodhisattva*, the equivalent of a Christian *saint*, who had created his own paradise. This Buddha promised his disciples that he would appear to them when they came close to death, so they could approach this transition without anxiety and prepare for paradise in their next rebirth into the *Land of Bliss*. Jewish mysticism also refers to what takes place at the moment of death. "We have further learnt that at the time of a man's death he is allowed to see his relatives and companions from the other world" (Zohar 1, 219a). In the ancient Sumerian myth of Gilgamesh, Enkidu also has a vision of an afterlife and journey to the land of the dead, where he is transformed into a bird by a bird-man figure.

Early pioneers investigating deathbed visions include Dr. James Hyslop, who published *Psychical Research and the Resurrection,* in 1908 and Sir William Barrett, a physics professor at the Royal College of Science in Dublin, who presented his findings in *Deathbed Visions,* published in 1926. Exhaustive contemporary studies on end-of-life visions undertaken by Karlis Osis and Erlendur Haraldsson contains testimonies from over a 1000 participants from both the United States and India, and so is based on both Western and Eastern cultural and mythological backgrounds, which are radically different. Although the research has a rigorous scientific aim, the experiential aspect of the dying process is extremely important. Both Osis and Haraldsson suggest death is not an intellectual problem to be solved, but rather presents a mystery that needs to be understood from the depth of the human being. Therefore, they obtained direct experiences whenever possible. Their research indicates certain patients approaching death have archetypal visions of a similar nature:

> They see apparitions of deceased relatives and friends. They see religious and mythological figures. They see non-earthly environments characterized by light, beauty and intense color. These experiences are transformative. They bring with them serenity, peace, elation, and religious emotions. The patients die a "good death" in strange contrast to the usual Gloom and misery commonly experienced before expiration.[31]

The results of earlier investigations and those concluded by Osis and Haraldsson reveal how the same mythological contents from deathbed visions also manifest in NDEs, even though religious images vary in cultural anomalies. The central component in both phenomena is a disembodied state, culminating in the sensation of passing through darkness into light and entering a heavenly realm of consciousness.

An elevation in the mood of the dying person is also observed, indicating some profound inner change, which is often alarming to medical witnesses. These mood shifts resemble cases of ESP, when an individual emotionally responds to some future event, without having conscious awareness of what has taken place. Research indicates that in the dying process, a psychic sensitivity is activated that operates outside of normal consciousness of the physical body and personality, transcending the fear of death and resulting in feelings of peace and serenity. John O'Donohue writes:

> You look at the dying and sense they are now beginning to belong more fully to the unseen world. Indeed they will often tell you that they have just glimpsed the countenance of some long-departed friend or family member. Already, their vision is altering. Now they are beginning to see the eternal tracings of the invisible world. It can be an incredible thing to really look into the eyes of the dying. Often you see such beauty dawning there. It is as if the whole tenderness and dispersed beauty of the person's life focuses in their eyes.[32]

The importance of experiential evidence is paramount in validating imaginings of a possible afterlife. R. M. Bucke, a late nineteenth-century Canadian psychiatrist, who studied mysticism, details a peak vision and the illumination of an altered state of consciousness. He describes a sense of the inner light, giving rise to feelings of immortality and the resulting loss of fear surrounding death; these core components are an integral part of the NDE. William James also gave many examples of mystical insights that are inexplicable through logic or intellectual debates.

A further example of paranormal, archetypal, religious experience bearing resemblance to deathbed visions and the NDE is that of the Christian mystic, Emanuel Swedenborg. Over a thirty-year period, he wrote prolifically on the subject, guided by his continuing psychic visits to the spirit realms. Swedenborg's commentary on life after death was generated by his apparent out-of-body experiences resulting in an *awakening*, similar to those described by NDE survivors. His visions led him to an irrefutable *belief* and strengthened his religious conviction that the spirit or soul inhabited the body up until the moment of death. He writes:

> I was brought into a state in which my physical senses were inoperative—very much, then, like the state of people who are dying. However, my deeper life and thought remained intact so that I could perceive and retain what was happening to me and what does happen to people who are being awakened from death. I was enabled to perceive and even to feel that there was a pull, a kind of drawing out of the deeper levels of my mind and therefore of my spirit from my body; and I was told that this was being done by the Lord and is what brings about our resurrection.[33]

Swedenborg's accounts received attention from theologians, because not only did they strengthen the faith, but contributed to debates on immortality that were of paramount speculation in Europe from about 1650, and carried on well into the next century. John Wesley, founder of the Methodist movement, was curious about Swedenborg's otherworldly encounters, as he believed it was possible to receive direct communication from angelic entities, either while awake or in the dreaming state. Goethe, considered an influential thinker in Western culture, thought Swedenborg to be an inspirational prophet and mystic, who had witnessed the reality of heaven and the nature of an afterlife. Jung also expressed interest in Swedenborg's subjective claims of accessing spiritual realms of existence that resulted in an emotional response, which was not only beneficial to Swedenborg, but humanity at large.

As Swedenborg's visions continued, he supposedly gained enhanced clairvoyant abilities. On one occasion, he informed a group of friends at a party that a fire had taken place in Stockholm, even though he was miles away from the city at the time. Jung comments that this type of enhanced perception could break through into awareness when the threshold of consciousness was lowered, thus enabling Swedenborg to gain knowledge of the fire "that was, in a sense, burning in him too."[34] Jung had many personal experiences of ESP and clairvoyant abilities. Many of his dreams and visions had prophetic qualities and in the autumn of 1913, he was forewarned of the future destruction and turmoil of World War 1, and *saw* the catastrophe of "mighty yellow waves, the floating rubble of civilization, and the drowned bodies of uncounted thousands. Then the whole sea turned to blood."[35] Following a two-week period, the vision returned, but more vividly than before, and he heard an inner voice telling him, "Look at it well; it is wholly real and it will be so."[36]

In his *Omega* study, Ring ascertains that spiritual development gained by NDErs provides a catalyst for enhanced psychic abilities, and he writes, "Finally, as a by-product of this spiritual development, NDErs tend to manifest a variety of psychic abilities afterwards that are an inherent part of their transformation."[37]

It has been established that the dying are more likely to experience deathbed visions when fully conscious and alert, rather than when their faculties and ability to communicate are impaired through medication or a state of delirium. Only a few patients included in the survey conducted by Osis and Haraldsson were on any form of drug therapy. "Those who had received medication had no greater frequency of afterlife visions than other patients. Whatever these drugs did, *they apparently did not generate deathbed phenomena suggestive of an afterlife*."[38] In many cases, the dying person was not consciously thinking of the deceased relative that appeared, but they were often supplied information detailing events that they had no prior knowledge of.

An interesting observation was made as to the nature of the visions, indicating that although people tended to translate archetypal energy into symbolic figures from their own religious belief systems, as with the NDE—this is not always the case. Osis and Haraldsson write, "Occasionally it is depicted in terms of the ancient mythology that the patient learned in school. For example, one man saw his wife standing beside a river, waiting for him. It seemed to be the 'River of Forgetfulness' which flows between the two worlds, as related in the Greek myth of Lethe."[39] This example indicates that symbolism or imagery encountered is not always dictated by religious orientation of the dying person, but may funnel into a 'collective' stored symbolism, depicting an afterlife state. However, the core components that include: feelings of peace, beauty, harmony, and serenity, remain the same for all who experience such visions, regardless of whether the person is Muslim, Christian, Jewish or Hindu.[40]

The most compelling testimony from those having a deathbed vision or near-death experience is that they view images of deceased relatives or religious entities as being transition guides. Osis and Haraldsson write, "The pilot survey revealed the most dramatic characteristic of deathbed apparitions: the ostensible intent to take the patient away to the other world. *This was again found to be the dominantly stated purpose of the apparitions of the dying, as well as of come-back cases, in both American and Indian cultures."*[41]

The most striking similarity between a deathbed vision and an NDE is that all those who have experienced such an event describe an intense emotional response. However, if deathbed visions confirm the possibility, or hope of an afterlife, why don't all people close to death recall such an overwhelming experience? Although the mystery of death is inexplicable to those who are merely witnessing the dying process, it could be that not all dying individuals consciously remember a deathbed vision. Furthermore, not all these visions manifest at the moment of death, but can occur some time before. St Augustine writes of an ecstatic vision that he shared with his mother, Monica. They had been discussing the afterlife when suddenly, they both experienced a great revelation bringing the profound realization of the rewards of heaven and how earthly pleasures paled in comparison. Shortly after, Monica fell ill and made her transition. Perhaps we all share such an inner or psychic experience that does not register in our conscious awareness, in the same way that the majority of us do not remember dreams that also emanate from altered states of consciousness

Mythological transition guides or psychopomps have been universally recognized and their role was to ensure safe transition for the newly deceased soul. They were depicted on funerary art and have often been associated with animals, including dogs and a variety of birds. For the ancient Greeks, Hermes was guide to the underworld after making a pact with Hades, in which he agreed to keep a register of the dead and assist souls to their final resting place. Roman myth recounts how Mercury, who shared many characteristics with Hermes, acted as the transition guide, and in ancient Egypt, the jackal-headed Anubis was the leader of souls. For the Etruscans, Charun, who was depicted with pointed ears and snakes around his arms, and sometimes shown with enormous wings, fulfilled this important function. In Hinduism, the deity known as Agni was known as the intermediary between mortals and the gods, and the Islamic Archangel of Death, Azrael, collected the souls of the dead. In contemporary Western deathbed visions and NDEs, the guides are often religious images, such as Jesus, heavenly angelic entities, or sometimes they can be deceased relatives or animals. Stanislav Grof and Joan Halifax write, "Mythological systems not only have detailed descriptions of afterlife realms, but frequently complex cartographies to guide souls on their difficult posthumous journey."[42]

The archetypal psychopomp appearing in a deathbed visions is also symbolized in fairy tale form. In *The Little Match Girl* that was originally written to illustrate the plight of child slave labor, Hans Christian Anderson simply encapsulates recurrent patterns, symbolic of an ancient wisdom.

The tale tells of a young girl out on the freezing streets selling matches on New Year's Eve. Stiff with cold, she dared to strike a few matches to warm herself, and suddenly saw images of a great feast, a Christmas tree blazing with lights, and candles that extended into twinkling stars. The girl then lit yet another match and night appeared to transform into day, as her grandmother, looking kind and loving appeared in the flame's circle. She lifted the child into her arms "and they soured into a halo of light and joy, far, far above the earth, where there was no more cold, no hunger, no pain, for they were with God."[43] The following morning, on New Year's Day, the body of the child was found, having, "Frozen to death on the last night of the old year."[44]

The motifs and numinous content of this simple tale is one of death and resurrection, portrayed through Christian symbolism that depicts what Marie-Louise von Franz describes as "unconscious life which renews itself and continues to exist eternally, after human consciousness has ceased to exist."[45] Imagery of ascension is also featured, together with the metaphor of the ending of the old year and beginning of the new, which humanity has celebrated for thousands of years. The deceased relative that appears to escort the child to the heavenly realms has similarities to transition guides described in contemporary deathbed visions. The halo of light is also a motif of a numinous, transpersonal encounter.

Archetypal imagery and symbolism contained in the tale can be described as both a thought pattern and an emotional experience that satisfy an unconscious emotional hunger within the human psyche. The archetypes that manifest appear in their purest form, but like those manifesting in NDEs and mystical states of consciousness, they still powerfully portray spiritual wisdom, encapsulated in an oral tradition.

Notes

1. Albert Heim, "Notizen uber den Tod durch Abstrz" (Remarks on Fatal Falls) *Swiss Alpine Yearbook*, 27 (Switzerland, 1892), 327-37).
2. See Elisabeth Kübler-Ross, *The Wheel of Life*, 188-92.
3. Ibid., 188.
4. See Raymond Moody, *Life After Life*, 25-98.
5. Kenneth Ring, *Life At Death*, 103.
6. Michael Sabom, *Light and Death*, 14.
7. Ibid., 41.
8. Ibid., 42-44.
9. Ibid., 45.
10. Ibid., 46.
11. Ibid., 50.
12. Margot Grey, *Return from Death*, 55.
13. Peter Fenwick and Elizabeth Fenwick, *The Truth in the Light: An Investigation of over 300 Near-Death Experiences* (New York: Berkley Trade, 1997), 168.
14. Michael Sabom, *Life and Death*, 200.

15. Margot Grey, *Return from Death*, 58.
16. Maurice Rawlings, *Beyond Death's Door* (New York: Bantam, 1979), 1.
17. Bruce Greyson and Nancy Evans Bush, "Distressing Near-Death Experiences." *The Near-Death Experience: A Reader*, 228.
18. Stanislav Grof, *The Ultimate Journey*, 122.
19. Malise Ruthven, *Fundamentalism: A Very Short Introduction* (Oxford: Oxford University Press, 2007), 5.
20. C. G. Jung, *Psychology and Religion based on the Terry Lectures delivered at Yale University* (New Haven: Yale University Press, 1938), 104.
21. Friedrich Nietzsche, *The Birth of Tragedy*, ed. Raymond Guess and Ronald Spears (Cambridge: Cambridge University Press, 1999), 6.
22. Lou Salome, *Nietzsche*, trans. Siegfried Mandel (Chicago: University of Illinois Press, 2001), 89.
23. Robert D. Romanyshyn, *Ways of the Heart* (Pittsburgh: Trivium, 2002), 90.
24. Aldous Huxley, *The Doors of Perception & Heaven and Hell*, 171.
25. C. G. Jung, *Memories*, 348.
26. Michael Sabom, *Light and Death*, 208.
27. C. G. Jung, 73.
28. F. W. H. Myers, *Human Personality and Its Survival of Bodily Death: Studies in Consciousness* (Charlottesville: Hampton Roads, 2001), 2.
29. J. B. Rhine, *Extra Sensory Perception* (Hagerstown: Kessinger, 2003), 5.
30. C. G. Jung, *Memories*, 190.
31. Karlis Osis and Erlendur Haraldsson, *At the Hour of Death*, 2.
32. John O'Donohue, *The Invisible Embrace of Beauty*, 208.
33. Emanuel Swedenborg, *Heaven and Hell*, trans. George F. Dole, int. Bernhard Lang (West Chester: Swedenborg

Foundation, 2000), 339-40).

34. C. G. Jung, *Structure and Dynamics of the Psyche: CW Vol. 8* (Princeton: Princeton University Press, 1971), 481.
35. C. G. Jung, *Memories,* 175.
36. Ibid., 175.
37. Kenneth Ring, *Heading Toward Omega,* 166.
38. Karlis Osis and Erlendur Haraldsson, *At the Hour of Death,* 189.
39. Ibid., 41.
40. Ibid., 41.
41. Ibid., 187.
42. Stanislav Grof and Joan Halifax, *The Human Encounter with Death* (New York,: E. P. Dutton, 1977), 2.
43. Hans Christian Anderson and Rachael Isadora Turner, *The Little Match Girl* (New York: Putnam, 1990), 25.
44. Ibid., 26.
45. Marie-Louise von Franz, *On Dreams and Death,* 25.

Chapter 5

The Realms of the *Imaginal* World

> I am certain about nothing but the holiness of the Heart's affections and the truth of the Imagination.
>
> John Keats (Letter to Benjamin Bailey, 1817)

Throughout human evolution, a vast array of mythical motifs and archetypal symbolism reflect *imaginal* visions of another reality beyond that of the sensory world, in which death and rebirth is a central affirmation. As far back as the Ice Age caves of France and Spain, the murals discovered may have illustrated prehistoric visionary near-death journeys that appear to depict beliefs in life after death.

The powerful and constant motif of an otherworldly journey can be found in the myths of ancient civilizations, as well as in the classic works of Plato, Homer, and Virgil. Religious texts and scriptures, including the Christian Bible, The Books of the Dead, and the Qur'an all make reference to a posthumous journey of the soul. However, are there possible explanations for the existence of an *imaginal* realm from which such supernatural perceptions arise? French scholar, Henry Corbin, put forward the idea of a *mundus imaginalis* and Jung hypothesized on *synchronicity*. Both concepts offer explanations beyond the rational and scientific conjectures of others, who contend that mystical states of consciousness accessed during near-death experiences are simply hallucinations of the dying brain.

The *imaginal* realm enables visions that translate symbolism, metaphor, and analogy. Early resurrection myths contain symbolic analogies and motifs of regeneration. That of Chiron, known as a sage, prophet, and mentor to the healing deities, including Asklepios, symbolized the human being as possessing both mortal and divine qualities, and underscored the effort required to integrate both the godly and shadow qualities of the psyche. Chiron suffered a mortal wound that could not be healed, which symbolized the dark shadow of his personality that feared death. To end his constant suffering, he surrendered his immortality to Prometheus and descended into the underworld and the realm of death. Chiron spent nine days and nights in Hades. The number nine symbolizes the culmination of a successful search and in Greek mythology; Demeter spent nine days wandering the earth looking for Persephone. In many early religions, this sacred number also corresponded to the spheres of both heaven and hell and represented an ending and new beginning, associated with decay and regeneration in Nature and the death and rebirth of the human being.

Chiron's gestation period in the underworld signified an initiation into death, for as he gazed into the darkness, he imagined a faint glimmer of gold and then remembered that Hades, Lord of the Underworld, was also known as Pluto, god of riches, because precious metals and crops manifested from his netherworldly kingdom. Intervention from Zeus resulted in Chiron ascending out of the darkness to reside eternally in the constellation of Sagittarius. The symbolic analogy of this myth reflects dynamic eternal regeneration, which is elusive to grasp without pivotal triggers, such as experiencing the challenges and wounds of life that can expand awareness.

The metaphorical language of myth was distinguished and understood by ancient Greeks, enabling them to differentiate between infinite and limited life without intellectualizing. In indigenous cultures, including that of the Native American Pawnee, physical death was considered a transition to a portal beyond space and time. An old Pawnee myth recounts a dead man manifesting as a ghostly presence, and saying, "I am in everything: in the grass, the water."[1] The dead are not thought to be leaving the world, but merely journeying to a land beyond the horizon, where the ancestors gather.

Much ancient architecture preserves a symbolic heritage, and cathedrals, mosques, and temples are central in many world cultures. Their doorways lead to images of God from many traditions and they are home to symbolic treasures depicting spiritual principles and ancient religious beliefs. Rouen Cathedral in northwestern France dates back to the twelfth century, but like many such sacred sites, continues to provide an inspirational source for integrating primordial affirmations back into consciousness. During the 1890s, Claude Monet painted a series of cathedral images captured at different times of day in changing weather conditions. Monet revealed illuminating changes in the cathedral's façade caused by natural light and brought inanimate stone to life, which is seen to be in state of perpetual change.

The Egyptian pyramids symbolized primordial archetypal motifs of death and renewal. The Giza plateau, located on the outskirts of Cairo, contains several magnificent ancient monuments, including the Great Pyramid of Khufu, the Pyramid of Khafra, and the Pyramid of Menkaura, together with the colossal sculpture of the Great Sphinx, which is carved from living rock and preserves the legacy of a heroic and transcendental vision. Known as one of the *Seven Wonders* of the ancient world, Giza still inspires feelings of wonder and awe, as it represents a portal to the underworld and Pyramid Texts from the fifth and sixth Dynasty are carved into the inner walls. These inscriptions held a magical ability to intercede with the gods and facilitate the Pharaoh's transfiguration and transition to the afterlife, and so pyramids symbolized the entrance to an *imaginal* realm, which incorporated the motif of death and renewal and united earthly and eternal life.

The annual flooding of the Nile, which the Egyptians were dependent upon, was seen to be a reenactment of the tears shed by Isis, when her husband, Osiris, was slain. Oxide sediments that give the river a reddish hue are still compared with blood that was miraculously changed to water and fertilized the land. The reemergence of the pyramids, as the water receded, symbolized rebirth and the mystery of creation was revealed when Osiris returned to the black earth, as green as the new valley crops.

The discovery of the ancient city of Caral, located in Peru, provided valuable clues into the evolution of human consciousness. The complex was as old as the Egyptian pyramids, dating back to 2627 BCE. Excavation of the site recovered remains of pyramids, temples, an amphitheatre, and small dwellings that were unearthed by archeologist Ruth Shady. The findings appeared to challenge an earlier consensus that warfare and fear were common denominators of all civilizations, for there was no evidence of weapons, battlements, or mutilated human remains. Instead, it was discovered that this early culture lived an almost paradisiacal existence that was firmly entrenched in peaceful trading and appreciation of the good life. Beautiful flutes were discovered that were formed from pelican and condor bones, and as with many ancient cultures, traces of drugs and aphrodisiacs that produced altered states of consciousness were unearthed, suggesting that inspiration for this ideal model was gleaned from an *imaginal* realm. Perhaps most striking was the discovery of the remains of a young infant lovingly buried with a precious necklace of stone beads, demonstrating this early culture's rituals and beliefs in the afterlife.

The *imaginal* world is a vast intermediary realm full of images and symbols that are just as real as representations from the world of the five senses and the intellect. Perception and awareness of this normally invisible dynamic is also accessible through works of art that stimulate evocative profound reactions, translated through the authentic voice of the psyche. Huxley suggests transcendence into alternate realms of reality can be accessed through primordial images of light and color:

> Light and color tend to take on a preternatural quality when seen in the midst of environing darkness. Fra Angelico's "Crucifixion" at the Louvre has a black background. So have the frescoes of the Passion, painted by Andrea del Castagno for the nuns of Sant'Appollonia at Florence. Hence the visionary intensity, the strange transporting power of these extraordinary works.[2]

Such creative endeavors contain powerful archetypal symbols encompassed in images, scenes, colors, and objects that remind observers of conscious or unconscious vague memories of the existence of an *imaginal* realm, inspiring a 'new' vision of greater possibilities, as they become focused and captivated by archetypal energies encoded in the works. These potent images continually provide an accessible gateway into an alternate realm through generating an intense *emotional* response, which can transport individuals from one state of being and perceiving to another of greater awareness.

The domain of the *imaginal* realm differentiates between fantasies and transpersonal experiences that appear to have an objective life of their own. Henry Corbin gave the *imaginal* realm a metaphysical definition and concurs that it does not exist as an empirical or observed reality in the physical world, for if this were the case, such manifestations would be perceived by anyone. It was also evident that such perceptions were unable to be incorporated into the spheres of the intellectual world, because they are made up of dimensions that are of no importance to the five senses, even thought they retain spatial and corporeal qualities. Such phenomena could not be placed in the category of the unreal, but needed a metaphysical explanation that placed them in an intermediary world known as the *mundus imaginalis archetypus.* Corbin also believed the Holy Scriptures originated from this realm and so represented the highest ability of the creative imagination.[3]

In short, Corbin theorized a classical distinction between an imagined realm, perceived in response to stimulus provided through the five senses, and an *imaginal* world that was real and accessed through the perceptions of a transcendent functioning of the imagination. Images from such a realm can complement rather than oppose logic, for the archetypes possess a logic that unveils the mystery and essential qualities of existence. Receptivity and openness to the *imaginal* enables the numinous to enter and the image of 'God' to appear.

Following his research into holotropic altered states of consciousness. Grof comes to a similar conclusion:

> The imaginal world possesses extensions and dimensions, forms and colors, but these are not perceptible to our senses as they would be when they are properties of physical objects. However, this realm is in every respect as fully ontologically real and susceptible to consensual validation by other people as the material world perceived through our sensory organs.[4]

For those who have not had a transpersonal experience and are deeply ingrained with the concept that consciousness is perceived through the five senses alone, such revelations could be overwhelming. However, expanding the mind to entertaining such possibilities is crucial for the ongoing development of the psyche.

Ritual and rites practiced by diverse cultures also facilitate entry into the realms of the *mundus imaginalis,* as participants leave historical time and enter mythological primordial time, known as *illud tempus,* which is eternal and never changes. Rituals provide the opportunity to transcend the profane to enter the sacred, as they consciously reveal unknown mysterious archetypal patterns and symbolism.

The ancient rituals and rites of *Samhain* meaning "summers end" saw a time when the structure of early Celtic tribes dissolved back into primordial chaos in preparation for a new order to begin, as they celebrated the New Year on the eve of 31 October. All hearth fires were extinguished and in the darkness, a huge bonfire symbolically represented the waning sun that would be 'magically' fortified through the fire, as the hearth fires were rekindled in preparation for the year ahead. Samhain was also believed to be the time when entities from other realms could make their presence felt. Such rituals and celebrations represented an initiation into death and rebirth through the symbolic lighting of the new fire in the presence of the dead.

During this festival, the profane met a sacred threshold. A liminal *imaginal* period existed where past, present, and future merged together and the cycles of Nature, which included that of human beings, were seen to have endings and new beginnings. Ancient civilizations, such as the Celts, were ritually structured and so gave form to human existence. Joseph Campbell writes, "A ritual is an organization of mythological symbols: and by participating in the drama of the rite one is brought directly in touch with these, not as verbal reports of historic events, either past, present, or to be, but as revelations, here and how, of what is always and forever."[5]

The slave-trade era saw a massive displacement of many thousands of Yoruba from the area now known as Nigeria and Benin. The slaves were stripped of their cultural identity, but their spiritual beliefs traveled with them to the New World and the archetypal images that remained in the collective, sustained and united those who were transported to a life of hardship and slavery.

The Yoruba believed in a Supreme Being known as *Olodumare*, whose powerful spiritual energy provided the source of life. Their mythology consisted of a pantheon of supreme living gods and goddesses known as the *orishas* that not only reflected the poetic and philosophical aspects of consciousness that encapsulated primordial wisdom, but also guided human destiny. Orally transmitted stories, known as *patakis*, preserved and retold the rich symbolic history of the deities, including that of the goddess of lightning and the wind, Oya, who, like the Egyptian Isis, presided over the dead and was symbolized by the colors of the rainbow. Oya was known as "gatekeeper of the cemetery," and her presence was invoked during ritual burials that encompassed both the living and the dead in a continuum of life.

The slaves were forcibly baptized into the Roman Catholic faith and to keep their religion alive, they amalgamated these beliefs and renamed their deities after Catholic saints and so continued to celebrate spiritually nourishing Yoruba rituals that invoked the intermediary transcendent deities in to daily life, while appearing to follow the new faith. The religion of Santería was born from this merging of Yoruba traditions with a Roman Catholic influence and the archetypes remained fluid, as they adapted to changing circumstances. Entering the sacred otherworldly domain of the *orishas* was facilitated through a wealth of rituals that included, dance and drumming and in ensuing trance-like states, human participants danced to divine rhythms and merged into the realm of their gods.

Through the archetypal images and symbolism of an *imaginal* world, the slaves transcended an existence filled with loathing and greed and built an inner harmonious *imaginal* realm of beauty, wisdom, and hope that sustained the community and enabled them to dream, imagine, and create their own sacred reality.

For Australian Aborigines, the *imaginal* realm of the *dreamtime* and the perception of immortality can be accessed through religious ritual, archetypal dreams, and psychic journeys. At the moment of death, the spirit is believed to leave the body and exist in a ghostlike form to follow the various routes taken by mythical ancestors that included: climbing a rope that appears from the sky, ascending on the rays of the setting sun, crossing an invisible border or bridge, or traveling across the Milky Way that extends from horizon to horizon. Burial rites are extremely important in helping the deceased accomplish this challenging transition, and also encourage the spirit not to linger in the threshold between life and death.

The realm of the ancestors is often described as being a sky dwelling or mythical island beyond the clouds, situated in the far west. The afterlife contains no judgment, reward, or punishment; for earthly life does not affect immortal existence and the Kingdom of the Dead is imagined as paradisiacal realm that resembles the earth, but is more fertile and lush. The deceased are expected to continue to influence human life and after successfully journeying to the afterlife, spirits can return and make their presence felt. The living can also contact the dead through waking dreams. Aboriginal medicine men visit the realms of the dead through out-of-body states to receive guidance and knowledge.

Some Aborigines are more open to the myth of reincarnation. They believe spirits of the deceased merge with the source of all creation—*the Dreaming*—and will eventually be reborn. Death, therefore, signifies entry into eternal life and rebirth into a sacred new form that can include that of a human being, animal, or an inanimate object from the natural world.

Celebrating the Day of the Dead takes place throughout Mexico at the end of October, and originated from myths of early Aztecs that worshipped the sun and believed deceased souls assisted the sun's journey across the sky and then reaped the rewards of a blissful eternity. Mixed with Christian mythological beliefs, these rituals evoke the duality of life, as the living create skeletal images of the dead and prepare for the return of departed spirits, symbolizing the affirmation of death and rebirth, in which human life parodies the decay and rejuvenation of the natural world. The living are often to be seen partying with images of the deceased in graveyards, and the afterlife state is celebrated with humor in the many little clay skeletons. These rituals of communication between the realms of the living and the dead continue to flourish in Mexico, indicating that the *imaginal* spirit world is still very much alive in the collective imagination.

Such rites and rituals portray death as an occasion for joyous festivities rather than sorrow and similar ancient imaginings were portrayed at the Etruscan tombs. The Etruscans were an early Italian civilization that believed all things manifested through the divine power of their pantheon of gods. In Rome, the Villa Giulia contains a collection of Etruscan artifacts that depict a heavenly afterlife, experienced as an eternal feasting. Visions of this paradisiacal realm were carved on walls of underground tombs and displayed images of dancers, animals, and lute players, all existing in a state of everlasting enjoyment. One of the most important pieces of Etruscan art shown at the villa, is the figurine of the "Sarcophagus of the Spouses," dating back to the late sixth century BCE. Molded from terracotta, it portrays a married couple reclining together at a banquet in the afterlife, symbolizing a celebration of death and new life in the image of a mystical marriage. Jung writes, "In the light of eternity, it is a wedding, a *mysterium coniunctionis.* The soul attains, as it were, its missing half, it achieves wholeness."[6]

Many homes in India feature artifacts related to the goddess, Kali, who personifies death, in her necklace made from human skulls. These images from an *imaginal* realm may horrify those in Western cultures, but for the Hindus, this depiction of Kali as a goddess associated with death is a stark reminder that death cannot be avoided, but rather should be incorporated into life, as Kali represents the illusion of linear time and so destroys the false sense of ego consciousness. Hindus believe that accepting mortality enables finding freedom in the realm of the gods, and so Kali's disturbing personification of death is clearly associated with the living.

Elaborate funeral and burial rites and rituals also open a threshold to the *imaginal* world of myth. Campbell writes, "A ritual is the enactment of a myth. By participating in a ritual, you are participating in a myth."[7] During rites of mourning, we are placed in an intermediary realm, and Arnold van Gennep writes that "the living mourners and the deceased constitute a special group, situated between the world of the living and the world of the dead, and how soon individuals leave that group depends on the closeness of their relationship with the dead person."[8]

The journey to the otherworld that the deceased was imagined to embark upon required certain rites that were firmly entrenched in the notion that the deceased must undertake such a voyage. During the Cro-Magnon era, rituals for the dead involved the corpses being bound and placed in fetal position, painted with red ochre, and decorated with shells. Provisions and icons of the Mother goddess were placed around them in order to ensure a safe transition to the otherworld. Excavation of ancient burial sites portrayed mythic beliefs in death symbolizing rebirth. Zaleski writes, "The ceremonial behavior toward the dead which we see embedded in the earth we excavate is nearly universal in historic times: and whenever one finds burial with grave goods or ritual cremation, sacrificial meals, or prescribed acts of mourning, such practices are but satellites of a much larger system of myths and rites that portray and sustain the cycles of life, death and rebirth."[9]

For the ancient Egyptians, Celts, Etruscans, and Greeks, this *imaginal* voyage was also the reason why dead were provided with a replica, or sometimes a real boat with oars, and given food, clothing, tools, and other essential items for the otherworldly passage. The Dogon of Mali in West Africa believe the 'dead' person to be impure and so perform sacred death rituals to release the soul from the body into the world of the living ancestors. Haitians also think that separation of the body and soul takes place at the moment of death and the most important death ritual frees the Divine Loa from the body. In both these traditions, an interim period exists that separates life from death and the deceased are known as the *living dead* that can cause disruption if the necessary rituals, including sacrifice, trance, initiation, and divination to convey them to their new status have not been observed. Life is viewed as a continuous cycle of regeneration, and as the living make offerings to the dead, the dead return to nourish the living.

The Greeks also often ritually placed silver coins in the mouths of the deceased to pay Charon to ferry them across the River Styx that separated the world of the living from the realm of the dead. A few mythological figures, including Orpheus, Psyche, and Aeneas took similar journeys with Charon, both to and from the underworld, and so transcended death. The name, Charon, originated from a Greek proper noun, translated to mean "flashing eyes" or "penetrating gaze," and some believe it represents a euphemism for death. The ancient Greek historian, Diodorus Siculus, however, suggested the ferryman and his name may have been inherited from Egyptian mythology and early Greek funerary vases depict scenes of the deceased clambering aboard Charon's boat. Dante also makes reference to Charon, who is the first mythological archetype that the pilgrim encounters on his journey through *Inferno*. Other representations of Charon include Michelangelo's depiction of a winged demonic character that carried an oar over his shoulder and threatened those who tarried.

The symbolic motif of supplying money for the afterlife transition has also been found in many other cultures: The Slaves gave monetary offerings to pay for the trip to the otherworld, and in Japanese Buddhism, coins were set aside to pay for the ferry trip across the Sanzu. Arnold van Gennep writes that such rituals initiated "a safe journey or crossing and a favorable reception, as they would a living traveler."[10] His research into funeral and burial rites also unearthed an interesting fact, for it was presumed that rites of separation would be the main focus of such ceremonies, but instead, rites of transition "which incorporate the deceased into the world of the dead are most extensively elaborated and assigned the greatest importance."[11]

Egyptian rites of mummification prepared the deceased for a dynamic nocturnal resurrection. The myth of the rebirth of Osiris/Ra symbolized the destiny of all individuals that had led a good life. Arnold van Gennep comments, "The death and rebirth, simultaneously, of Ra, Osiris, the king, the priest, and every deceased man who was 'pure' certainly constitutes the most extreme case known to me of a dramatic representation of the death and rebirth theme."[12]

Symbols from the natural world, including many flowers, also vividly enable an avenue to encounter archetypal energies and affirmations of the *imaginal* realms. In Persian images of the afterlife, every divine deity is associated with its own special flower, symbolizing the mandala of wholeness. The god, Vohuman, is depicted with white jasmine translated to mean "gift from God," Shrativar is portrayed with the basil plant, which is also associated with burial rituals in Europe where basil leaves are often placed in the hands of the deceased to ensure a safe passage.

The Rose has a long history of symbolism, personifying wisdom or truth. For the Greeks, the flower represented love and beauty and was dedicated to the goddess of love, Aphrodite. Thirteenth-century iconography also depicts the Virgin Mary holding a rose and she was often referred to as 'The Mystic Rose.' The Roman Catholic devotion of The Rosary originates from the Latin *rosarium*, translated to mean a rose garden or garland of roses. The fourth Sunday in Advent is known as Rose Sunday and symbolizes a time of rejoicing. The somber purple vestments worn by the priests throughout Lent are replaced by rose-colored ones, as the congregation is urged to *look up* beyond the

Crucifixion and Calvary to imagine the first rays of the newly born Easter sun and the risen Christ, the messenger of light that will bring redemption and joy, who exemplifies new life emanating from a mystical dimension beyond time and space.

The red anemone is associated with the death of Adonis, and appeared where his blood was spilt. Christians translate the symbology of the anemone to symbolize the blood of Christ shed at the Crucifixion. In Buddhism, the lotus symbolizes the potential of the human being to flower into divine essence and manifest the qualities of the Buddha, who is often shown to be sitting on a lotus in full bloom. As well as being associated with the Buddha, Egyptian monuments built on the banks of the Nile display images of the lotus, which is also featured in the adornments of headdresses of various deities. Isis, who held the secret to immortality, was depicted as having been born from a lotus flower and the Egyptians positioned lotuses into the hands of the mummified deceased, representing the afterlife that dead souls were entering. The lotus was also symbolic of the sun, because it closed its petals at night after becoming submerged in water, but then in the morning, it rose to the surface to bloom again.

The Aztecs acknowledged flower symbolism in their goddess of fertility, Xochiquetzal, depicted wearing a floral garland on her head and carrying a bouquet of flowers. Fragments of ancient Aztec poetry and texts suggest these ancient people also believed flowers to be motifs of death and new life. The Greeks also honored the floral goddess, Chloris. Her Roman equivalent, Flora, was honored each spring in the festival of the Floralia that took place in April or May, symbolizing the renewal of life. Later, Christianity adopted the month of May to honor and revere the Virgin Mary.

Stunning symbolic archetypal images from the natural world are found in crop circles that are associated with ancient stone monuments including, Stonehenge, which comprises of a structure of enormous standing stones that are engraved with prehistoric hieroglyphs and stand within a circular bank. Although the exact purpose of this sacred site remains unclear, it is thought to have been erected as a temple or sacred burial ground that was constructed about five thousand years ago during the Neolithic period and is aligned almost exactly with the sunrise that takes place at the summer solstice. Many ancient monuments, including the pyramids of the ancient Egyptians, are said to incorporate a form of sacred geometry that placed these shrines on the earth's energy grids, enabling communication between the mortals and the gods. Robert Lawlor writes, "Geometric diagrams can be contemplated as still moments revealing a continuous, timeless, universal action generally hidden from our sensory perception. Thus a seemingly common mathematical activity can become a discipline for intellectual and spiritual insights."[13]

During the Cartesian era, interest in ancient monuments and crop circles waned. However, during the later part of the twentieth century, the mysterious crop circles began to manifest once more in fields of wheat, barley, and canola and although the plants have their stems bent and are swirled and flattened, they remain undamaged. The ancient myths of dying and resurrected gods and goddesses were associated with the crop cycles. Both Demeter and Persephone were depicted in ancient art as wearing crowns of corn and holding stalks of corn in their hands, symbolizing cycles of regeneration. A ritual that included a dead-looking barley stalk containing seeds of the following year's crops was a motif of eternity and part of the Eleusinian Mystery rites.

The giant crop circles or mandalas remain as living symbols that appear to facilitate remembrance of ancient messages and affirmations. They attract thousands of pilgrims, who witness the elaborate geometrical patterns that can enable numinous shifts in consciousness and open a portal to the *imaginal* realm of the archetypes. For many, these ancient symbols speak in the poetic language of the soul, which is inseparable from the imagination and so generates a highly emotive response of awe, prayer, and contemplation that has a transformative effect. Freddy Silva writes, "Like Egypt's hieroglyphs, today's crop glyphs are cryptic and generally require an understanding of the meaning concealed beneath the first outward layer of expression. They are multilayered, ambiguous, metaphorical, instructional, even inspirational, containing myths not so much to be read but absorbed subconsciously."[14]

The symbolic language of ancient civilizations, who understood and deciphered the relationship between mortals and the gods has been richly preserved in rock carvings, art work, pottery, mythology, and places of worship that include temples and monuments. These sacred symbols continue to flourish and in the latter part of the twentieth century over 10,000 crop circles were recorded in various countries, although a staggering ninety percent of these manifested in the United Kingdom. There have been many hoax circles that do not contain the beauty or precision of the originals, but they are still valid examples of an unconscious motivation to open a channel of communication between the visible and invisible realms.

Plato's hypothesis of 'forms' implied qualities, such as beauty, have an eternal essence containing primordial *forgotten* knowledge. As in all mystical states of consciousness, including that of the NDE, the eternal perfection of beauty and light is a powerful reminder of an ancient affirmation. Images in crop cycles emit an eternal beauty, enabling the creative imagination to flow as a modern-day catalyst for initiation, which nourishes the soul. Silva writes, "They are harmonic creations of light, sound and magnetism, and so they are the mirrors of humanity, guiding us to reflect within, unlocking ancient memories and reminding us that we are not egocentric, but cosmocentric."[15]

Corbin's theory of a *mundus imaginalis* may well throw light on the enigma of NDE's and deathbed visions. He writes:

> Some of these testimonies cannot be entertained let alone understood except on the condition of having at one's disposal an ontology of the *mundus imaginalis* and a metaphysics of the active Imagination as an organ inherent in the soul and regulated by its own right to the world of subtle corporeity.[16]

Archetypal realms exist outside of time and space, but manifest in the psyche, as organized images from the unconscious. Jung describes an archetype as "rich in secret life, which seeks to add itself to our own individual life in order to make it whole."[17] He was fascinated by clusters of 'meaningful' coincidences containing a psychic element, beyond that of causality and believed archetypes were responsible for these manifestations in which both inner and outer events existed simultaneously, in a principal that he named ***synchronicity***.

Jung hypothesized that synchronistic clusters and their psychic, archetypal qualities hint at an alternate dimension of reality. An early example of synchronicity is found in divination practices of ancient, Greek, Egyptian, Indian, Scandinavian, Tibetan, and West African cultures, in which intermediary priests or medicine men interpreted divine signs and omens and contacted the ancestors. Greeks who wished to communicate with deceased spirits would visit the Oracle of the Dead at Acheron and entered an underground chamber where Persephone and Hades were believed to reside. After purification and initiation, prayers and invocations were recited in preparation for after death communication.

The Chinese *I Ching, or Book of Changes* is an ancient book of wisdom that comprises of 64 hexagrams, arranged in pairs. Each of these hexagrams has a name, number, and portion of text that symbolizes archetypal associations and the possibility of change. Jung was captivated in the principles of the *I Ching* that appeared to link physical and psychic sequences or patterns of events and was also enriched by the quest for individuation that was a central tenet of Zen Buddhism and Taoism. He spent an entire summer consulting the *I Ching* and was preoccupied in discovering whether the answers proved meaningful. He writes, "Time and again I encountered amazing coincidences which seemed to suggest the idea of acausal parallelism (a synchronicity, as I later called it)."[18] This great philosophical work and sacred heritage of China still represents a symbolic mirror for transformative spiritual practice.

Another form of divination that we are all familiar with is that of consulting the *Tarot* that is associated with early Egyptian symbolism and the Mystery Cults of Mithras, a mystery religion practiced in Rome from the first to fourth century AD. Early Tarot decks were originally used in card games throughout fifteenth-century Europe, but during the latter Renaissance period, they became associated with divination purposes, as this era was one that saw a return to ancient methods of communication with the gods through meditating or contemplating ancient symbols that connected the soul with a larger universe. However, regardless of their origins, the Tarot activates the power of the imagination. Sallie Nichols writes, "The essence of their importance for us is that a very real and transforming human emotion must have brought them to birth. It seems apparent that these old cards were conceived deep in the guts of human experience, at the most profound level of the human psyche. It is to this level in ourselves that they will speak."[19]

Christianity suppressed divination practices and viewed Tarot images as originating from the 'pagan' world and representing satanic forces, but Jung believed these images originated "from the archetypes of transformation."[20] The Cartesian era of scientific enlightenment alienated all forms of mystical consciousness and by the nineteenth century, the Tarot had disappeared and was associated with the occult. Modern Tarot decks have been influenced by ancient magical practices, myths, and legends, but they still retain a universal archetypal symbolism, providing patterns of meaningful coincidences or synchronicities. The seemingly random choice of cards encompasses the totality of inner and outer events into a meaningful whole, through the representation of archetypal energies.

Perhaps the most well-known form of divination today is astrology that originated in ancient Babylonia and spread to Greece and Rome sometime during the fourth century BCE. Although the Arabs further developed the ancient art from the seventh to thirteenth century BCE, many early civilizations, including that of the Maya, had developed astrological alignments. Early astrologers were priests and seers that believed the will and intervention of the deities in human destiny were closely linked with omens in the heavens. Interpretations were gathered and formed the basic foundation of modern-day astrological forecasts.

A great surge of interest in astrology manifested during World War 1, when newspapers started to publish daily horoscopes that still interpreted symbolic planetary influences as a means of accessing hidden timeless knowledge from an *imaginal* realm. Astrology has also been closely associated with the ancient art of alchemy, as the planets in the solar system were associated with various alchemical metals.

Jung believed synchronistic clusters could also manifest in the dreaming state and so inform an individual of another's death. He describes waking one night to feel a pain, as if someone had struck him on the forehead, and then again in the back of his skull. The next day, a telegram arrived informing him that one of his patients had shot himself and committed suicide. It was later ascertained that the bullet had become lodged in the back of this person's skull.[21] Jung suggests that the archetypal content of this synchronistic experience dissolved the barriers of time and space, enabling him to simultaneously experience the death of his patient, through direct contact with the collective unconscious:

> This experience was a genuine synchronistic phenomena such as is quite often observed in connection with an archetypal situation—in this case, death. By means of a relativization of time and space in the unconscious it could well be that I perceived something which in reality was taking place elsewhere. The collective unconscious is common to all; it is the foundation of what the ancients called the "sympathy of all things". In this case the unconscious had knowledge of my patient's condition.[22]

He also recounts how one of his pupils appeared to psychically experience near-death phenomena in a prophetic dream that occurred two months before her actual death. In the dreaming state, Jung concurs that the woman in question had entered an alternate reality:

> She had entered the hereafter. There was a class going on, and various deceased woman friends of hers sat on the front bench. An atmosphere of general expectation prevailed. She looked around for a teacher or lecturer, but could find none. Then it became clear that she herself was the lecturer, for immediately after death people had to give accounts of the total experience of their lives. The dead were extremely interested in the life experiences that the newly deceased brought with them, just as if the acts and experiences taking place in earthly life, in space and time, were the decisive ones.[23]

The projected image of the hereafter was extremely helpful to this woman, who experienced anxiety about the dying process, as it provided her with a prophetic "myth about death."[24] Jung stresses the importance of such a myth that can dispel the rational fear of death as being more than a descent into a darkened pit and, he says, "Myth, however, can conjure up other images for him, helpful and enriching pictures of life in the land of the dead."[25] That the woman should have such a dream at this transitional period in her life reflected the individuation aspect and unifying nature of synchronicity.

Synchronistic events are archetypal and symbolic, indicating a numinous connecting principal that produces an intense emotional response, enabling transcendence of perceived human limitations. The hypothesis of synchronicity adds credence to Corbin's theory of a *mundus imaginalis,* as mystics, including Swedenborg, perceive these heightened states of reality. Jung writes, "Synchronicity postulates a meaning which is *a priori* in relation to human consciousness, and apparently exists outside man."[26] He also acknowledged that the manifestation of synchronicity could not be fully substantiated, but he believed that both his mystical experiences and his observations of other out-of-body states and visions provided validation for the idea that synchronicity could enable "temporary access to 'absolute knowledge.'"[27] This extended perception also indicated a potential *other* world to the empirical world existed, and that the *unus mundus* (one world), encompassed the totality.

The realm of the *unus mundus* is one in which various types of incidents seem to form themselves into clusters. Although the archetypes manifest separately, at the same time, they are connected in what Marie-Louise von Franz describes as being a "unified multiplicity."[28] The uniting principle of the *unus mundus* occurs during synchronistic events, in which the duality of 'outer' and 'inner' become harmonized as one within the psyche.

The concept of synchronicity did much to shed light on near-death phenomena and mystical states of consciousness. In providing an example illustrating his theory, Jung recounts (what was later to be named a near-death experience by Moody) of one of his patients. The woman was in labor and suddenly, her pulse became undetectable. As worried medical staff gather around her bedside, the lady in question could still see them even though she started to sense an out-of-body sensation:

> She had the feeling that she was sinking through the bed into a bottomless void . . . . The next thing she was aware of was that, without feeling her body and its position, she was *looking down* from a point in the ceiling and could see everything going on in the room below her; she saw herself lying in the bed, deadly pale with closed eyes. Beside her stood the nurse. The doctor paced up and down excitedly, and it seemed to her that he had lost his head and didn't know what to do. Her mother and her husband came in and looked at her with frightened faces. She told herself it was too stupid of them to think she was going to die, for she would certainly come round again. All of this time she knew that behind her was a glorious, park-like landscape shining in the brightest colors, and in particular an emerald green meadow with short grass, which sloped gently upwards beyond a wrought-iron gate leading to the park . . . . The sloping meadow was flanked on both sides by dark green trees. It gave her the impression of a clearing in the forest, never yet trodden by the foot of man.[29]

The woman then describes a gateway to another dimension and 'knows' that if she walks through the portal, she will be stepping out of her life, but senses that if she turns back, she will reenter her body and earthly life. This narrative contains core components of the near-death experience: the out-of-body state, scenes of great beauty, a barrier to cross, and the decision to return to the body. The woman later related what she perceived had taken place during her 'unconscious' phase and medical staff confirmed her story mirrored events just as they had taken place in reality.

Such an example of NDE synchronistic patterning suggests

that even when conscious awareness is not functioning, perceptions and sensations continue to manifest. Altered states of awareness correspond to synchronistic phenomena that represent events that have no causal correlation with organic processes. Such a concept may be difficult to fully master, but this conflict stems in a rigid belief in causality, resulting in intellectual barriers. However, Jung writes that "we must regard them as *creative acts*, as the continuous creation of a pattern that exists from all eternity, repeats itself sporadically and is not derivable from any known antecedents."[30]

Integration into the realm of the *unus mundus* is perceived to take place at the moment of death. The ancient imagining that death is a transcendent phase of development appears to be confirmed by NDE survivors. At the beginning of the near-death journey, a sense of dual awareness exists, but as the experience unfolds, there is an awareness of another dimension that the NDEer becomes drawn into it. During an archetypal otherworldly journey, a sense of 'oneness' is experienced, which culminates in an individual's entire existence appearing to have been woven together into a meaningful whole and the resulting sense of unity transcends everyday differentiation between object and subject. Similar perceptions also manifest during a *peak* mystical experience, as the person no longer feels the duality of mind and body, but expresses a sensation of wholeness in an ecstatic merging with 'God' and the entire universe, giving rise to feelings of bliss, joy, and an inner serenity.

Notes

1. See David Abram, *The Spell of the Sensuous* (New York: Vintage, 1977), 219.
2. Aldous Huxley, *The Doors of Perception*, 117.
3. See Henry Corbin, *Alone with the Alone* (Princeton: Princeton University Press, 1969), 248.

4. Stanislav Grof, *The Ultimate Journey,* 141.
5. Joseph Campbell, *Myths to Live By* (New York: Penguin Compass, 1993), 97.
6. C. G. Jung, *Memories,* 314.
7. Joseph Campbell with Bill Moyers *The Power of Myth,* ed. Betty Sue Flowers (New York: Doubleday, 1988), 82.
8. Arnold van Gennep, *The Rites of Passage,* trans. Monika B. Vizedom and Gabrielle L. Caffee (Chicago: University of Chicago Press, 1960), 147.
9. Carol Zaleski, *Otherworld Journeys: Accounts of Near-Death Experiences in Medieval Times* (New York: Oxford University Press, 1987), 12.
10. Arnold van Gennep, *The Rites of Passage,* 154.
11. Ibid., 146.
12. Ibid., 160.
13. Robert Lawlor, *Sacred Geometry: Philosophy and Practice* (London: Thames & Hudson, 1982), 7.
14. Freddy Silva, *Secrets in the Fields: The Science and Mysticism of Crop Circles* (Charlottesville: Hampton Roads, 2002), 148.
15. Ibid., 309.
16. Henry Corbin, *Spiritual Body and Celestial Earth* (Princeton: Princeton University Press, 1977), xviii.
17. C. G. Jung, *Memories,* 304.
18. Ibid., 374.
19. Sallie Nichols, *Jung and the Tarot: An Archetypal Journey* (New York: Weiser, 1980), 5.
20. C. G. Jung, *The Archetypes and the Collective Unconscious,* 38.
21. See C. G. Jung, *Memories,* 138.
22. Ibid., 138.
23. Ibid., 305.
24. Ibid., 306.
25. Ibid., 306.
26. C. G. Jung, *Structure and Dynamics of the Psyche, CW Vol. 8,* 503-04.

27. Anthony Storr, *The Essential Jung* (Princeton: Princeton University Press, 1983), 26.
28. Marie-Louise von Franz, *Alchemical Active Imagination: Revised Edition (C. G. Jung Foundation Books)* (Boston: Shambhala, 1979), 148.
29. C. G. Jung, *Structure and Dynamics of the Psyche*, 508.

Chapter 6

The Mythological and Archetypal Imprint of Near-Death Journeys

The myths are metaphorical of spiritual potentiality in the human being, and the same powers that animate our life animate the life of the world.

Joseph Campbell, *The Power of Myth*

From the moment of birth, the power of story is paramount in shaping an individual and collective identity. Mythic stories of ancestors and cultural backgrounds inspire a sense of 'belonging,' as this heritage comprises of belief systems that instill a sense of our origins and links to a particular society. Equally important to understanding our place in the material world, is the quest to find a deeper sense of purpose and spiritual connection that proves to be an elusive task, as we continually strive to fill the painful void that manifests in the "dark night of the soul." Robert Romanyshyn writes, "Always in that deep hour of solitude we understand that, in spite of love, success, achievement, we are restless, beckoned beyond ourselves, called to another place. Before each morning's sun banishes these shadows of night, we feel in the deepest chambers of our hearts that we are still so far away from *home*."[1] However, illumination can be found in the mythic world of symbols that expand the imagination beyond the confines of objective reality and provide a spiritual compass to rediscover the sense of a divine more authentic identity. Joseph Campbell writes:

What is a God? A god is a personification of a motivating power or a value system that functions in human life and in

> the universe—the power of your own body and of nature. The myths are metaphorical and spiritual potentiality in the human being, and the same powers that animate our life animate the life of the world. But also there are myths and gods that have to with specific societies or the patron deities of the society . . . . There is the mythology that relates you to your nature and to the natural world, of which you are a part. And there is the mythology that is strictly sociological, linking you to a particular society.[2]

Mythic representations weave in and out of our lives preserving a numinous thread, which encompasses the history of primordial experience that not only instills a sense of the eternal nature of being, but also determines a pattern for the future. While there are various definitions explaining the function of myth, certain core characteristics illustrate how myths seek to convey spiritual values. William G. Doty refers to topics that frequently appear in this type of debate, which include: "subject matter having to do with the gods, an 'other world,' making universals concrete or intelligible, explicating beliefs, collective experiences, or values, 'spiritual' or 'psychic' expression."[3] Through their psychic nature, myths convey stories of the soul in archetypal images and symbolic metaphors, often reflecting analogies to the continual cycles of the natural world. Some, including that of Persephone, explain the origins of the seasons, and also allude to the cycles of human nature. The powerful symbolism that is associated with the forces of Nature reveals an unconscious, hidden, esoteric knowledge. Jung writes:

> All the mythological processes of nature, such as summer and winter, the phases of the moon, the rainy seasons, and so forth, are in no sense allegories of these objective occurrences; rather they are symbolic expressions of the inner, unconscious drama of the psyche, which becomes accessible to man's

consciousness by way of projection—that is mirrored in the events of nature.[4]

It may also be possible that early cultures, such as ancient Egyptian civilization, also had knowledge of the mystical elements of near-death journeys, when making assumptions of an eternal soul. Egyptian funerary rites and terminology certainly implied communication between the living and the dead, and the vast collection of funerary texts was originally named *Coming Forth by Day*, as the deceased made the nocturnal voyage with Osiris/Ra through the dark underworld, before being reborn into the light of a new existence. Ruth Schumann Antelme and Stephane Rossini write, "The parallel that exists between this 3500-year-old text and the stories of modern experiencers needs no commentary."[5]

Near-death researcher, Melvin Morse also believes *The Egyptian Book of the Dead* gives a clear description of the NDE. "This book is simply a detailed description of the near-death experience. It starts with a judgment scene and goes on to reveal how many gods and various voices, continue on a long boat trip through a dark tunnel, and ends with union with a bright light."[6]

Rediscovering the divine dimension of eternal life cannot be manufactured, but can be accessed through mythic representations and rituals that symbolically propel individuals into mythic time, where relics of sacred knowledge hover on the edge of consciousness. The enduring archetypal and symbolic qualities of near-death journeys that contain an otherworldly vision have been recorded for thousands of years and continue to manifest today, inspiring the *same* imagining of what transpires beyond physical death. These narratives manifest as *living* myths that endorse sacred principles and affirmations of diverse religions, even in a world that is often consciously alienated from such teachings.

But why do humans continue to seek out images of the dead,

imagined realms of an afterlife, and the stories of those on the threshold of death for guidance? Perhaps the reason can be traced to the ancient belief that only the dead can illuminate the darkness of death for the living. Robert Pogue Harrison writes:

> The primary reason why the dead have an afterlife in so many human cultures is because it falls upon them—the dead—to come to the rescue and provide counsel when that debilitating darkness falls. Why this special authority? Because the dead possess a nocturnal vision that the living cannot acquire. The light in which we carry on our secular lives blinds us to certain insights. Some truths are glimpsed only in the dark. That is why in moments of extreme need one must turn to those who can see through the gloom.[7]

The powerful archetypal content of mythological stories and illuminating states of mystical consciousness represent a quest for enlightenment rather than being a product of ancient or 'primitive' wishful imaginings. Jung made this point very clear:

> It is commonly assumed that on some given occasion in prehistoric times, the basic mythological ideas were "invented" by a clever old philosopher or prophet, and ever afterwards "believed" by credulous and uncritical people. It is said that stories told by a power-seeking priesthood are not "true," but merely "wishful thinking." But the very word "invent" is derived from the Latin *invenire,* and means to "find" and hence to find something by "seeking" it. In the later case the word itself hints at some foreknowledge of what you are going to find.[8]

Jung related his many mystical visions, including his transformational near-death account, into a world where many dispute the validity and authenticity of such experiences and believe 'mythologizing' to be a pointless conjecture. But he believed humanity needed to move beyond the limitations of science and the intellect and investigate myths of the psyche that although cannot be proven, can bring healing and broach inexplicable matters, such as death and immortality, of which we have no real knowledge. Through clues manifesting from the archetypal and metaphorical world, there lie potentials for enlightenment.

Having explored Jung's concepts on the nature and origins of archetypes, an important question to be considered is: does the NDE represent an archetype that is specifically connected with death and illumination? Near-death research uncovers the universal, paranormal, mystical, and recurring characteristics of the phenomenon, which manifest in primordial images that form patterns of psychic energy within the collective unconscious, and so validate the transpersonal quality of the experience. Michael Grosso claims that a specific archetype is evident during the NDE. He names it as being the *"archetype of death and enlightenment"*[9] that fits into an archetypal pattern associated with a specific situation in life—that of physical death. During an NDE, a formation of events manifest at the brink of death, hinting that such a pattern resides in the deeper layers of the psyche. Archetypal energies are not static, but remain fluid to reveal an abundance of recurring motifs and affirmations associated with near-death journeys, as defined by Moody. Grosso enumerates an archetypal definition in this context:

> The term *archetype* does not here denote a single thing or a simple static formula: it is shorthand for a constellation of recurrent, though fluid, motifs. We find not one thing but a family of psychic processes. In the near-death experience we find personifications, guides, light beings, deceased relatives, religious and mythical figures, voices and presences. We also observe situations, ways and places, such as coming to a border, beholding heavenly (and sometimes infernal)

> landscapes and cities, hearing the music of the spheres, passing through tunnels, cones, whorls, caves, soaring through darkness into the light, having prophetic visions of global catastrophe and new age. The common thread of the various elements of the near-death archetype is the theme of transformation.[10]

Near-death narratives, like many myths, illustrate how archetypal sequences address human experience and the essential key elements of life—through clearly defining how the individual is a finite creature that is separated from the numinous sacred, but continually strives to achieve individuation and find a spiritual identity in the mysterious realms of the cosmos.

The following part of this chapter explores narratives of NDE survivors that have been well-documented and brought to the attention of leading researchers in the field of near-death studies. Through contemplating and comparing the archetypal symbolic content of these accounts, it is possible to assess whether these people appear to have experienced the archetype of death and enlightenment.

The first sequence of events to be considered is the sensation of an out-of-body state, passing through a dark tunnel or void, and a vision of heavenly realms and encountering a "being of light." This 'light' being is often perceived in NDEs of Western culture to manifest in the image of Christ and symbolizes an encounter with the Self archetype, giving rise to feelings of immortality. Ancient hero myths also encompassed a meeting with eternal deities, and various rituals and rites commemorating these figures reenacted the imagining of liberation from death. Invoking such an apparition was also the prime objective of ancient Mystery cults. Rites of deification projected archetypal images, including Dionysos and Persephone, and participants believed they had encountered the deities and so experienced a perception of eternal life. Jung writes:

> The universal hero myth, for example, always refers to a powerful man or god-man who vanquishes evil in the form of dragons, serpents, monsters, demons and so on, and who liberates his people from destruction and death. The narration or ritual repetition of sacred texts and ceremonies, and the worship of such a figure . . . grip the audience with numinous emotions (as if with magic spells) and exalt the individual to an identification with the hero.[11]

Religious imagery, such as Christ, manifesting in contemporary NDEs is not that surprising, given that the roots of Christianity are steeped in Egyptian mythology and the 'god-man,' who originated from the myth of Osiris and his son, Horus. Many contemporary near-death experiencers believe they witness the form of Christ, projected through the image of pure light. Jung also relates that one night he awoke and at the foot of his bed, surrounded by a glowing light, he saw a beautiful vision of Christ on the Cross, symbolizing alchemical transformation. The figure was of a greenish gold hue and Jung states that he "had an essentially alchemical vision of Christ."[12] The green gold represented the living essence that the alchemists thought was contained in all things, and the emphasis on metal in Jung's vision emphasized "the undisguised alchemical conception of Christ as a union of spiritually alive and physically dead matter."[13]

While the image of the Self is often envisioned through a masculine vision of Christ, it is important to remember that he was both the son of God *and* the Divine Mother, Mary, who suckled and gave him life-sustaining energy. Within the collective unconscious, the Christ archetype is associated with feminine qualities of compassion and love. Works of art, including Leonardo da Vinci's, *The Head of Christ*, and Simeone's, *Sacred Heart of Christ*, depict these nurturing qualities. Similarly, Bellini portrays Christ in a long white robe in the *Transfiguration of Christ.* Known for performing miracles and providing guidance on how to live more consciously through parables, the masculine image of Christ is seen to encompass feminine attributes, thus making him 'whole.' Certain individuals encounter a female projection of the Self during their NDEs, often in the form of the Virgin Mary that also appears in a bright light.

Margot Grey describes the threshold of death, often envisaged by NDErs as a dark tunnel, representing "a passage between one state of being and another, leading on to other realms of perception."[14] The motif of the tunnel, cave, hole, or similar entry point that leads to an alternate realm, symbolizes enlightenment, as illustrated in Plato's allegory of release from the dark cave, when the prisoner realizes that "what he's seen before was inconsequential, but that now—because he is a bit closer to the things that are and is turned towards things that are more—he sees more correctly."[15]

Mythic beliefs in the deceased undertaking a journey are borne out of the elaborate preparations, scrolls, and prayers found surrounding the remains of the dead in many early cultures, including that of the ancient Egyptians. The sensation of an out-of-body state, commonly described in the NDE, also symbolizes an alchemical transformation, attained through relinquishing the restraints of an embodied existence. This state of *disembodiment* and an initial image of darkness are also associated with the states of death and rebirth in the *bardo of becoming,* described in *The Tibetan Book of the Dead.* Sogyal Rinpoche writes:

> The final phase of the dissolution process of the bardo of dying . . . is when the black experience of "full attainment" dawns "like and empty sky shrouded in utter darkness." At this point, the teaching speaks of a moment of bliss and joy. One of the main features of the near-death experience is the

> impression of moving "at a terrific speed" and "feeling weightless" through a black space, "a total, peaceful, wonderful blackness," and down a "long, dark tunnel."[16]

One of the most widely publicized accounts of an NDE is that of Betty J. Eadie, who describes feeling her spirit rise from her dead body and rapidly moving through a dark tunnel feeling calm and serene, as she passed through what she perceived to be "the valley of death". At the end of the tunnel, she saw a brilliant light and noticed a man radiating in the light:

> There was no questioning who he was . . . . He was Jesus Christ . . . . He was life itself, love itself . . . . I knew that I had known him from the beginning, from long before my earth life, because my spirit *remembered* him.[17]

Historically, light emerging from darkness symbolizes a universal primordial image of the rising of consciousness. This symbol is found in many mythologies and is referenced in the Christian Bible: "And the light shines in the darkness" (John: 1-5). The NDE pattern, which involves coming forth from the darkness into the light, is also found in many creation myths from diverse cultures. Grosso writes:

> We find a similar sequence in many creation myths: in the *Rig-Veda.* Hesiod's *Theogony,* the Old Testament and the Scandinavian *Eddas.* For Jews, Arabs, Germanic peoples Celts and many others, a day begins with night; darkness precedes the dawning of the light. Light is a primordial image of consciousness; it always rises from the depth of darkness.[18]

In *The Tibetan Book of the Dead,* the deceased also encounters the image of clear light shining in all its magnificence. Sögyal Rinpoche writes:

> At the moment of death, the Ground Luminosity or Clear Light dawns in all its splendor. The *Tibetan Book of the Dead* says: "O son/daughter of an enlightened family . . . your Rigpa is inseparable luminosity and emptiness and dwells as a great expanse of light; beyond birth or death". It is, in fact, the Buddha of unchanging Light.[19]

In 1975, following a lightning strike and being determined clinically dead, Dannion Brinkley told of an NDE during which, after passing through a dark tunnel, he came into a brilliant light and encountered a higher being:

> The being of Light stood directly in front of me. As I gazed into its essence I could see prisms of color, as through it were composed of tiny diamonds, each emitting the colors of the rainbow. Although I refer to the Being of Light as a "he," I never saw this Being as either male or female.[20]

Brinkley also 'saw' energy fields resembling light prisms and passed through lush landscapes, as he flew like a bird—an ancient symbol of the soul—over the realms of a Chrystal City of cathedrals that reminded him of similar ancient French monuments. Such visions of alternate realms and landscapes are also experienced by the deceased in the *bardo of becoming*. Following a heart attack, a few years later, Brinkley reported a second NDE in which he met the same formless image of the Being of Light that he believes represented a higher power.

Near-death researcher and experiencer, P. M. H. Atwater, describes a vision of light and all things existing in a shimmering curtain of energy. She then had an apparition of Jesus, who suddenly appeared in front of her. "He instantly appeared without any effort on my part. When he stood before me, there was no feeling to bow down or worship him: rather, I felt him to be more of an elder brother, long absent, whose return was joyous and a cause for celebration."[21]

Mellen-Thomas Benedict had an NDE in 1982, when a hospice nurse declared him clinically dead. Rigor mortis was starting to set in, when he eventually revived and he had been 'dead' for at least an hour and a half. Benedict describes how he seemed to fall asleep and then darkness surrounded him, as he had an out-of-body experience. He then saw a light shining and as he turned toward the light, he sensed a variety of archetypal religious images. Having no particular religious affinity, Benedict witnessed many images of the archetypal guise of 'God.' "The Light kept changing into different figures, like Jesus, Buddha, Krishna, mandalas, archetypal images and signs . . . . As the Light revealed itself to me, I became aware that what I was really seeing was our higher-Self matrix."[22]

Jung's narration of his NDE that took place in 1944, following a heart attack, describes a disembodied sensation of hovering above the earth that was outlined in vibrant blue light. While feeling that he was floating through the universe, he saw a large dark stone rather than passing through a tunnel. This huge rock had steps leading to an opening:

> An entrance led into a small antechamber. To the right of the entrance, a black Hindu sat silently in lotus posture upon a stone bench. He wore a white gown, and I knew that he expected me. Two steps led up to this antechamber, and inside, on the left, was the gate to the temple. Innumerable tiny niches, each with a saucer-like cavity filled with coconut oil and small burning wicks, surrounded the door with a wreath of bright flames.[23]

Perhaps as a result of his life-long fascination with Eastern mythology, Jung imagined the presence of a Hindu image of the Being of Light. A few days before his death, Jung recounted a dream in which he again encountered the image of the stone, and although it manifested in a slightly different form, he saw the following words engraved upon it, "And this shall be a sign unto you of wholeness and oneness."[24] He also saw trees that had golden threads sparkling in their roots, as they enveloped him in the embrace of alchemical transformation.

Such powerful meetings with a numinous being, often projected by the archetypal light, symbolize an extended conscious awareness that leads experiencers to believe they are reunited with the archetype of 'God.' Although in Christianity, identifying the Self with God may be viewed as blasphemous, Eastern philosophies are not reticent to form this equation. Hindus speak of the oneness of *Brahman* and *Atman*, and Tibetan Buddhists believe the divine light is in fact a projection of the Self. Ring proposes the divine reality is, in reality, *oneself*. He further comments that this archetypal image of the Self "is not merely a projection of one's personality, however, but one's *total self*, or what in some traditions is called the *higher self*."[25]

The second sequence of events includes: a life review, feelings of wholeness, gaining enlightened wisdom, and reentry into the physical body. An integral part of the NDE sequence is a life review, similar to those described in great detail in *The Egyptian Book of the Dead*, when a confrontation with shadow aspects of the psyche is revealed. Those reliving the actions and stories of their lives tend to judge themselves harshly, but also appear to be initiated into the possibility for change. Eadie writes, "I understood that I had to let go of the past. If I had broken laws or sinned, I needed to change my heart, forgive myself, and then move onward."[26]

Brinkley describes how he witnessed a review of his entire life. "This life review was not pleasant. From the moment it began until it ended, I was faced with the sickening reality that I had been an unpleasant person, someone who was self-centered and mean."[27] However, as the burden of guilt lifted, he realized this self-reflection gave him the knowledge of how to improve his life.

Jung describes an unfamiliar feeling, as all of earthly existence was stripped away, but he sensed that what remained was the sum entity of his entire life. "The experience gave me a feeling of extreme poverty, but at the same time of great fullness. There was no longer anything I wanted or desired. I existed in an objective form; I was what I had been and lived. At first the sense of annihilation predominated, of having been stripped or pillaged; but suddenly that became of no consequence."[28]

Following an almost fatal accident, Ginette Paris experienced core components of the NDE, including a sensation of golden light filling the room, absolute radiance, and a life review. "It is the first time I am honestly willing to confront my shadow in its full dimensions, wide and long....I see my faults not through guilt. I am being led to understand that, try as we may to love well, we also do harm, even to, especially to, those we love; having a shadow is part of the world of the living. The grace is that the divinity of love seems ready to absolve me."[29]

Atwater also describes a life review. "For me it was a total reliving of *every* thought I had ever thought, *every* word I had ever spoken, and *every* deed I had ever done; *plus* the effect of each thought, word and deed on everyone and anyone who had ever come within my environment or sphere of influence whether I knew them or not . . . ."[30]

During their life reviews, these individuals became aware of the totality of their actions and thoughts, both positive and negative, which are then reconciled as a unified whole in a timeless, eternal dimension. The bi-polar aspect of archetypes can enable a glance into the future, as well as a past review. Brinkley had his future mission revealed that would involve helping others rediscover spiritual meaning, as he was led to a series of therapy rooms that appeared to be the equivalent of modern-day oracles, similar to those of ancient Greece:

> I know that each of these rooms represents a modern form of an ancient oracle, the temples of spirit and mystery that were popular in ancient Greece. For instance, what takes place in the bed is similar to the dream incubation that took place in the temples of Asklepios. The reading area represents the temple of Delphi, where people used to talk to the spirits. The reflection chamber is the "necromanteum" of Ephyra, where the ancients went to see apparitions of their departed loved ones.[31]

The dissolution of space and time that projects both the past and future possibilities is described as an overwhelming sensation. Jung writes, "How can I imagine that I exist simultaneously the day before yesterday, today, and the day after tomorrow? There would be things which would not yet have begun, other things which would be indubitably present, and others again which would already be finished—and yet all this would be one."[32]

Feelings of 'wholeness' are also imagined during an NDE, and even individuals with life handicaps find them to be gone in the spiritual realm. Moody describes a case history:

> A man I knew fell from a billboard onto some high-voltage wires. He lost his legs and part of one arm from the burns. He had an out-of-body experience in the operating room. While looking down at his own body, the first thought that came to his mind was, "Look at that poor man." He didn't even recognize the body on the table as being his own. When he finally realized that badly damaged body was his, he noticed something else peculiar: his spiritual body was not handicapped in any way.[33]

Benedict had a spiritual sense of wholeness during his NDE, which he believes, culminated in a physical healing. When he went back to his doctor for a check up, he was told that all signs of his former illness had miraculously vanished:

> Within three days I was feeling normal again, clear yet different than I had ever felt in my life. I remember the doctor at the clinic looking at the before and after scans, saying, "Well there is nothing here now." I said, "Really it must be a miracle!" He said, "No, these things happen they are called spontaneous remission." He acted very unimpressed. But here was a miracle, and I was impressed.[34]

Spontaneous remission in cancer patients said to have experienced an NDE have been recorded in near-death studies, and some researchers believe that such a 'miracle' could be the result of exposure to the brilliant light that may change the body chemistry in some way. This theory echoes with the sentiments of ancient Greeks and Egyptians, who thought healing took place through divine intervention in the sanctity of the healing temples.

One of the primary characteristics of mystical state of consciousness is gaining profound spiritual insights and esoteric wisdom. Benedict writes:

> The Light explained to me that there is no death; we are immortal beings. We have already been alive for ever! I realized that we are part of a natural living system that recycles itself endlessly.[35]

Eadie had existential questions during her NDE, and believes she received answers. "His light now began to fill my mind, and my questions were answered even before I had fully asked them. His light was knowledge. It had power to fill me with truth . . . .This knowledge was more like remembering. Things were coming back to me from long before my life on earth."[36]

Brinkley believes his NDE transported him to a place of higher learning. "Now more than ever I knew that this was a place of learning. I would be steeped in knowledge, taught in a way that I had never been taught before . . . . I would become knowledge and know everything that was important to know . . . . It was like being a drop of water bathed in the knowledge of the ocean, or a beam of light knowing what all light knows."[37]

Paris sensed a meaningful wisdom, as she hovered in the threshold between life and death, bathed in the image of light that surrounded her and her daughter. "I have never seen anything as beautiful as the light that flows from the bed on which my daughter and I lay, never felt the bond of love with such simplicity, imperfection and all. It is a miracle happening, a very simple and common one: I have ceased to find fault with the world, even if it is delivering death to me."[38]

Jung describes how he reentered the enchanted states of ecstasy of his NDE and had mythological visions that imparted the wisdom of creation. "All these experiences were glorious. Night after night, I floated in a state of purest bliss, 'thronged round with the images of all creation.'"[39]

The new ineffable insights, imparted during NDEs are experienced as a wisdom that language alone cannot fully articulate upon return to everyday reality. Many try to recreate their rapturous visions through painting or drawing, but the colors are simply not vibrant enough to recapture the vividness of the landscapes, images, and symbolism. But, rather than gaining wisdom, the individuals concerned often sense a *remembering* of ancient knowledge. Waking up to regain lost primordial understanding is a theme of many world religious traditions, ancient Gnostic and Hellenistic philosophy, Buddhist and Hindu scriptures, and Sufi poetry.

For NDE survivors reentering the physical body causes much anguish, for there is a reluctance to leave such a blissful state. Some feel anger and frustration at having to return. However, these people also sense that they have a unique mission to complete in their earthly carnations. Eadie, says, "Although I would hate to leave the glorious world of light and love for one of hardship and uncertainty, the necessity of my mission compelled me to return."[40]

Brinkley felt resistance at leaving the archetypal realms. "After coming here, going back to earth would be as confining as living on the head of a pin. Still I was given no choice . . . . And then I came back."[41]

As Jung prepared to enter the rock temple of his vision, an image of his doctor appeared, framed by a gold-colored laurel wreath or gold chain. He seemed to be in his primal form, as king of a Greek region known as Kos, which was famous for being the site of the renowned healing temple of Asklepios. Jung recalls feelings of deep dismay, as the doctor communicated that he must return to earth. "Dr. H. had been delegated by the earth to deliver a message to me, to tell me there was a protest against my going away. I had no right to leave the earth and must return. The moment I heard that, the vision ceased."[42] Jung was saddened at this news. "I was profoundly disappointed, for now it all seemed to have been for nothing . . . . I was not allowed to enter the temple, to join the people in whose company I belonged."[43]

Paris had a vision of a delicate butterfly fluttering above her head, perhaps acting as a transition guide to a realm beyond, as she is "waiting, still and focused, ready for a plunge into death."[44] The butterfly is a motif for the psyche or soul in ancient mythology. Ancient wall paintings discovered in Pompeii depict Psyche as a young girl with butterfly-wings. The ancient Egyptians saw a metaphor in the wrappings of the mummy and the chrysalis of the butterfly, and the Greeks also placed golden butterflies in the tombs of the deceased. This symbolism was also contained in a metaphor used by St. Teresa of Avila to explain the destiny of the soul following her ecstatic visions of the kingdom of God. Kübler-Ross also often used this imagery to illustrate how the soul left the body at the moment of physical death. The image of the butterfly stays with Paris, as she hovers in that liminal space of transition. As she asks the question, "Am I coming or going?" The butterfly signifies that she must return to the land of the living. She describes how it "folds its wings into a cocoon, and takes refuge in my heart, as if to say: "We shall meet again, but not just now."[45]

During the NDE, experiencers sense a border or barrier and individuals either choose, or are instructed, to return to earthly life. In the *bardo* states there is no return to earth, as the person remains 'dead.' However, in Tibet, a tribe of people known as *deloks* traditionally experience a phenomenon that much resembles accounts of near-death narratives, when ordinary people, usually women of great spiritual faith, 'die' and then return to life with a message for the living. Sögyal Rinpoche writes:

> In Tibetan *de lok* means returned from death," and traditionally deloks are people who seemingly "die" as a result of an illness, and find themselves traveling in the bardo. They visit the hell realms, where they witness the judgment of the dead and the sufferings of hell, and sometimes they go to paradise and the buddha realms. They can be accompanied by a deity who protects them and explains what is happening. After a week the delok is sent back to the body with a message from the Lord of Death for the living, urging them to spiritual practice and a beneficial way of life.[46]

This ancient ritual tradition continues to flourish in modern-day Tibet and delok women experience out-of-body states for several hours on certain commemorative days in the Buddhist calendar. The major purpose of this otherworldly journey is for the women to act as intermediaries between the living and the dead.

Children also have NDEs and the image and symbolism of the 'child' was central in the ancient Eleusinian Mystery rites and personified in the demi-god, Iakkhos, known as the attendant of Demeter. He was depicted as a young man adorned with a myrtle wreath, holding the twin torches of the Mysteries that symbolized the contrast between darkness and light. He led the procession of initiates in the ritual cry of joy on the sixth day of the celebration, as they made the pilgrimage along the Sacred Way to Eleusis.

In contemporary cultures, children narrating near-death journeys, often describe a similar out-of-body state, moving through a tunnel, and seeing the same archetypal imagery and heavenly realms that adults report, even though their imaginings are often much simpler. Children's NDEs include many of the core components described by Moody. However, perhaps due to their more pure and innocent state, young children do not appear to have a life review. These near-death journeys are very valid to NDE research, because they are often free from cultural conditioning, yet still tap into the mythic pool of the collective unconscious. The messages these children bring back repeat those of adults having the experience and echo the same powerful affirmation of resurrection.

Morse has collected many narratives of children's NDEs, which include that of a young patient who 'died' on the operating table. The boy was later resuscitated and told his mother that he had "been climbing a staircase to heaven. It was such a good and peaceful feeling. I felt wonderful. I was on a staircase and it was dark, and I started climbing upward. I got about half way up the staircase and decided not to go any higher. I wanted to go on up, but I knew I wouldn't come back if I went too high."[47] The boy then turned and went back down the staircase and reentered his body.

A sixteen-year-old boy, Dean, told Morse what happened after his heart stopped beating during a cardiac arrest. He found himself disembodied and moving through a dark tunnel at great speed. "At this point I also noticed there was someone with me.

He was about seven feet tall and wore a long white gown with a simple belt tied at the waist. His hair was golden, and although he didn't say anything, I wasn't afraid because I could feel him radiating peace and love."[48] Dean then suddenly sensed himself back in his body. He referred to this profound experience as being 'supernatural.' It was only some time later, when he saw a television documentary on NDEs that he realized what had happened to him.

Children also describe deathbed visions in which they sense archetypal transition guides. Morse tells of a young boy who was close to dying and started to imagine landscapes from *another world*. These visions became more frequent and intense in the six days prior to the child's death; they included images of bright lights, transpersonal realms, and the image of God. Morse comments, "From the time I met him, Mike looked forward to becoming "one with God" in his visions. 'When I become one with God, the dreams will be over and I will be dead.' That finally happened. Peacefully. It made glad I hadn't taken those visions away from him."[49].

What is most fascinating about these narratives is that young children describe the Light in the same way as enlightened spiritual teachers. Their imaginings also contain the main characteristics of a religious or mystical experience, as defined by William James, who wrote extensively of the noetic, transient, and passive qualities of transcendent visions.

The myth of Er contained a reminder of the primordial vision of pure light "that stretched over the whole of heaven and earth."[50] Part of the human being's earthly incarnation may involve the need to rediscover the core meaning of such a vision, which manifests during the mystical state of the NDE.

For some NDErs, however, the total sum of their experiences are said to consist of disturbing visions of hellish realms and apparitions of terrifying creatures or images. But, these shocking imaginings may represent incomplete NDEs, rather than alternatives. Some survivors describe these dark realms vanishing into heavenly ascents and the light, but what could be the reason for such fearsome archetypal manifestations? Some fervent Christians believe negative near-death experiences are a judgment call—illustrating the concept of eternal damnation for those who do not obey the will of God. Others suggests hellish experiences offer a chance of religious conversion, similar to that described in Bede's early near-death narrative.

The theory of a 'collective' fear of ego-death rather than a merely personal one has been overlooked in previous near-death studies, but is extremely important in illustrating the full spectrum of archetypal experience stored in the collective unconscious. For those having a fearful experience, this theory offers an interesting avenue of inquiry, for the myth of death may also express itself as a collective experience. Should individuals enter this collective imagining during an NDE, it could result in them being drawn into previously unimaginable realms of intense awareness and perception. A negative otherworldly journey does not necessarily reflect an unworthy life. Christopher M. Bache suggests archetypal images of painful suffering may manifest, as a result of engaging with these dimensions that are alive in the collective unconscious.[51]

The metaphor of the personal confronting the collective reservoir of suffering that ultimately results in transformation and transcendence is portrayed in the myth of Christ who, during his Crucifixion, suffered the sins of the world, but then ascended to the heavenly realms. The myth of Inanna psychologically symbolizes the need to integrate both the light and shadow aspects of the Self, as Inanna is required to "journey towards, and to encounter the fierce, forbidding and terrifying queen, Ereshkigal—Inanna's other self."[52] In hero myths, battles with entities, including fearful dragons, serpents, and demons have to be faced for the hero to triumph and free his people from death and destruction. There is also a parallel in the images of wrathful deities appearing in *The Tibetan Book of the Dead* that are encountered by the deceased, who is unable to fully merge with the image of clear light. Due to a lack of understanding of 'pure' awareness, moving on to the second *bardo* state of *Chonyi Bardo* contains encounters with both peaceful and enraged entities. This frightening initiation is one of purification. Sögyal Rinpoche writes, "The spiritual task is to know that these are merely the radiance of one's own intrinsic nature. This realization frees the awareness to merge inseparably with the Light of wisdom."[53]

In Donegal found in the northwest of Ireland there is a small island on the Lake of Lough Derg, known as *Saint Patrick's Purgatory* that myths and legends describe as being the entrance to the underworld, as opposed to previous beliefs that this portal was to be found in ancient Greece or Asia, because this geographical area is the nearest to where the sun sets into the western ocean. A Benedictine monk, Henry of Saltry, recounted underworld journeys that emanated from this holy shrine, including that of the medieval Irish knight Owen, who served under King Stephen of England.

Owen wanted absolution from some of his transgressions and asked that he be allowed to do the most dangerous penance of St. Patrick's purgatory. Having fasted for many days, on the sixteenth morning, he was permitted to enter the cave that led to the underworld. He survived and returned from this perilous undertaking to recount encountering dark archetypal energies, including howling spirits, grotesque demons, and stinking abysses. Through keeping the image of God in mind, as he confronted these terrors, Owen successfully navigated his way through the underworld of hell, and eventually arrived at a far more beautiful landscape, surrounded by glass with a golden gate that was embedded with precious jewels. He realized this was heaven and begged to enter, but was told that he could only pass through after death and was led back to the cave entrance. However, his place in paradise was now guaranteed, as the descent into the dark death realms had resulted in absolution. As the story swept throughout Europe, many curious pilgrims flocked to the scene seeking similar forgiveness through penance and prayer.

People living in this era were curious and fascinated by accounts of otherworldly journeys depicting visions of heaven and hell, just as we are today. Although traces of the mysterious cave have vanished, pilgrimages to the site still continue and many take part in three day vigils at the island basilica and, as in ancient initiation rites, sleep deprivation, and fasting play a major part in rituals that also include prayer and chanting, symbolic of death and spiritual rebirth, to prepare pilgrims to face death in a pure state.

In Dante's *Inferno,* the pilgrim has a vision in which a dark demon "had slung a sinner, upward from the thighs, in front the demon gripped him by the ankles" (XX1: 35-36). The image of hell has been recorded in many world religions and although descriptions of this realm vary, the common characteristic is that hell represents a place of alienation and estrangement from 'God,' resulting in painful suffering. The Jewish concept of hell is known as Gehenna, described as being a fiery pit of torment. For the ancient Greeks and Romans, Tarturus was the part of Hades where evil spirits were punished. In Hinduism, the deity Yama is known as the Lord of Death and Justice and weighs good and bad karma that has accrued throughout an individual's lifetime. Those who have transgressed must atone and endure punishment in a lower realm known as *naraka,* a Sanskrit term for the underworld. However, this realm is not permanent, but only a temporary phase in the cycle of reincarnation according to the law of karma. In Christian mythology, hell is described as being eternal and a second death for unrepentant sinners. "This is the second death, the lake of fire; and anyone whose name was not found written in the book of life was thrown into the lake of fire" (Revelation 20:14-15).

Negative archetypal manifestations in near-death journeys may simply be a rite of purification necessary for the continuation of a spiritual journey. Bache writes, "Though difficult and painful to confront, their intent is simply spiritual purification. Paradoxically, *the severity of our pain in this confrontation is a measure of how much more we are becoming than we have yet managed to be, both individually and collectively.*"[54]

George Ritchie had an NDE when he was a young serviceman. He describes an out-of-body sensation and found himself searching for his body that he eventually discovered covered with a sheet, and then realized that he was 'dead.' Suddenly, he saw an incredibly bright light and sensed that the light was formed of a Man of light that he recognized as being Jesus. The image symbolized "power itself, older than time and yet more modern than anyone I had ever met."[55] Ritchie knew immediately that the 'Man' loved him unconditionally, as he had a life review. He then experienced a journey through hell, which was a place of dire misery and suffering, but this was followed by a heavenly vision, where inhabitants were not self-absorbed and wallowing in their misery, but rather diligently working and involved in a higher purpose. He says, "Jesus could only reveal as much as my mind could grasp. He had first shown me a hellish realm, filled with beings trapped in some form of self-attention. Now behind, beyond, through all of this I began to perceive a whole new realm."[56]

Ritchie, like Brinkley, believes he was shown vast libraries filled with books of knowledge and sensed there was still a higher reality. He was transported to a huge void and saw a shining city in the distance, which appeared to be made from the light. He then felt as though the image of light accompanied him back to the hospital room and back to his body. He remembers the anguish he felt as the darkness of the hospital room closed around him, and consciousness slipped away.

Ritchie's otherworldly narrative is definitely steeped in a

Christian mythological background and there are parallels with Bede's early account of Drycthelm's near-death journey and Dante's description of the wise guide leading the pilgrim through the darkness of hell to eventually ascend to the heavenly realms of light. Like the pilgrim, Ritchie also believes that his sight was not clear enough to keep a lasting impression of paradise. "My imperfect sight could not now sustain more than an instant's glimpse of this real, this ultimate heaven."[57]

Howard Storm was an atheist with no spiritual values, and describes his life prior to his NDE as being one of meaningless self-absorption. Storm was totally unprepared when, following a medical emergency, he felt himself disengage from his body and journey into complete darkness, where hundreds of frenzied people began to push and shove him around. Alone and terrified, he started to pray and, to his amazement, his tormentors started to back away from him, as he experienced a life review in which he sensed, "My life was building a monument to my ego . . . my illusions of power, were all an extension of my ego . . . . All those things that I had lived for were lost to me, and they didn't mean a thing."[58] Through the darkness, he saw a bright light and a luminous being that he believed to be Jesus, who took him out of the depths of hell and into a vast illumination of the light.

Storm was then told he must return and found himself back in his hospital bed. The fact that a pronounced atheist should experience visions of 'hell' and a projection of the Christ image during his NDE does much to validate the theory that archetypes function independently and compensate for lack of affinity with the unconscious realms. Grosso writes, "So atheism would be an extreme state of one-sidedness and alienation from the powers of the unconscious. A vision of Christ might well occur to such an atheist."[59]

There are also accounts of 'shared' NDEs when a person who is not dying, but has a close relationship with someone nearing death, enters an altered state of consciousness and shares part of the near-death journey. These narratives are fascinating and help to dispel the theory that near-death imagery is either caused by medication administered to a person close to death or the dying brain hypothesis. Although it is feasible to suggest that people close to each other may share common thoughts and emotions, the concept that the mind is not confined to the brain, enables consideration of a more literal sharing of experiences and the possibility that a psychic sensitivity activated during the transitional phase of death, may enable out-of-body states and archetypal imagery to be experienced by those attending the dying. Moody writes, "Dozens upon dozens of first rate individuals have related to me that, as a loved one died, they themselves lifted out of their own bodies and accompanied their dying loved upwards towards a beautiful and loving light."[60]

Research into empathetic NDEs includes, reports from doctors, nurses, and hospice workers, who strongly believe they have witnessed the spirit leaving the body at the moment of death. These bystanders are convinced that they simultaneously experience a transcendent state. The powerful message people in these shared experiences narrate is the same as that in "first-person" NDEs—the importance of, and all engulfing, feelings of unconditional love.

In *Parting Visions,* Morse recounts such an incident that took place during World War II:

> Kari Skala was one of Germany's most noted poets. During World War II, he had an NDE. He and his best friend were huddled together in a foxhole during an artillery bombardment. The shells hit closer and closer until one finally hit close to Skala's friend and killed him. Kari felt his friend slip forward into his arms and go limp with death. Then a strange thing happened to Skala. He states that he felt himself being drawn up with his friend, above their bodies and then above the battlefield. Skala could look down and see

himself holding his friend. Then he looked up and saw a bright light and felt himself going toward it with his friend. Then he stopped and returned to his body. He was uninjured except for a hearing loss that resulted from the artillery blast.[61]

Experiences, including the above, suggest NDE imagery is not just limited to the personal, but is also a collective imagining that we can all share. During this turbulent period in history, it was not unusual for many to experience heightened states of awareness, and there were numerous accounts of ESP abilities that enabled apparitions of deceased loved ones, before telegrams announcing death or 'missing in action' arrived. Such experiences would appear to validate Jung's theories on synchronicity and reaffirm the hypothesis that rather than seeking literal truth, there is more value in discovering mythic, psychological, or spiritual meaning.

There are also occasions when groups of people, often following natural disasters, share disembodied states. Sometimes, individuals witness others leaving their bodies; they then communicate their observations of the NDE, as it takes places. Following the Tangshan earthquake in 1976, doctors found that forty of the eighty-one survivors narrated a near-death journey. P. M. H. Atwater writes that these descriptions contained "feeling estranged from the body as though it belonged to someone else, unusually vivid thoughts, loss of emotions, unusual bodily sensations, life seeming like a dream, a feeling of dying, a feeling of peace or euphoria, a life review or 'panoramic memory' and thinking unusually fast."[62] She adds that Chinese accounts of NDEs vary from their Western counterparts, leading physicians conducting the study to determine that diverse cultural backgrounds and religious mythologies appeared to account for anomalies in the content of such narratives.

In 1989, a fire-fighter described a shared NDE. He was part of an elite fire-crew fighting a blaze that got out of control, and as the crew struggled for oxygen, he felt he was about to die and immediately went into an out-of-body state, looking down at his lifeless body. Suddenly, he found himself at peace and saw his colleagues in a similar state, hovering above their bodies. One of his crew had a defective foot, but in this disembodied state, the man was free of this impediment. He then described seeing a bright light and his deceased great-grandfather appeared as a guide throughout his NDE. Through wordless communication, he was told to choose whether to return to his body, but was reluctant to do so and wanted to stay in the peaceful and beautiful paradise. He was also afraid of reentering a badly burned body, but was assured that both he, and his crew members, would suffer no ill effects.

Finding himself back in his body, he saw that metal tools had melted in the intense heat and despite the fire that continued to rage; he was able to walk to the surrounding hilltop, feeling insulated in some kind of protective bubble. He then met up with other members of the crew, who also escaped the fire with no lasting injuries. The group knelt in prayer, full of awe at what had taken place and all described similar out-of-body sensations, encountering a deceased relative, and being given the choice of whether or not to return.[63]

Shared stories of near-death journeys are a fairly new observation in near-death studies. However, such shared imaginings were part of Mystery Cult otherworldly projection. In the Eleusinian rites, a number of initiates shared archetypal images and beatific visions of Persephone. Plato also made reference to groups witnessing such wondrous visions, "This did we celebrate in our true and perfect selves . . . when as initiates we were allowed to see perfect and simple, still and happy Phantoms" (33: 58-62).

All the near-death narratives referenced, present very similar accounts that can enrich our myths about dying, as the archetypal and symbolic patterns definitely tap into mythic content of the collective unconscious. These powerful stories give expression and meaning to particular archetypal images, and reaffirm the religious and spiritual belief that death can be considered a great adventure and transition from earthly to transcendent reality. Grosso writes, that "what we call death is archetypally portrayed as the road to a greater and more fulfilling reality than what we know in life."[64]

Great relevance can be discovered in recognizing the existence of an archetype of death and enlightenment, which can compensate for the narrow ego view of death, resulting in the lessening of human fear and anxiety of the unknown. Cognitively, the archetype points to an expanded realm of consciousness and metaphysically, it suggests the reality of an eternal spiritual realm. As illustrated, this archetype of death and enlightenment does appear to manifest during near-death journeys, resulting in a new sense of Self and purpose.

Jung stresses the continuing importance of archetypal images and believes they highlight higher values of the psyche. In a letter to Dr. Kristine Mann, he writes:

> Behind this veil, he wrote, there is a sense of peace and fulfillment such that one does not wish to return. He advised her: "Whatever you do, if you do it sincerely, will eventually become the bridge to your wholeness, a good ship that carries you through the darkness of your second birth, which seems to be death to the outside.[65]

Countless other survivors express similar joy and ecstatic feelings of peace, resulting in spiritual epiphanies. While such otherworldly journeys remain a mystery and cannot be scientifically proven experiencers are so convinced of the validity of an illumined voyage into an altered states of consciousnss that they appear to need no further validation from outside sources.

Notes

1. Robert R. Romanyshyn, *Ways of the Heart*, 36.
2. Joseph Campbell with Bill Moyers, *The Power of Myth*, 22-23.
3. William G. Doty, *Mythography: The Study of Myth and Rituals* (Tuscaloosa: Alabama University Press, 2000), 29.
4. C. G. Jung, *The Archetypes and the Collective Unconscious*, 7.
5. Ruth Schumann Altelme and Stephane Rossini, *Becoming Osiris: The Ancient Egyptian Death Experience*, trans. Jon Graham (Rochester: Inner Traditions, 1998), 112.
6. Melvin Morse, with Paul Perry, *Closer to the Light* (New York: Ivy Books, 1991), 90.
7. Robert Pogue Harrison, *The Dominion of the Dead* (Chicago: Chicago Press, 2003), 158-59.
8. C. G. Jung, "Approaching the Unconscious," *Man and His Symbols*, 69.
9. Michael Grosso, "The Archetype of Death and Enlightenment." *The Near-Death Experience A Reader*, eds. Lee W. Bailey and Jenny Yates (New York: Routledge, 1996), 129.
10. Ibid., 132.
11. C. G. Jung, "Approaching the Unconscious," 68.
12. C. G. Jung, *Memories, Dreams, Reflections*, 211.
13. Ibid., 211.
14. Margot Grey, *Return from Death*, 41.
15. Plato, *Republic*, V11: 515 d).
16. Sogyal Rinpoche, "The near-Death Experience: A Stairway to Heaven." *The Near-Death Experience A Reader*, 164.
17. Betty J. Eadie, with Curtis Taylor, *Embraced by the Light* (New York, Bantam, 1994), 41-42.
18. Michael Grosso, "The Archetype of Death and Enlightenment."*The Near-Death Experience A Reader*, 141.
19. Sogyal Rinpoche, "The Near-Death Experience: A Stairway

to Heaven." *The Near-Death Experience A Reader,* 164.
20. Dannion Brinkley, with Paul Perry, *Saved by the Light: The True Story of a Man Who Died Twice and the Profound Revelations He Received* (New York,: Harper Paperbacks, 1994), 10-11.
21. P. M. H. Atwater, *Coming Back to Life* (New York: Dodd, Mead & Co., 1988), 33.
22. Mellen-Thomas Benedict, "Through the Light and Beyond." *The Near-Death Experience A Reader,* 42.
23. C. G. Jung, *Memories,* 290.
24. Marie-Louise von Franz, *Jung: His Myths in Our Time* (New York: Inner City, 1975), 287.
25. Kenneth Ring, *Life at Death,* 240.
26. Betty J. Eadie, with Cutis Taylor, 71.
27. See Dannion Brinkley, *Saved by the Light,* 12-25.
28. C. G. Jung, *Memories,* 291.
29. Ginette Paris, *Wisdom of the Psyche* (New York: Routledge, 2007), 12.
30. P. M. H. Atwater, *Coming Back to Life,* 37.
31. Dannion Brinkley, *Saved by the Light,* 60-61.
32. C. G. Jung, *Memories,* 296.
33. Raymond Moody, *The Light Beyond* (New York: Bantam, 1988), 86.
34. Mellen-Thomas Benedict, "Through the Light and Beyond." *The Near-Death Experience A Reader,* 48.
35. Ibid., 46.
36. Betty J. Eadie, with Curtis Taylor, *Embraced by the Light,* 44.
37. Dannion Brinkley, *Saved by the Light,* 36.
38. Ginette Paris, *Wisdom of the Psyche,* 12.
39. C. G. Jung, *Memories,* 294.
40. Betty J. Eadie, with Curtis Taylor, *Embraced by the Light,* 118.
41. Dannion Brinkley, *Saved by the Light,* 61.
42. C. G. Jung, *Memories,* 292.
43. Ibid., 292.

44. Ginette Paris, *Wisdom of the Psyche*, 3.
45. Ibid., 12.
46. Sogyal Rinpoche, "The Near-Death Experience: A Staircase to Heaven." *The Near-Death Experience A Reader*, 173.
47. Melvin Morse, with Paul Perry, *Closer to the Light*, 31.
48. Ibid., 33.
49. Ibid., 66-67.
50. Plato, *Republic*, X: 616, c.
51. See Christopher M. Bache, 116.
52. Diane Wolkstein and Samuel Noah Kramer, *Inanna: Queen of Heaven and Earth*, 169.
53. Sogyal Rinpoche, "The Near-Death Experience: A Stairway to Heaven." *The Near-Death Experience A Reader*, 158.
54. Christopher M. Bache, *Dark Night*, 64.
55. George G. Ritchie, with Elizabeth Sherrill, *Return from Tomorrow* (Waco: Chosen Books, 1978), 49.
56. Ibid., 68-69.
57. Ibid., 73.
58. Howard Storm, *My Descent into Death* (Forest Row: Clairview, 2000), 25.
59. Michael Grosso, "The Archetype of Death and Enlightenment." *The Near-Death Experience A Reader*, 133.
60. Raymond Moody, *The Last Laugh: A New Philosophy of Near-Death Experiences, Apparitions and the Paranormal* (Charlottesville: Hampton Roads, 1999), 4.
61. See Melvin Morse, with Paul Perry, *Parting Visions: Uses and Meanings of Pre-Death Experiences* (New York: Villard, 1994), 45-46.
62. P. M. H. Atwater, *The Big Book of Near-Death Experiences: The Ultimate Guide to What Happens When We Die* (Charlottesville: Hampton Roads, 2007), 251.
63. See Arvin S. Gibson, *Fingerprints of God, Evidences from Near-Death Studies, Scientific Research on Creation and Mormon Theology* (Hammond: Horizon, 1999), 129-131.

64. Michael Grosso, "The Archetype of Death and Enlightenment." *The Near-Death Experience A Reader*, 142.
65. See C. G. Jung, *Jung on Death and Immortality*, 7 (from *Letters, Vol.* 1, 358-359.

Chapter 7

The After-Effects of Near-Death Journeys

Deep, unspeakable suffering may well be called a baptism, a regeneration, the initiation into a new state.
Ira Gershwin

While proof that NDEs manifest from a spiritual eternal realm of consciousness cannot yet be scientifically corroborated, we can observe the resulting full spectrum of important changes in the future lives of survivors. People having an NDE undergo an initiation, similar to those described in ancient rituals when initiates glimpsed mythic dimensions of their future existence, as they transcended everyday consciousness to experience non-duality that extended a sense of unity and 'wholeness.' Such illuminating visions can also manifest during the dreaming state. Shortly after Jung completed building the Bollingen Tower, he had recurring dreams of a complete replica of the tower standing on the other side of the lake. Shortly before his death, he was to dream again of the tower, which was formed of gold, an ancient alchemical symbol. He held the key to the entrance and a 'voice' informed him his new home was now ready. This dream symbolized the 'otherworldly' residence of the immortal Self that was now complete and awaited him. Marie-Louise von Franz writes, "When Jung dreamed of the golden tower in the Beyond, the unconscious furnished him with a primal, eternal image, a copy of which he had built for himself on earth."[1]

Ancient death rituals and ceremonies culminated in a rite of passage, but even though a soul had been separated from the living, it was believed that it could change direction and reappear once more among the living.[2] The three stages of separation, transition, and incorporation, consist of: parting from a former world, an intermediary liminal phase, and integration into a new state of being. These three hallmarks of initiation seem to also take place during the NDE when, during an out-of-body state, there is a sense of having sacrificed the physical body to enter a liminal threshold of the light, which simultaneously appears to exist between the duality of the physical and non-physical worlds. Upon returning to the earthly body, the survivor senses and feels some kind of mysterious transformation has taken place.

Understanding the enigma of otherworldly journeys is a difficult task, but many indigenous tribes look to find the meaning of archetypal transcendent experiences with the wisdom of hindsight. Victor Turner writes how the Ndembu people of northwestern Zambia believe that it is only "when the symbolic path from the unknown is completed that we can look back and comprehend its final form."[3]

Having completed the NDE sequence, survivors either decide to return to their bodies, or they are instructed to do so, but they usually have no memory of their reentry. In Plato's myth, Er "didn't know how he had come back to his body, except that waking up suddenly he saw himself lying on the pyre at dawn."[4] However, many experiencers land back in their bodies with an agonizing jolt, or wrenching sensation.

Integrating the magnitude of the NDE can be extremely difficult. Following his near-death experience, Jung spent three weeks clouded by depression and disappointment. "I felt weak and wretched, and scarcely dared to stir. Gloomily I thought, 'Now I must go back to this drab world.'"[5]

After deciding to return, Eadie was told to 'sleep' by heavenly spirits and woke up to find herself "back in the pain and sickness of my body again… I became inconsolably depressed. After the joy of spiritual freedom, I had become a prisoner to the flesh again."[6]

Brinkley returned in agonizing pain and wished he could go back to the Chrystal City of his vision. His subsequent recovery was long, slow, and painful. However, although his family doubted his near-death journey, they also noticed a strange 'glow' about him. A cousin commented that Brinkley "has a sort of glow, like Jesus must when they took him down from the cross."[7] This type of aura often emanates from survivors. Atwater writes, "There was a marked change in appearance of each person afterwards. They would seem to glow and have a light around them."[8] The halo or bright light surrounding religious imagery depicts an outer symbolic manifestation of the numinous. A similar 'glow' surrounding NDE survivors, therefore, appears to indicate the mark of a mystical transcendent encounter.

Ritchie begged to stay in the light, but was told to return. But the trace of his experience radiated through his being. When Moody met him, he was to state, "I was struck from the beginning with his warmth, kindness and humor. It came as a great surprise to me when I later learned a very interesting fact about him, namely, that he had been dead . . . and that he had given a most fantastic account of what happened to him while he was 'dead.'"[9]

After a period of painful reintegration, both physically and psychologically, *transformation* seems to be the key element resulting from a near-death journey. These changes are central components in evaluating whether the NDE provides both a mythic model for conscious living and a powerful affirmation to make sense of death. Fenwick and Fenwick's research with over three hundred and fifty NDE survivors considers the far reaching magnitude and consequences of the phenomenon:

> For most people, the near-death experience is one of the most profound they will ever have. It is vividly remembered for years—often for a whole lifetime. And very often the person

> who has had it reports that he or she returned changed in some way, often, though not always, permanently. Virtually everyone reports that afterwards they have no fear of death, though they don't particularly want to die—it's as if they value life even more and have a renewed sense of purpose. Their attitudes change. If they already have some religious faith the experience tends to confirm it. Even if they have no particular religious faith, many, probably most, return believing that death is not the end.[10]

Initiates of the Eleusinian Mysteries experienced similar revelations and transformation. Depictions on Apulian vases illustrate that the transcendent essence of the rites were based on a mythical reenactment of the death of a mythological figure, in order to glimpse everlasting life. This can be equated to NDE survivors dying to their former self projections and encountering what is believed to be the archetypal image of the eternal Self, mirrored in religious imagery. The ancient paintings also accentuated the benefits for society through living life in a conscious manner, linking mortals to the divine, through the analogy of the immortality of vegetation. The object of both the Eleusinian and Dionysian Mystery cults was to dispel the illusion of death, which was believed to be merely a transition to the eternal realm of the gods. In the rites of Dionysos, the animal quality of the image appeared to possess 'godlike' features, projected in a human face.

The Eleusinian Mysteries comprise of a main trinity of deities—Persephone, Hades, and Eubouleus, a mysterious demigod, often referred to as either a son of Demeter or Zeus, who presided over the sacred swine of the Mysteries and was depicted as a torchbearer that illuminated the path back from the underworld. His role in this triad was clearly thought to represent wisdom that would not only perfect the world, but also help individuals to die confidently, through having lived an exemplary life. Persephone's marriage to Hades, Lord of the Underworld, appeared to symbolize death, but also hinted that through death, life was enriched by the experience and so gave hope for the human condition, initiated by the reality of a beatific vision of the goddess. Kerényi writes, "This hope would not have had such great religious value for those who cherished it if they had not, already here on the earth, attained certainty of the goddess's existence, certainly conferred by the beatific vision they had of her. In addition, they possessed a myth to which the experience of the Mystery Night gave a peculiar credibility."[11]

NDE survivors are certain of the reality of their visions, which foster hope in a fresh sense of meaning. Jung writes, "A good many of my principal works were written only then. The insight I had . . . gave me the courage to undertake new formulations."[12]

Eadie became certain that service, compassion, and kindness was what life was all about, "The details of my experience are important only to the point that they help us to love. All else is an appendage to that."[13] Brinkley discovered a unique new mission through hospice work and seeks to educate people on the lessons that can be learned through the NDE, "When our human experiences are rooted in love and compassion, our outcomes are destined to be filled with spiritual grace. From this perspective, it is easy to find our true purpose in life."[14] Brinkley also discovered a new spiritual quest to connect with his inner divinity.

Ritchie noticed that when he narrated his NDE to others, it had a profound effect on them. He slowly integrated the experience into his life and ceased trying to recapture the love manifesting in the image of Jesus, but started searching for him in the faces of others and went on to train as a medical doctor and psychiatrist. Moody answers the central question: what kind of a difference did a near-death experience make in George Ritchie's life? He writes, "As will be obvious from his account, Dr. Ritchie's experience has had an enormous—indeed central effect on the life he leads . . . . Those of us who know him as a friend can truly sense the depth of kindness, understanding, and loving concern for others which characterize this remarkable man."[15]

Storm believes his near-death journey dismantled all his prior belief systems and demanded "a rebuilding of my entire life."[16] Prior to his NDE, depression ruled his life and to self-medicate, he drank heavily. However, he ceased using alcohol altogether, because for the first time in his life, he felt happy and at peace. As his religious convictions began to emerge and strengthen, like St. Paul on the road to Damascus, Storm believes he experienced a conversion and epiphany, which led him to also investigate other faiths to discover further inspiration. He sensed the importance of narrating his story to others, believing it reinforced ancient spiritual beliefs:

> In the telling of my story, I have been telling you and old, old story. The story goes back before history. The story makes visible the invisible in our lives. What we have been blind to, we now see. When you get it you will never let go. The message has never changed. The message is how much God loves us and cares about us. The message is how we can respond to this great love. I give you my story in the hope that you will find, or more fully appreciate, where God is in your story.[17]

Storm believes his visions of both heaven and hell manifested from the conflict and isolation that was raging within him that symbolized a spiritual crisis, resulting in physical illness. He says that his near-death experience did not make him a perfect person, but one who was making progress in his spiritual development, through relating in love toward others. As with many similar 'conversion' NDEs, what appears to be merely a narrative of otherworldly landscapes and images, emerges as being a catalyst for deep inner change, as the 'convert' shares profound new insights with others.

The NDE also illustrates how humans both create and are linked to images from the collective. Accepting this fact does not enhance skeptic attitudes toward the phenomenon, but rather *validates* the near-death journey, through acknowledging that the religious imagination searches for ultimate truth. Zaleski writes that through "recognizing the imaginative character of other-world visions, we move beyond the merely defensive posture of arguing against reductionism."[18]

The messages and affirmations brought back by NDE survivors bear similarity to mythological teachings of world religions, including Buddhism. Sögyal Rinpoche writes, "The central message that the near-death experiencer brings back from their encounter with death, or the presence of "being of light," is exactly the same as that of Buddha and of the bardo teachings: that the essential and most important qualities in life are love and knowledge, compassion and wisdom."[19]

Benedict became far less judgmental towards his fellow beings. Like Jung, he claims he was able to reenter the *imaginal* realms and believes others can do the same, without having to 'die,' through practicing deep meditation. He contends that the archetypal history of human beings is revealed during contemporary near-death journey and he states, "human beings are already legendary throughout the cosmos of consciousness. The little bitty human being of Earth/Gaia is legendary."[20]

Atwater became guided by the insights she received, "I have always been guided by revelations made to me while on 'the other side' of death, revelations that gave me a purpose: clarifying and giving perspective to soul awakenings."[21] She devotes her life to near-death studies and has interviewed over 3,000 individuals from different nationalities and cultures, purported to have an NDE. Her research supports the belief that archetypal imagery and symbolism provide a blueprint for living life in the highest possible manner and "challenges us to reconsider our very *aliveness* and the existence of *spirit*."[22] Although each NDE is unique and no single testimony is more powerful than any other, the unilateral affirmations emerge to benefit humanity as a whole.

Psychological after-effects following a near-death experience have also been well-documented by leading researchers and reveal that the phenomenon underscores the importance of living a conscious life, rather than simply focusing on death. However, the mystery of how archetypal images and symbolism bring the affirmation of death and rebirth to life remains unanswered. But, it is evident that embedded in archetypal patterning and symbolic metaphors is the foundation for codes of religious morality, without which, humans would have no spiritual compass or direction. Zaleski writes that "the main conclusion we can draw, is that the other world—in its literal or metaphoric forms—plays a significant role in our imaginative appropriation of moral and religious ideals."[23]

In speaking of the psychological impact of her NDE, Paris believes that she was offered the opportunity to gain wisdom. She writes, "Life's ordeals offer an opportunity to penetrate the outer shell of our persona and to plunge into the core of our being, the place where our own psychological intelligence is waiting our arrival . . . . It does now show up as a wisdom in full bloom, but as a seed ready to germinate . . . . Wisdom is a destination rather than a destiny, a goal rather than a state."[24]

As children, we begin life in a vulnerable state and if initial needs are not met, adulthood necessitates addressing the resulting problems, which is one of the prime motivating tasks of psychotherapy, and it has been suggested that some people could have an NDE, because they have a psychological need for direction and enlightenment.

Psychological impacts following near-death experiences culminate in a pattern of change, as survivors experience spiritual or religious awareness, resulting in a sense of freedom manifesting in the second 'gift' of life. However, this opportunity for transformation is reliant on the person's psychological interpretation of the experience. Ring ascertains that to begin with, the experience must appear to be *real*. Second, there are *spiritual* or *religious* connotations. Third, there is a *belief* in a joyous life after death. Fourth, the individual has been given another chance to *live*. Fifth, these impressions are *compelling* and *vivid* and are subjectively authentic. He writes that if these criteria have been met, "life seems more grounded in a sense of purpose and is more consciously shaped by the spiritual values of love, compassion, and acceptance?"[25]

Acquiring the ability to live life in a state of creative freedom is the psychological goal of individuation and discovering a deeper inner meaning to life is imperative in this process. The value of NDEs can be psychologically adapted to demonstrate that if one individual reaches a stage of individuation, this transformation can have a beneficial effect on others. Ring describes experiencing a sense of inner emptiness in his life. He remembers the sense of feeling lost and spiritually adrift and began searching for some clue that may enable him to find a way to conquer "spiritual death."[26] Upon reading Moody's *Life after Life*, he was intrigued and stimulated by the accounts and found the answer he was looking for contained in these stories that changed his life and instilled a spiritual awakening. He consequently complied and undertook his own research into the phenomenon and comments:

> The effect, combined with a certain quality of luminous serenity, which many near-death survivors display, made me feel that I myself was undergoing an extended spiritual awakening. In any event, as my interviews continued, I found that I was no longer oppressed by the spiritual deadness that had, ironically, provided the initial impetus to my research. In

fact my feeling was becoming just the opposite."[27]

Overcoming the fear of death features very highly in psychological after-effects of NDEs, as survivors claim that they are no longer afraid that this transition means the annihilation of consciousness, or the eternal Self; this new perspective also encourages a greater appreciation of life and many believe they are actually *living* for the first time. This conviction is also shared by those who have an NDE, but do not have strong spiritual or religious convictions.

Atwater writes, "Death loses all meaning and relevance. The individual now *knows* death does not end anything. Some individuals explained that death is like a birth into another plane or level of life, and that birth into this plane is like death from the other; that death itself is nothing but a change of awareness."[28]

The sense of transformation and renewal is described by survivors as being exclusively connected to the experience of dying and returning to life. Eadie sensed a new alchemical understanding of the dying process. "When we 'die', my guides said, we experience nothing more than a transition to another state. Our spirits slip away from the body and move to a spiritual realm. If our deaths are traumatic, the spirit quickly leaves the body, sometimes even before death occurs . . . . The body may actually appear still alive for some moments, but the spirit will have already left and be in a state of peace."[29] These powerful new convictions and affirmations regarding death continue to be experienced throughout the lifetime of the individual.

Jung sensed the everlasting quality of his NDE, saying, "We shy away from the word "eternal" but I can describe the experience only as the ecstasy of a non-temporal state in which present, past, and future are one."[30] In addressing the concept of an afterlife, Jung could only 'mythologize,' and relate stories that he believed in, as to speak openly about death requires the experience of being close to death, and so the only opinion he offered came from "the myth itself."[31]

Benedict describes how the NDE changes imaginings on death. "We are actually going to see the wisdom of life and death and enjoy it. As it is now, we have already been alive forever. This body, that you are in, has been alive *forever*. It comes from an unending stream of life, going back to the Big Bang and beyond. This body gives life to the next life, in dense and subtle energy."[32]

Osis and Haraldsson's research into deathbed visions, containing similar archetypal imagery and symbolism encountered in the NDE, suggests that these visions also alleviate human concern with death. "All your ideas are inadequate approximations, something like dry leaves of yesteryear in your earthly garden. Soon you will see more clearly, for now it is still 'through the glass darkly,' but 'then your eyes will be opened.'"[33]

In Western cultures, Christian mythology endorses an afterlife, not only in the resurrection of Christ, but also in the raising of Lazarus of Bethany, who after being dead for four days and lying in a dark cave, came back to life. Jesus asked for this miracle to show the crowd the reality of rebirth as, "The dead man came out" (John 11: 44). Jesus says, "Did I not tell you that if you believed, you would see the glory of God" (John 11: 40). In narratives of deathbed visions and NDEs, religious motifs imbue individuals with mythic affirmations of an afterlife, and these recurring messages warrant our attention.

It has also been established that those attempting suicide often recall no near-death experience, or only a partial one. However, individuals that do have a core experience *may* be less likely to consider suicide again, but conversely, it has also been noted that the resulting loss of fear surrounding death could encourage further attempts, simply because death is no longer terrifying. A full-blown NDE can act as a powerful deterrent to people repeating this drastic course of action..Atwater writes, "They resolve to stay alive and often use their near-death event as a source of courage, strength and inspiration."[34] There are cases when suicide related NDEs include negative archetypal visions and images. Although initially of a shocking nature, these disturbing events can provide a vehicle for change. Atwater comments, "This kind of devastation *can* be transforming if used as a catalyst to help him or her make changes that comprise constructive, long-term solutions."[35]

Research indicates that individuals do not make changes simply because they feel they must do so during their NDEs, but rather that transformation manifests as a direct result of sensing purity, wholeness, and goodness that inspire a goal to live differently. Moody writes, "You have to understand that the being of light isn't telling them that they have to change. My summation, after hearing of hundreds of these cases, is that people change willingly because they are in the presence of the standard of goodness, which makes them want to change their behavior radically."[36]

The results of witnessing negative archetypal images can have a similar transformational effect. Ritchie had visions of both hell and heaven, but it was the feelings of overwhelming unconditional love that imbued him with a new spiritual understanding. However, witnessing the fate of those who had led unworthy lives filled him "with a lifelong terror of any attitude, habit, priority that would shape me for an existence like some of those I had seen . . . . Every minute of everyday since that time, I've been aware of the presence of a larger world."[37]

The importance of love is paramount in the lives of survivors, Moody comments, "Upon their return, almost all of them say that love is the most important thing in life. Many say it is why we are here. Most find it the hallmark of happiness and fulfillment, with other values paling alongside it."[38] Brinkley had the following realization, "I was elated, I knew the simple secret to improving mankind. The amount of love and good feelings you have at the end of your life is equal to the love and good feelings you put out in your life. It was just that simple."[39] Ginette Paris says, "Through her arms, the Great Mother rocked me in a silence filled with the light shed by particles of love made visible."[40]

Sabom's "Atlanta Studies" also validate the importance of love following an NDE. "The Life-Changing Questionnaire further documented a consistent overall increase in the eight capacity-for-love items following the near-death experience."[41] Forty percent of participants also reported a greater involvement in family life. Sabom also interviewed people who had been close to death, but did not have an NDE, and these life changes were not reported. This research proposes that near-death experiences independently affect individual meaning to life.

A fresh sense of interconnectedness with all life forms also emanates from an NDE, often manifesting in a newly acquired respect for the natural world, which reflects the beliefs of many ancient cultures. Moody refers to a man, described prior to his NDE, as a hard-driven business man, who was subsequently to state "One big thing that I learned when I died was that we are all part of one, big living universe. If we think we can hurt another person or another living thing without hurting ourselves, we are sadly mistaken. I look at a forest or a flower or a bird now, and say, 'That is me, part of me.'"[42]

NDE symbolism remythologizes spirituality for survivors, who believe they have shifted from a personal/ego/body perception to one of an eternal consciousness or soul, which is reflected in new occupations that provide service to others, as illustrated in the cases of Brinkley, Ritchie, and Storm. For countless others, including Eadie, the transformational effects of the NDE are incorporated into everyday life, family values, and relationships, resulting in tasks like bringing up children being accomplished with the divine direction of wisdom, love, and compassion.

In Morse's "Transformations Study," 350 adults took part, including: those who had an NDE, individuals close to death with no NDE, people expressing New Age values that had not been seriously ill or had an NDE, people that only had out-of-body experiences, and normal middle-class individuals, who reported none of the above. NDErs scored the highest in living a well-balanced life, determined by the their healthy lifestyles, strong spiritual foundations, and regard for others.[43]

Striking personal transformation following a transcendent NDE strengthens the belief that the phenomenon is *not* caused by chemical and physiological changes that may take place in the brain at the moment of death, as side-effects could cause brain malfunction rather than enhanced memory and abilities.

Many NDE survivors also claim to have gained psychic talents. For some, these new abilities seem to originate from the life review sequence. Brinkley imagined future events and subsequently discovered that not only did these premonitions come true, but that he also developed a psychic gift, which other survivors shared. "I have yet to meet a person who has a near-death experience who doesn't have flashes of precognition or very-well developed intuitive powers."[44] Morse discovered that individuals having had a childhood NDE are four times more likely to experience psychic manifestations and he "honors the spiritual mystery that they imply."[45]

Increased psychic sensitivity may arise from expanded changes in perception, as a door of new awareness opens to a different imagining of life and the cosmos. The visionary poet, Blake, writes, "If the doors of perception were cleansed everything would appear to man as it is, infinite. For man has closed himself up, till he sees all things thro' chinks of his cavern."[46] Once this new state of consciousness has imbued the individual, it becomes enhanced and can include the manifestation of psychic abilities.

That the manifestation of new psychic 'gifts' reported by survivors should be dismissed is strange in a Judaeo-Christian society, for the Bible contains many mythic accounts of prophetic dreams and paranormal psychic abilities, including Jesus "walking on the sea" (Matthew 14:25). The transfiguration of Christ was witnessed by the disciples, James and Peter, "He was transfigured before them, and his clothes became dazzling white, such as no one on earth could bleach them. And there appeared to them Elijah with Moses, who were talking with Jesus" (Mark. 9:2-5). The Gospel of Mark also makes reference to Jesus casting out an unclean spirit from a young boy who "appears like a corpse . . . but Jesus took him by the hand and lifted him up" (26: 27). The greatest psychic phenomenon recorded in the gospels is the resurrection of Christ. Religious scholar, S. Ralph Harlow, writes, "One cannot be acquainted with this field without concluding that the dawn of Christianity is associated with psychic phenomena on an unprecedented scale. Not to understand this closes the door to insights into accounts of the Resurrection."[47]

Belief in a 'magical' otherworldly power was of paramount importance in ancient world mythologies and religions. Virgil refers to a prophetic vision experienced by Aeneas, in book VI of the *Aeneid*, when the hero descends to the underworld to contact the spirit of his dead father, Anchises, and is given a vision of the future splendor of Rome, before leaving the nether realms to rejoin his ship:

> And when Anchises from end to end
> Guided his son, and fired his soul with love
> Of future fame, thereafter he makes known
> What wars must next be waged, and teaches him.[48]

The Egyptians also looked to supernatural forces to improve life conditions and their religious rituals, rites, and ceremonies comprised of a sacrosanct and unchanging 'magic.' The principal deities, Seth, Thoth, Isis, and Ra were thought to be imbued with magic spells and formulas, which manifested in healings, the casting out of malign spirits, and alchemical change of the corruptible body into the incorruptible soul. The forces of Nature were also considered to be under the power of the divinities 'magical' control. The Vedic religion of India ritually invoked the help of supernatural beings, and the Greeks facilitated healing either through direct divine intervention or indirectly through oracles, visions, dreams, and omens.

The transcendent visionary state of the NDE and revelations of a divine wisdom can be considered to be a supernatural event, and so survivors may well notice an increase in their 'magical' or ESP abilities, which is a feasible outcome, when viewing the otherworldly journey as a merging with the light of supreme consciousness. Ring writes that during an NDE, many experience "a direct transmission of the light's energy into themselves and that which is absorbed in that encounter with the light in that moment outside of time remains with them when they return to the world of time."[49]

After gaining profound truth, following a journey to the divine realm of the gods, the mythic hero returns having 'boons' to bestow on humanity. NDE survivors believe they have undertaken such a voyage to an alternate realm of consciousness and reenter earthly existence with similar gifts, including new ESP abilities, and their inspirational stories, as Joseph Campbell writes, "attempt to make plausible, or even interesting, to men and women consumed with passion, the experience of transcendental bliss."[50]

Those who experience the primordial affirmation of death and rebirth as a living reality, consequently live life differently, and can even direct change in society as a whole. Jung believes that the enlightening and transformational rites of the Eleusinian Mysteries "expressed together with the Delphic oracle, the essence and spirit of ancient Greece."[51] The NDE mirrors the illumination of the Mysteries, which Grosso proposes is "reminiscent of the classic NDE. Like the NDE, it made an indelible impression on the celebrant's consciousness . . . . What makes this model of group experimentation so interesting is that celebrants emerged with a wider and more vibrant sense of their present embodied life."[52]

Contemporary near-death narratives express a novel way to repeat an ancient story that lies within the historical collective unconscious. Many diverse religious traditions, including Islam, Buddhism, and Hinduism contain myths that reinforce the affirmation of death and rebirth. In the sixth-century Lao Tzu, translated to mean "old man," was said to be the author of the *Tao Te Ching* or *The Way and It's Power*, which recorded the central principles of Taoism. Like the Prophet Muhammad, Lao Tzu was also said to have an out-of-body state when he journeyed throughout the universe and entered the nine heavens. Zaleski writes, "These traditions also see death as a journey whose final goal is the recovery of one's true nature, even if its immediate effect is a temporary sojourn in paradise or hells or a return to existence in a new body, they agree, moreover, that awareness of death is a precondition for wisdom and that it is necessary to prepare—morally, spiritually, or imaginatively—if one is to die well."[53]

Ring's *Omega Study* proposes that the growing number of similar out-of-body states being reported in NDEs may *"collectively represents an evolutionary thrust towards higher consciousness for humanity at large,"*[54] as such a profound spiritual epiphanies expand boundaries of human perception, instilling survivors with the goal to fully appreciate life. The value of these powerful mythic stories, like those of the past, is that they can instill similar motivation in everyone. Campbell amplifies how "all mythologies, all great poetries, and all mystic traditions are in accord; and where any such inspiring vision remains effective in a civilization, everything and every creature within its range is fully alive."[55]

Notes

1. Marie-Louise von Franz, *On Dreams and Death*, 131.
2. Arnold van Gennep, *The Rites of Passage*, 62.
3. Victor Turner, *The Ritual Process: Structure and Anti-Structure* (New York: Aldine de Gruyter, 1995), 20.
4. Plato, *Republic*, X: 621, b.
5. C. G. Jung, *Memories*, 293.
6. Betty J. Eadie, with Curtis Taylor, *Embraced by the Light*, 124.
7. Dannion Brinkley, with Paul Perry, *Saved by the Light*, 57.
8. P. M. H. Atwater, *Coming Back to Life*, 117.
9. Raymond Moody, *Life After Life*, 14.
10. Peter Fenwick and Elizabeth Fenwick, *The Truth in the Light*, 11.
11. Carl Kerényi, *Eleusis*, 169.
12. C, G. Jung, *Memories*, 297.
13. Betty J. Eadie, with Curtis Taylor, *Embraced by the Light*, 147.
14. Dannion Brinkley, with Kathryn Brinkley, *Secrets of the Light: Lessons from Heaven* (New York: Harper One, 2008), 141.
15. Raymond Moody int. *Return from Tomorrow*, by George Ritchie, with Elizabeth Sherrill, 10.
16. Howard Storm, *My Descent into Death*, 59.
17. Ibid., 87.
18. Carol Zaleski, "Evaluating Near-Death Testimony." *The Near-Death Experience A Reader*, 354.
19. Sogyal Rinpoche, "The Near-Death Experience: Stairway to Heaven." *The Near-Death Experience A Reader*, 174.
20. Mellen-Thomas Benedict, "Through the Light and Beyond." *The Near-Death Experience Reader*, 51.
21. P. M. H. Atwater, "What is Not Being Said About the Near-Death Experience." *The Near-Death Experience A Reader*, 232.
22. Ibid., 232.
23. Carol Zaleski, *Otherworldly Journeys*, 201.
24. Ginette Paris, *Wisdom of the Psyche*, 14.

25. See Kenneth Ring, *Life at Death*, 203.
26. Ibid., *Life at Death*, 17.
27. Ibid., 17.
28. P. M. H. Atwater, *Coming Back to Life*, 115.
29. Betty J. Eadie, with Curtis Taylor, 83.
30. C. G. Jung, *Memories*, 296.
31. Ibid., 304.
32. Mellen-Thomas Benedict, "Through the Light and Beyond." *The Near-Death Experience A Reader*, 51.
33. Karlis Osis and Erlendur Haraldsson, *At the Hour of Death*, 213.
34. P. M. H. Atwater, *Coming Back to Life*, 18.
35. Ibid., 18.
36. Raymond Moody, *The Light Beyond*, 39.
37. George G. Ritchie, with Elizabeth Sherrill, *Return from Tomorrow*, 85.
38. Raymond Moody, *The Light Beyond*, 41.
39. Dannion Brinkley, with Paul Perry, *Saved by the Light*, 26.
40. Ginette Paris, *Wisdom of the Psyche*, 12.
41. Michael Sabom, *Light and Death*, 93.
42. Raymond Moody, *Life After Life*, 42.
43. See Melvin Morse, with Paul Perry, *Transformed by the Light*, 223.
44. Dannion Brinkley, with Paul Perry, *Saved by the Light*, 120.
45. Melvin Morse, "Parting Visions: A Scientific Paradigm." *The Near-Death Experience A Reader*, 21.
46. See William Blake, *The Marriage of Heaven and Hell*, plate 14.
47. S. Ralph Harlow, *A Life After Death* (New York, 1961), 249.
48. Virgil, *The Aeneid*, trans. James Rhoades, ed. Robert Maynard Hutchins (London, 1952), V1: 888-91.
49. Kenneth Ring, *Heading Toward Omega*, 88.
50. Joseph Campbell, *The Hero with a Thousand Faces*, 217.
51. C. G. Jung, "Approaching the Unconscious." *Man and His Symbols*, 68.

52. Michael Grosso, "Parapsychology and Religion: Afterlife and Spirituality". <http://www.parapsi.com/psi_survival .htm>, 11.
53. Carol Zaleski, *Otherworld Journeys*, 24.
54. Kenneth Ring, *Heading Toward Omega*, 255.
55. Joseph Campbell, *Myths to Live By*, 257.

Chapter 8

The Affirmation of Death and Rebirth in Contemporary Western Cultures

The night kisses the fading day whispering to his ear,
"I am death, your mother. I am to give you fresh birth."
Rabindranath Tagore, Stray Birds

The affirmation of death and rebirth manifested constantly in ancient cultures, symbolized in natural phenomena, visionary states of consciousness, and myths of death and resurrection that established the practices of early worship. Similar primordial images are characterized in contemporary near-death journeys and deathbed visions, and they also continue to flourish in religious rituals, film, literature, poetry, music, and works of art that emanate from fantastic voyages into the deep recesses of the collective unconscious. The modern-day pilgrimage into an *imaginal* realm reflects the way humanity maintains the quest to conquer new horizons of consciousness, through accessing an ancient wisdom on how to embrace the shadow of Thanatos as a motivating force to both live consciously and well in the present moment and to enrich myths of death.

Ancient myths and the Mystery traditions fulfilled a powerful role in the evolution of consciousness and as we struggle with religious discord, reminders of a legacy inherited from archetypal figures, such as the Egyptian Osiris, continue to impact the collective unconscious through echoing the importance of embracing tolerance and immortalizing the human quest for beauty and wisdom. Mojsov writes:

> The most important bequest of the ancient religion is found in its pluralism, its accommodative spirit, the happy coexistence

> of the One and the Many . . . . The ancient gods appear almost as secular, invisible gods. Their humanity, travails, errors, and acts of reparation reveal a world of genuine tolerance. Hence their adaptability to the dynamic changes of the world.[1]

Ancient monuments, temples of worship, and sacred sites found throughout the world preserve a legacy of sacrosanct ideals, opening a portal to *imaginal* landscapes and celebrating human rites-of-passage, initiations, and communal worship. A palpable energy is stored in these holy shrines, often renowned for their fabulous art treasures that reflect human yearning to merge with the divine through the numinous significance of archetypal symbolism.

Archetypes embodied in many Christian saints provide a means to access transcendent realms of consciousness. These revered figures act as guides to our imaginings and luminous experiences, for like mythic heroes, they personify souls who have completed the cycle of death and rebirth and entered the pure light. These archetypal images act as intermediaries between the fleeting conscious and eternal unconscious realms of existence and maintain connection and continuity to the past. They also exemplify perfect role models that exert influence in our lives, and intercession through prayer and rituals make them readily accessible. Myths of saints reflect their various archetypal personalities, and convey spiritual messages that are reaffirmed on feast days that commemorate these venerated beings. In Roman Catholicism, the many symbolic holy days provide a foundation for spiritual enlightenment and practice.

The Buddhist Bodhisattvas, including Avalokitesvara, who embodies compassion, and Manjursi, representing transcendent wisdom, exert a similar influence and represent the human quest for enlightenment. In Hinduism, the ancient Sanskrit word *sant* is translated to mean "one who knows truth or has experienced ultimate reality." Widely revered figures include Raghavendra

Swami, who was believed to perform miracles and continues to bless devotees, and Paramahansa Yogananda, who spread Eastern wisdom throughout North America and Europe. For Hindus, different days of the week are also associated with various deities and worship. Native Americans observe the sanctity of harvest festivals that are celebrated to give thanks to the Great Spirit and to Nature for the continuance of the crops and life. The many archetypal images commemorated by varying religious traditions on holy days enable intercession with the divine, and are constant reminders that enlightened wisdom emanates from a mystical dimension of consciousness.

Philip's gospel from the Gnostic Bible states:

> Truth didn't come into the world naked
> but in types and images. Truth is received only
> that way. There is rebirth and its image.
> What is the resurrection?
> Image must rise again through image.
> The bridegroom and image enter through image
> into truth, which is restoration....
> You are no longer a Christian but Christ[2]

The *imaginal* world of film provides an extension to the ancient art of story, resulting in the ability to transpose the symbolic affirmation of death and regeneration on to the big screen. This medium enables us all to share and become submerged in images seeking a creative outlet in the collective unconscious, as movies transcend the barriers of time and space and create a fresh mythic version of communication between the 'gods' and humans. Campbell writes, "There is something magical about films. The person you are looking at is also somewhere else at the same time. This is a condition of the god."[3]

Films that contain either a core near-death experience or some of the principal elements have flourished during the past decades. *Resurrection*, made in 1980, tells the story of a woman, Edna, who has an NDE and returns to her body to discover a new ability to heal others. The final scenes of the movie see her ostracized from her home town, as people become suspicious as to the origin of her psychic 'gift,' and she moves to a solitary existence in the desert. The scenes that depict the burned red earth and bleached white rocks can be imagined to reflect an alchemical container for illumined beings, such as Edna, who are often unwelcome in main-stream society.

In 1995, Brinkley's NDE was adapted into a television movie. The film exhibited many of the central characteristics of the phenomenon, including that of personal transformation.

Movies that contain the life-review sequence of the NDE include several versions of *A Christmas Carol*, based on the novel by Charles Dickens, and in *It's a Wonderful Life*, made in 1946, and directed by Frank Capra, a man facing hardship attempts suicide and is shown by heavenly beings what would happen to his family if they were without him. Through the transformational effect of the life review, he realizes that taking his life is no longer an option, and remembers just how much he values his loved ones and family. *Defending Your Life*, a 1991 comedy, portrays the victim of a car accident having an out-of-body experience and finding himself in "Judgment City," where he is on trial to determine whether he will proceed to the afterlife, or return to his body. In 2009, *Ghosts of Girlfriends Past* includes the life review of a selfish and uncaring man, who ultimately undergoes a transformation.

The movie, *Ghost*, became a blockbuster in 1990 and follows the story of an individual who dies and finds himself in the afterlife. The scenes that depict separation from the body contain many special effects and correlate with Moody's description of such a disembodied state. *Wizard of Oz*, based on the children's novel, *The Wonderful Wizard of Oz*, by L. Frank Baum, became a classic and depicts a fantastic journey, as Dorothy, falling unconscious, is sucked through the power of a great cyclone into the realm of Oz. Her adventures are marked by many mythic NDE motifs that include: passing through a vortex or portal, encounters with strange beings that she somehow recognizes, and directions to the "Emerald City" where the 'god-like' image of the great Wizard lives. Eventually, Dorothy returns to everyday consciousness, profoundly altered by her experience. The archetypal content and popularity of this movie illustrates how near-death imagery lingers on the borders of consciousness and it was announced in 2009 that a new version will be produced. One of the songs featured, *Over the Rainbow*, tells of a paradisiacal realm beyond earthly dimensions and continues to be considered a classic.

The Chronicles of Narnia, written by C. S. Lewis during the 1950s have also been adapted into movies and tell the exploits of four young children, who through the back of a dark wardrobe, which can be viewed as representing the tunnel motif of the NDE, are transported to the fantasy "World of Narnia" where they have many adventures. Such representations, including the *Wizard of Oz*, start off as children's stories, but find a large and eager adult audience.

Between Two Worlds made in 1944 attempts to answer the question of what happens at the moment of death, as passengers on board a cruise liner sail through a mist-filled ocean and meet with the mysterious Examiner, who reviews their lives and deaths and issues tickets for the next destination. This movie tries to deal with the anxiety surrounding death during World War II, and is an updated version of *Outward Bound* that was produced in 1930. In *Black Orpheus* (1959), the myth of Orpheus and Eurydice is retold, as a young musician from Rio de Janeiro attempts to find his missing girlfriend. On this quest, he is led to a voodoo ritual and initiation that tests his faith. This movie is set against the background of carnival celebrations and features dancing sirens and villains wearing skeleton masks, and it endorses the central message of the ancient Orphic Cult—the threshold of death can be successfully navigated by those who have the right attitude.

In 2009, James Cameron wrote and directed *Avatar*, which projects the archetypal hero's journey in a new, but familiar dimension. The story, which is set in the year 2154, is full of alchemical and mythic motifs. The term *Avatar* is associated with Hinduism and the belief that a single energy (Brahman or God) imbues all things. In the movie, the Na'vis are blue—the color that symbolizes Hindu deities and the nature of the infinite. They inhabit the lush planet of Pandora and live in harmony with Nature, worshipping the mother goddess, Eywa. The Na'vi society respects and communicates with plant and animal life forms sharing the planet, Pandora, and the universal motif of the Tree of Life is depicted in the Hometree, which harnesses the sacred life force. In order to become 'one' with this energy, the Na'vi practice a ritual of circling the tree and holding hands, but the atmosphere of this gentle compassionate planet is toxic to humans.

The protagonist, Jake Sully, a paraplegic and former marine is able to enter an out-of-body state and is seen to lose his handicap each time he temporarily enters the body of a Na'vi-human hybrid, symbolizing the ancient teachings of myths including that of *Gilgamesh*—humans comprise of both mortal and divine dimensions. This ability to transcend everyday consciousness and access a mystical state of illumined awareness is part of religious or spiritual experience and in Hinduism; *Parakaya Pravesham* is translated to mean temporarily entering the body of another person to gain knowledge. The large flying bird that Jake tames is symbolic of the *Garuda*, a mythical creature found in both Hindu and Buddhist mythology. In Hinduism, the bird-like being is known as the mount of the deity Vishnu. In Buddhism, similar birds are thought to combine the characteristics of animals and divine beings.

The human presence on Pandora is fuelled by the desire to plunder a precious metal from its core. For the ancient alchemists, the planets were associated with metals and their search for a *golden* wisdom was the aim of chemical experiments. However, the greed of the futuristic exploiting force on Pandora threatens to create the opposite effect and result in the Hindu concept of *Adharma*, whereby evil and wrongdoing threaten the natural order. The scenes of mass destruction and war that take place are metaphors, symbolizing the volatile state of the world that we find ourselves in, brought about by disregard for others and the hunger to accumulate material possessions.

Like many of the heroes in ancient myth, Jake Sully undergoes an initiation. As a result, he becomes transformed and rejects his former ideals. After the sacred Hometree is destroyed in a violent attack, Jake prays to the mother goddess, Eywa for her divine intervention through the Tree of Souls. It appears that Eywa answers his prayer, as all the Pandoran wildlife rises up and joins in the battle and the perpetrators are defeated. The motif and affirmation of death and rebirth are the central components of *Avatar*. Not only does the hero, Jake, undergoes a spiritual rebirth in which he is seen at the end of the movie permanently changed, but he also depicts the god-like man of many ancient myths and religious traditions, who through dying to his former self, facing many trials, and aligning himself with a higher order, saves the world. At the end of the movie, he is transformed into a Na'vi avatar and leader of the Omaticaya clan, but he has also found love and the spiritual home of the divine feminine, in the form of Neytiri, who initially rescued him as he wandered, lost and dazed, through the forest. A scene that is reminiscent of the opening to Dante's epic *The Divine Comedy*, as the pilgrim discovers he has lost the true path.

The movie also symbolizes our yearnings for an eternal harmonious state of existence, reflected when Grace dies, but at the moment of death is elated to see a powerful vision of the mother goddess. This scene echoes apparitions of Persephone invoked during the Eleusinian Mystery rites and archetypal images glimpsed in both deathbed visions and the near-death experience. Perhaps most important, is the fact that Cameron was inspired to write *Avatar* following a dream that his mother had of a tall blue-skinned woman. This image stayed with him and resulted in this archetypal figure being brought to life. The fact that this movie has been so successful all over the globe reinforces how symbolism of death and renewal from the collective unconscious continually seeks creative outlets to emerge into the full consciousness of humanity.

Hereafter, directed by Clint Eastwood, tells the story of three characters that are all touched by death in different ways: A blue-collar American is shown to have psychic abilities to communicate with the dead, through touching the hands of the living. He believes this gift to be a curse and so refuses to help others and is considered mentally ill by the medical establishment. A French journalist, who has a near-death experience and discovers her previous perception of reality, has been shaken to the core, and a London school boy that has lost his brother and is desperately seeking answers. The lives of these three people are woven together, bound by death and their experiences of an afterlife. As with ancient sacred texts, however, this movie is not solely concerned with what happens at the moment of death, but illuminates the personal transformation of all concerned and the joy and beauty that can be experienced in life.

Poetic musing reflects an intense awareness of an expanded mystical state of consciousness that focuses on an outer image to reveal an inner sacred meaning. Although style and language vary between eras, authentic poetry always ignites a new imagined perception into reality and reflects human aspirations to reach the divine, which is meaningful for both the poet and society as a whole.

In ancient Greece, mythological poetry emanated from the

muses, who inspired the creative arts and were considered the source of a profound wisdom that was related orally for centuries in stories and poetic lyrics. Calliope, the daughter of Zeus and Mnemosyne (the goddess of memory), inspired epic poetry, including Homer's *Iliad* and the *Odyssey*. She was also the mother of Orpheus, the priest, singer and poet, and taught him to sing his transcendent melodies. Depicted with a writing tablet or book in her hand and wearing a golden crown, Calliope was considered to be the wisest and oldest of the muses. The mythical affirmation of death and resurrection is often the focus of transcendent poetry and Joseph L. Henderson writes, "Poets more than prose writers express clearly and poignantly the mythological theme of death and its archetypal corollary, rebirth, of the quest for the certainty of an after-life, namely resurrection."[4]

William Wordsworth, one of the great English Romantic poets, was inspired to create a new kind of poetry that originated from intuition, rather than reason and intellectual logic. His genius was stimulated by his sensitivity to the divine power found in the natural world. Wordsworth's timeless words embodied the hallmark of illumined mystical states of consciousness, as they sprang forth spontaneously in outpourings of powerful emotions that he experienced in the beauty of rivers, woods, streams, mountains, rocks, and flowers. Transcendent communion with Nature inspired imaginary encounters with the god-image and enabled Wordsworth to have intuitive flashes of understanding that he transcribed in his "Poems of the Imagination". He writes:

> Do I behold these steep and lofty cliffs,
> That on a wild secluded scene impress
> Thoughts of more deep seclusion; and connect
> The landscape with the quiet of the sky.[5]

Wordsworth believed the power of poetry imparted spiritual revelations and reminded people that the deeper meaning of life was not to be found in conflicts of the material world, but rather through journeying inward and leading a contemplative pastoral existence that enabled the formation of real character to emerge through communing with Nature and hearing the 'voice' of God. He advocated that redemption could be found in the *imagination* that reconciled the individual to the *absolute*. For a number of years, he lived quietly in Grasmere, a village in Cumbria, and this period spent in the majestic beauty of the Lake District produced some of his greatest work. His simple home, Dove Cottage, became the main literary shrine in England and still attracts thousands of pilgrims every year. Many of his poems revolve around death and imaginings of a world beyond:

> Our birth is but a sleep and a forgetting:
> The Soul that rises with us, our life's Star,
> Hath had elsewhere its setting,
> And cometh from afar:
> And not in utter nakedness,
> But trailing clouds of glory do we come
> From God, who is our home:
> Heaven lies about us in our infancy.[6]

Walt Whitman cultivated a great interest in mythology, especially that of the ancient Egyptians. He explored these narratives to gain an intellectual awareness of religious beliefs of ancient people and many of his poems, accessed through his mythic imagination, repeat the ancient message of transcendence over death.

> Allons! To that which is endless as it was beginningless,
> To undergo much, tramps of days, rests of nights,
> To merge all in the travel they tend to, and the days and

> nights they tend to,
> Again to merge them in the start of superior journeys.
>
> To know the universe itself as a road, as many roads, as roads for traveling souls.[7]

Whitman writes of the connectedness of all beings and conjures up images of the mythical ferry crossing of souls returning home:

> On the ferry-boats the hundreds and hundreds that cross, returning home, are more curious to me than you suppose.[8]

He was inspired to a new philosophy on death that arose from reconnecting to ancient archetypal energies, in which life becomes fluid and transcends time.

The poems of Emily Dickinson also contain many metaphors and motifs of death and rebirth, and her work continues to be appreciated by many. She was not only influenced by Christian mythology, but also by an independent inner myth that recognized and understood how life was being stripped of its supernatural and sacred meaning. Dickinson used symbolism from the natural world to illustrate the pain this alienation reflects:

> A Color stands abroad
> On solitary Fields
> That Science cannot overtake
> But Human Nature feels
>
> Then as Horizons step
> Or Noon report away
> Without the Formula of Sound
> It passes and we stay—

A quality of loss
Affecting our Content
As trade had suddenly encroached
Upon a Sacrament[9]

The presence of universal archetypal patterns intermingles with Dickinson's personal symbols in this poem, suggesting that she wrote poignantly on the subject of death, but that the meaning of her work included her individual access to the *imaginal* realms. As she approached death, her creative imagination focused on the mythic life of Jesus, whom she felt, personifies the merging of the finite and the infinite. The simple, but miraculous life which Christ lived amongst humble people, fired Dickinson with the concept that just by living on earth—Christ touched all of humanity, past and present. She found faith and hope in this ancient oral message of death and rebirth:

Death is a Dialogue between
The Spirit and the Dust.
"Dissolve" says Death—The Spirit "Sir
I have another Trust" –

Death doubts it—Argues from the Ground—
The spirit turns away
Just laying off for evidence
An Overcoat of Clay[10]

While the poet's *imaginal* 'knowing' is fleeting, the insights retain an eternal quality. Rupert Brooke narrates how a perfectly ordinary afternoon tea-party gave rise to a glimpse of mystical understanding:

I saw the immortal moment lie.
One instant I, an instant, knew

As God knows all. And it and you
I, above Time, oh, blind! could see
In witless immortality.[11]

The writer and poet D. H. Lawrence is described as a mythological poet. Having visited the Etruscan tombs in Italy, he describes how entering the dark caves became symbolic of death, which he acknowledges without protest or bitterness. In one of the burial sites of an Etruscan prince, Lawrence saw the elaborate preparations for the journey to the afterlife, which included a small bronze ship. The archetypal image and symbolism of this miniature vessel were alive for Lawrence and transported him to a transcendent imagining, as he approached the end of his life:

The floods subside, and the body, like a worn sea-shell
emerges strange and lovely.
And the little ship wings home, faltering and lapsing
on the pink flood,
and the frail soul steps out, into her house again
filling the heart with peace.[12]

In one of his final poems, he captured a mythological representation of death heralding a mystical marriage:

Let me guide myself with the blue, forked touch of a flower
down the darker and darker stairs, where blue is darkened
on blueness down the way Persephone goes, just now in
first-frosted September, to the sightless realm where
darkness is married to dark and Persephone herself is but a
voice, as a bride, a gloom invisible enfolded in the deeper
dark of the arms of Pluto as he ravished her once again.

Give me a flower on a tall stem, and three dark flames,

for I will go the wedding, and be wedding-guest
at the marriage of the living dark.[13]

In this poem, Lawrence refers to a flower as symbolizing the mandala of wholeness, representing a 'mythological' torch on the journey to the underworld, where Persephone embraces Hades. Persephone represents the soul meeting death, which is not a dreadful fate, but rather, a god-like and sacred encounter.

Works of inspirational literature also continue to repeat the primordial the affirmation of death and resurrection. In the novella, *The Death of Ivan Ilyich,* Leo Tolstoy narrates the fate of an individual, spiritually unprepared to accept death as a living reality. Although written in 1886, this work reflects an attitude to death and dying in which the language of denial has not changed much over the last century, and portrays death as a social tragedy. However, the story also symbolizes how numinosity can shine even in the darkest realms of the psyche as death approaches, resulting in transformation and a vision of 'God.' As Ilyich struggles through a process of transition, his family collude in the harmful deception that he will make a recovery, and, "Nothing did so much to poison the last days Ivan Ilyich's life as this falseness in himself and in those around him."[14] In desperation, he calls out for an absent God and has a life review, during which, he realizes that perhaps his life has been "a dreadful, enormous deception that shut out both life and death."[15]

Screaming in terror for three days, he feels himself drawn into a black hole (a motif of the NDE), which he resists. On the evening of the third day, a tremendous force crushes his chest and he falls into the sinister opening to discover that at the "bottom, something was shining."[16] A similar allegory was made in the ancient myth of Chiron. In this moment of illumination, Ilyich experiences redemption and salvation. His agony vanishes and he cannot detect his accustomed fear of death. "Where was death? What death? There was no fear because there was no death. Instead of death there was light."[17]

The story of Ivan Ilyich not only encompasses the anxiety and denial surrounding death, but also highlights the resulting emptiness when imagination, intuition, and emotions have been devalued and disconnected from the deeper layers of the Self. Fundamental in this story, is the mythological symbolism: Ilyich's agony and suffering, which lasted for three days, mirrors the agony and Crucifixion of Christ who "rose again" on the third day from the dark cave to be reunited with his heavenly father. The spiritual awakening of Ilyich is similar to that described in many deathbed visions, and led him to rediscover 'God." This theme of separation and reunification that takes place in the dying process is central in many cultural myths. Corbin writes, "Death enters the world as humankind is estranged from God or the gods . . . thus estrangement is perceived to be overcome only through death."[18]

In the play, *Sheppey*, novelist and playwright Somerset Maugham describes the changes that occur in the life of hairdresser, Joseph Miller, (nicknamed Sheppey) after he wins the Irish lottery. The protagonist is ultimately visited by the inevitability of death and unsuccessfully tries to avoid this encounter. Maugham draws on an ancient Arabic myth to illustrate the futility of this action, as Death tells Sheppey:

> There was a merchant in Baghdad who sent his servant to market to buy provisions and in a little while the servant came back, white and trembling, and said, "Master, just now when I was in the marketplace I was jostled by a woman in the crowd and when I turned I saw it was Death that jostled me. She looked at me and made a threatening gesture. Now, lend me your horse, and I will ride from this city and avoid my fate. I will go to Samarra and there Death will not find me." The merchant lent him his horse, and the servant mounted it, and he dug his spurs in its flanks and as fast as

> the horse could gallop he went. Then the merchant went down to the market place and he saw me standing in the crowd and he came to me and said, "Why did you make a threatening gesture to my servant when you saw him this morning?" "That was not a threatening gesture," I said, "it was only a start of surprise. I was astonished to see him in Baghdad, for I had an appointment with him tonight in Samarra."[19]

Other works of literature that contain reference to NDE motifs, include *Pale Horse, Pale Rider*, by the Pulitzer Price winning author, Katherine Anne Porter. The novella centers on the narrow border-threshold between life and death. The character, Miranda, has an out-of-body experience while seriously ill and describes the oblivion of death: "She lay on a narrow ledge over a pit that she knew to be bottomless . . . . There it is, there it is at last, it is very simple; and soft carefully shaped words like oblivion and eternity are curtains hung before nothing at all . . . . There it is, that is death and there is nothing to fear . . . . Look don't be afraid, it is only eternity."[20]

The story then relates Miranda's encounter with the image of light and the beautiful landscape of otherworldly realms:

> At once it grew, flattened, thinned to a fine radiance, spread like a great fan and curved out into a rainbow through which Miranda, enchanted, altogether believing looked upon a deep clear landscape of sea and sand, of soft meadow and sky, freshly washed and glistening with transparencies of blue. Why, of course, of course, said Miranda, without surprise but with a serene rapture.[21]

Miranda is then told to return to her body. The NDE sequence is said to be based on the author's personal experience when she became seriously ill during the often fatal outbreak of influenza, which swept through the harsh winter of 1918.

The short story, *The Snows of Kilimanjaro,* by Ernest Hemingway also contains a description of a life review and out-of-body sequence. The main character, Harry, has wasted his writing talents and squandered his gifts in a life of decadence, and the knowledge that he is shortly to die "came with a rush; not as a rush of water nor of wind; but of a sudden evil-smelling emptiness."[22] As he feels the touch of death come yet still closer, he sees a plane coming to rescue him and describes a journey in which he flies over forests above the earth. Suddenly, he can see standing out in the white sun "the square top of Kilimanjaro. And then he knew that this was where he was going."[23] Kilimanjaro is highest mountain peak in Africa and is known as the "Masai," translated to mean the House of God. The tale opens with a description of the frozen carcass of a leopard close to the summit and, "No one explained what the leopard was seeking at that altitude."[24] However, the image of the 'frozen' creature was believed to symbolize the need to search at a higher level for one's true nature and find 'God,' and the leopard had ascended close to the mountain peak on this pilgrimage of discovery. Jung writes, "The mountain stands for the goal of the pilgrimage and ascent, hence it often has the psychological meaning of the self."[25] Hexagram 17, *Sui* or "Following" from the *I Ching*, describes how:

> The king introduces him
> To the Western Mountain.[26]

Although Hemingway's creative vision enabled archetypal portrayals of the deeper layers of death, and he purportedly experienced an NDE when he was seriously wounded in during World War I, he never reconciled the conflict that raged within him, and much of his writing symbolized a struggle with death. He recounted his near-death experience in *A Farewell to Arms,* in which the central character, Frederic Henry, is wounded and feels himself:

> Rush bodily out of myself and out and out and out and all the time bodily in the wind. I went swiftly, all of myself, and I knew I was dead and that it had all been a mistake to think you just died. Then I floated and instead of going on I felt myself slide back. I breathed and I was back.[27]

Similarities with Moody's central components of an NDE can clearly be seen in this description—an out-of-body state, the sensation Frederic has of knowing that he has died, the realization that consciousness still exists beyond death, and the return to the body. Hemingway's conscious battle with accepting death and his paradoxical unconscious archetypal insights into myths of a possible afterlife were often depicted in his novels and stories, through the many war scenes that reflected his inner turmoil.

Most recently, Dan Brown's novel, *The Lost Symbol*, published in September 2009, sold over five million copies. The plot consists of a voyage through a labyrinth of ancient rituals, symbols, and recurring archetypes. Brown also reminds us how the symbol of the Unfinished Pyramid, featured on the reverse side of the dollar bill, remains a powerful symbol in the collective psyche:

> [A] symbolic reminder that man's ascent to his full human potential was always a work in progress. Though few realized it, this symbol was the most widely published symbol on earth. *Over twenty billion in print.* Adorning every one dollar bill in circulation, the Unfinished Pyramid waited patiently for its shining capstone, which hovered above it as a reminder of America's yet-unfulfilled destiny and the work yet to be done, both as a country and as individuals.[28] (161)

The symbolic eye in the pyramid reflects the powerful presence of an ancient Mystery Cult motif, portraying the all-seeing eye of the resurrected Osiris that was placed in the pyramid containing the tomb of the Pharaoh Khendjer, ruler of Egypt, during the thirteenth dynasty. Either the Freemasons or Rosicrucians may have imported the image that remains fully visible on the reverse side of the dollar bill, which is the most powerful world currency, yet the metaphorical interpretation of new order springing from the legacy of ancient archetypal symbolism is often banished to the realms of the collective unconscious. Depicted opposite the pyramid is an American eagle, reminiscent of an ancient Egyptian head-dress or crown, and bunches of wheat depict the immortality of ancient vegetation deities. The eagle holds a scroll with the words *e pluribus unam*, translated to mean "One from Many." Above the eagle is a configuration of stars, representing ancient Egyptian beliefs that following death, the deceased becomes a shining star in the realms of the sun god. Both archetypal images are encompassed in a circle or mandala, symbolizing a unifying wholeness.

Works of art achieve a visual splendor that unites universal beliefs with the power of the creative imagination. James S. Perkins writes:

> In the world of Art are mysteries and strange passages to be negotiated if a rendezvous with the unknown is to be reached, where there are toll-gates that open beyond—toll-gates that are to be opened at a price. In that beyond, the artist has traffic with his *immortal* Self . . . .The engagement is with genius and the passage is into the noumenal sphere, the world of the Real.[29]

William Blake was not only a prophetic poet, but also a great artist. His ongoing fascination with mythology began as a child, when he started to sketch copies of Greek antiquities, and he greatly admired the ancient Greek poets. His own poetry and art contained a mystical undercurrent and he thought the imagination was capable of embracing and producing images of God and the mysterious source of human existence. He was influenced by both Boehme and Swedenborg and produced a great many visual images and symbols of death and resurrection emanating from his mythic imagination, coupled with those of the ancient world.

Blake's, *The Soul Hovering Above the Body*, depicts a young woman watching her lifeless body, capturing an out-of-body state and reflecting alchemical belief in the soul leaving the body at death, and illustrates how the imagination can change perception. His vision of *Hecate* portrays the Greek goddess, who was associated with the supernatural and known as the guardian of the entrance to the spirit world. Shortly before his death, Blake was commissioned to illustrate Dante's *Divine Comedy* and the pilgrim's journey through the afterlife realms. Although this work remained incomplete, the Dante Watercolors are examples of his finest work. Blake also experienced a deathbed vision, as he made his transition. A letter written by his friend, George Richmond, shortly after Blake's death describes how the poet's "countenance became fair—His eyes brighten'd and He burst out Singing of the things he Saw in Heaven."[30]

The distinguished Indian writer and poet, Rabindranath Tagore, was considered a mystic and visionary, who maintained that all of Nature symbolized and affirmed resurrection. He became a prolific artist in later years and his paintings and sketches depict haunting landscapes of a primordial *imaginal* world, containing mystical motifs that reflect collective unconscious archetypal patterns. Many of these artworks portray death as a form of renewal.

Salvador Dalí used extensive symbolism in *Christ of Saint John of the Cross*. The work was inspired by the drawing Saint John of the Cross completed, following a mystical vision of Christ. In this surreal painting, Dali appears to present the Crucifixion from

God's view, as he depicts Jesus Christ on the cross, suspended in a darkened sky. Symmetry is based on a triangle symbolizing the trinity, and a circle, encompassed in the head of Christ, representing the center of the universe and wholeness.. The image is shown to be looking down and floating over an earthly landscape, containing a lake with a boat and fisherman—signifying Christ as an intermediary between the mortal and immortal realms. This use of darkness surrounding the cross forms an image of death, but the figure of Christ is illuminated, symbolizing resurrection.

The transcendent power of music plays a major part in numerous spiritual practices. Buddhists, Muslims, Christians, Hindus, and Native American rituals involve chanting, often considered to be a heightened from of speech, accompanied by a set of notes that can be simple or highly complex and inspire enhanced awareness. Over time, chants evolved into song and formed the roots of contemporary Western music that contains a pattern of tension and release, dating back to the Medieval Church, and mirroring natural cycles of death and rebirth. Death is embodied into the structure of many compositions, characterized by the somber mood and slow tempo. The Russian-American composer, Sergei Rachmaninov, produced *Isle of the Dead,* inspired by Arnold Böcklin's painting of the same title, which opens with a slow funeral march that gives way to the gentle lapping of waves and the sound of Charon's oars, skimming across the waters of the river Styx. A long crescendo symbolizes the boat approaching the Isle of the Dead, as it passes through the mist, separating earthly life from the realms of the dead. The tone then switches to a sweet melody depicting the rest of death, and then rises to a crescendo with the eerie chant of the *Dies Irae* taken from the Latin Mass. A sudden change in tempo follows, as woodwind instruments mimic bliss. The sounds of the waves then return as Charon, having completed his task, departs from the Isle of the Dead.

The sound produced by bells has also been important in religious rites throughout antiquity. Archeological excavations have unearthed small hand bells used for this purpose in ancient Babylonian, Egyptian, Greek, and Roman civilizations, and bells feature prominently in Eastern religions, including Hinduism and Buddhism. Larger bells were described by early Christian historians to be an integral part of every church, as they not only summoned and united the faithful in rituals of worship, but also signified the joy or solemnity of baptisms, weddings, and funerals. In Roman Catholicism, the ringing bell focuses attention and heralds the climax of the mass, as offerings of bread and water are miraculously transformed into the body and blood of Christ.

The bell is formed through an alchemical practice of shaping and transforming molten metal from the earth, which then becomes symbolic of the divine feminine energy in its final appearance. In Hinduism, bells are found in all temples and used for invoking the participation of the gods, as the bell produces the primordial holy sound of *Om*, an all encompassing consciousness, reflecting an unchanging, eternal, and absolute reality. In Buddhism, wind bells proclaim the sacred transcendent teachings of the Buddha. A fourth-century Buddhist monk, Fo-t'u-teng, was revered as a pioneer missionary monk, who traveled to China and was said to perform miracles and spoke, as if divinely inspired, by the sound of accompanying bells. He used his 'magical' powers to illustrate the potency of Buddhist teachings and burned incense, as he filled his begging bowl with water and recited an incantation over it. Immediately, blue lotus flowers sprang from the bowl and the vibrant color of the blooms dazzled spectator's eyes.[31]

Nature also produces many bell-shaped flowers and bellbirds, known for their bell-like call, also produce highly evocative sounds. On his travels, while contemplating the dawn break into a new day, Jung writes, "The cry of the bellbird rang around the horizon. At such moments I felt as if I were inside a temple. It was the most sacred hour of the day. I drank in this glory with insatiable delight, or rather, in a timeless ecstasy."[32]

In Meditation 17, the metaphysical poet, John Donne, invokes an image of the tolling bell:

> No man is an island, entire of itself; every man is a piece of the continent, a part of the main....never send to know for whom the bell tolls; it tolls for thee.[33]

One of the most important functions of music is utilized in assisting the dying during their transition from earthly life, as the power of music, symbolized in the ancient myth of Orpheus and practices of the Orphic Cult, facilitates a mystical shift in consciousness that calms the mind and stimulates the imagination. Music vigils for the dying are journeys of spiritual awareness and often feature harp music, which soothes and guides individuals to a transcendent peaceful state of consciousness that replaces feelings of fear and anxiety and supports the liberation of the eternal soul from the corruptible body.

The contradictory conflict of preparing for death while living life is familiar to all humans and causes immense anguish and uncertainty. However, it is also evident that the recurring primordial affirmation of decay and regeneration, visible in Nature and our creative imagination, indicate an archetypal pattern that is similar and sometimes identical to ancient esoteric beliefs and resurrection myths, which give death another meaning as a rite of passage.

Recognizing hints in recurring archetypal imagery symbolizing death to be a transition rather than a final ending, results in an enormous difference in both our psychological and biological endeavors to lead a more conscious life, and in drastically changing end-of-life care to value individuals as being a multi-dimensional beings. For those close to death, NDE spiritual affirmations restore the sanctity of the dying process, allowing grace to enter and make its presence felt, rather than the sterile isolation experienced in many modern-day care facilities.

Imparting the therapeutic value of deathbed visions to those in the final stages of transition enables many barriers to be crossed, for both the dying person and loved ones. The essence of these numinous visions can also help reevaluate society's response to approaching death, encouraging people to view the process as an evolution into the realms of the eternal Self, rather than a final ending. The living can greatly assist the dying through implementing the ancient art of death 'midwifery' that focuses on empowering individuals to make the transition with peace and serenity, rather than fear. Many practitioners have produced transition guides that seek to make order out of the chaos surrounding death, returning to examples detailed in *The Tibetan Book of the Dead* and the *Ars Moriendi*, whereby priests or transition guides accompanying the dying is an integral part of the dying process. The spells, prayers, and ritual preparations for the dying, detailed in *The Egyptian Book of the Dead* also created a 'passport' on the journey from one world to the next.

The power of the NDE is that survivors continue to convey an ancient alternative preparation for death to others. Ernest Becker reminds us that indigenous cultures celebrate this transition "*because* they believe that death is the ultimate promotion, the final ritual elevation to a higher form of life, to the enjoyment of eternity in some form."[34] Most of us in Western culture have lost this belief and so have no resources to deal with either our own mortality or the death of a loved one. However, near-death survivors help restore this essential mythic container through narrating 'stories' reflecting ancient beliefs and hopes of an afterlife, heralding what could be a return to the old-fashioned deathbed scene that enables a person to die with dignity, peace, and grace, surrounded by loving friends and relatives.

We can clearly see how the primordial motif of death and

renewal remains *alive* in the collective unconscious. This powerful affirmation continues to emerge into consciousness in many guises, opening up new paradigms to express an ancient universal blueprint that awakens the dormant spiritual aspect of the psyche and provides guidance on how to live and die more consciously.

Notes

1. Bojana Mojsov, *Osiris Death and Afterlife of a God*, 126.
2. *The Gnostic Bible: Revised and Expanded Edition*, eds. William Barnstone and Marvin Meyer (Boston: Shambhala, 2009), 235.
3. Joseph Campbell, with Bill Moyers, *The Power of Myth*, 15.
4. Joseph L. Henderson and Maud Oaks, *The Wisdom of the Serpent: The Myths of Death, Rebirth and Resurrection* (New York: Collier, 1963), 261.
5. William Wordsworth, *The Poetical Works of William Wordsworth, Vol. 2* (Boston: Adamant), 145.
6. William Wordsworth, *Ode: Intimations of Immortality From Recollections of Early Childhood* (Whitefish: Kessinger, 2010), 23.
7. Walt Whitman, *Leaves of Grass* (New York: New American Library, 1955), 142.
8. Ibid., 144.
9. Cynthia Griffin Wolff, *Emily Dickinson* (New York: Alfred A. Knopf, 1987), 446.
10. Ibid., 456.
11. Rupert Brooke, *The Collected Poems* (New York: John Lane, 1915), 90.
12. D. H. Lawrence, *The Complete Poems*, 20.
13. Ibid., 960.
14. Leo Tolstoy, *The Death of Ivan Ilyich*, trans. Lynn Solotaroff, int. Ronald Blythe (New York: Bantam, 1981), 105.

15. Ibid., 127.
16. Ibid., 132.
17. Ibid., 133.
18. Henry Corbin, *Spiritual Body and Celestial Earth*, 21.
19. John O'Hara, *Appointment in Samarra* (New York: Vintage 2003), xvii.
20. Katherine Anne Porter, *Pale Horse, Pale Rider* (Orlando: Harcourt, 1990), 199.
21. Ibid., 199.
22. Ernest Hemingway, *The Complete Short Stories of Ernest Hemingway: The Finca Vigia Edition* (New York: Scribner, 1998), 47.
23. Ibid., 56.
24. Ibid., 39.
25. C. G. Jung, "The Phenomenology of the Spirit in Fairytales." *The Archetypes and The Collective Unconscious*, 219.
26. Richard Wilhelm, *The I Ching or Book of Changes*, trans. Cary F. Baynes, (Princeton: Princeton University Press, 1967), 74.
27. Ernest Hemingway, *A Farewell to Arms* (New York: Scribner, 1957), 55.
28. Dan Brown, *The Lost Symbol* (New York: Anchor, 2009), 161.
29. "Mysticism in Art." *The Silent Encounter Reflections on Mysticism*, ed. Virginia Hanson (Wheaton: Quest, 1974), 155-56).
30. See G. E. Bentley, *A Stranger from Paradise: A Biography of William Blake* (New Haven: Paul Mellon Center, 2003), 509-510.
31. See A. F. Wright, *Fo-t'u-teng: A Biography*, (Harvard Journal of Asiatic Studies, X1, 1948), 321-71.
32. C. G. Jung, *Memories*, 268.
33. John Donne, *The Works of John Donne, Vol. 111*, ed. Henry Alford (London, 1839), 574-75.
34. Ernest Becker, *The Denial of Death* (New York: Free Press, 1973), ix.

Chapter 9

Eternity—A Living Reality

Hold infinity in the palm of your hand
And eternity in an hour
William Blake, *Auguries of Innocence*

Through tracing interconnecting threads of mystical states of consciousness, we can fully appreciate how these illuminating, ineffable encounters with the inner Self, preserved in myths, Holy Scriptures, and the narratives of mystics, visionaries, and many ordinary people, reflect the human quest to glimpse timeless universal truths and bring them fully alive into a more expansive present. Experiential vivid accounts of such enlightening wisdom suggest having bypassed limited logical thought processes to powerfully reconnect with a divine legacy that enriches the goal of living a more altruistic life, embedded in the essential qualities of love and compassion.

Mystical experiences stimulate the intuition and creative imagination, resulting in deeply evocative emotional responses that enable a liberating *awakening* or spiritual epiphany through lifting the veil of the normally invisible transcendent realms of consciousness. C. S. Lewis writes, "Therefore, mysticism is, by empirical evidence, the only real contact man has ever had with the unseen. The agreement of the explorers proves that they are all in touch with something objective. It is therefore the one true religion."[1]

The growing interest in mystical states heralds a *remembering* of an ancient wisdom that lies dormant in the collective unconscious, indicating human yearnings to sidestep beliefs and theories blocking spiritual development. We all have profound insights that appear to manifest from some fleeting inexplicable supernatural source, yet leave the stamp of an indelible 'knowing' that we are indeed multi-dimensional beings and part of a far larger tapestry of cosmic consciousness. Such other-worldly knowledge manifests in various sensation, perceptions, symbols, and archetypal images and while it remains impossible to solve the 'mystery,' these revelations can imbue us with a sense of wholeness that colors, nourishes, and sustains the inner landscape, for, as Capra writes, "Our spiritual moments are the moments when we feel most alive."[2]

The belief that there is an unseen guiding force, often projected through the archetype of the 'guardian angel,' dates back to ancient Babylonian times and was also alluded to in Plato's *Phaedo*; as well as in Zoroastrian, Christian, Islamic, and Jewish mythologies. The guardian angel appears in the Old Testament books of Genesis, Exodus, and Daniel. In the New Testament, angels are depicted as providing mediation between mortals and God. Most notably is the account of the guardian angel that liberated St. Peter from prison. The angel, surrounded by a shining light, told Peter to wrap his cloak around himself and to follow him, as they then passed the guards keeping watch and escaped through the prison gates that opened of their own accord. As they walked down a lane, the angel mysteriously vanished, and Peter says, "Now I am sure that the Lord has sent his angel and rescued me from the hands of Herod and from all that the Jewish people were expecting" (Luke 12:11).

For Native Americans and many indigenous cultures, spirit guides offering protection and guidance manifest through the ancestors or various animal forms. In vision quests that include rites of initiation, young people are introduced to their particular guide, who will help them through the challenges of life.

Jung's many mystical experiences led him to concur that it was possible to interact and communicate with spirit guides that he believed manifested as archetypes from the collective unconscious. Much of his work was inspired through conversations with his guide or guru, Philemon. Jung says, "Psychologically, Philemon represented superior insight. He was a mysterious figure to me. At times he seemed to me quite real, as if he were a living personality. I went walking up and down the garden with him, and to me he was what the Indians call a guru."[3]

Awareness of an invisible presence manifesting in times of dire stress or mortal peril to offer support and comfort is well-documented and may have originated from Biblical accounts of the resurrected Jesus appearing to two of his disciples on the road to Emmaus. T. S. Eliot, who was inspired by early Greek writers and Christian, Buddhist, and Hindu religious scriptures, hauntingly writes:

> Who is the third who walks always beside you?
> When I count, there are only you and I together
> But when I look ahead up the white road
> There is always another one walking beside you.[4]

A well-known account of this phenomenon was recorded by explorer, Sir Ernest Shackleton, as he attempted to cross the Antarctic via the pole. Disaster struck when his ship was crushed by ice floes and marooned his team on the polar ice. During a treacherous journey for survival, Shackleton was convinced that an unseen benign presence accompanied him and two of his team on the final part of the journey:

> When I look back at those days I have no doubt that Providence guided us, not only across those snow fields, but across storm-white sea that separated Elephant Island from our landing place on South Georgia. I knew that during that long and racking march of thirty-six hours over the unnamed mountains and glaciers of South Georgia it seemed to me often that we were four, not three. I said nothing to my

> companions, but afterwards Worsley said to me, "Boss, I had a curious feeling on the march that there was another person with us." Crean confessed the same idea. One feels "the dearth of human language, the roughness of mortal speech" in trying to describe things intangible, but a record of our journeys would be incomplete without a reference to a subject very near to our hearts.[5]

Widely publicized is the similar experience of Ron DiFrancesco, who, during the catastrophic events of 9/11, was fighting his way through the devastation after the second plane hit the South Tower. He was the last person to escape the building alive and his miraculous survival was aided by an invisible rescuer 'telling' him to get up and then leading him down the stairs and through the burning fires to reach safety, just as the building began to collapse.

Although current neurological research offers a biological explanation, many consider such accounts to be genuine examples of 'otherworldly' guidance, as they contain the hallmark of numinous encounters and generate hope for the assurance that we are not alone. A young man, Jay, recounts:

> I had a friend come over from the UK to visit and we decided to go into town and have a few drinks to celebrate his arrival. We met up with some people who were partying and things just got a bit out of hand. The last thing I remember is ending up at someone's house close to a nearby lake and passing out. At some point in the early hours, I suddenly woke up and through the corner of my eye, I could see the door to the room was open and there was the figure of a man standing there. He appeared to be elderly and was wearing some kind of hat, although I didn't get to see his face. I knew instantly that I had to get up and follow him. It was pitch black and I had no idea where I was going, but I simply placed my footsteps in those

of the old man, who led the way. We walked quite a way around the lake and then I could see car lights in the distance and knew we must be near the main road and then mysteriously, the figure just vanished.

I started to walk along the road back to town when a friend, who had been out early at a garage sale, saw me and picked me up. I felt very disorientated when I got home. I realized that I had drunk so much that there was a strong possibility that something really serious could have happened to me if I hadn't been led to walk off some of the alcohol in my system—I could even have died—a very sobering thought. This was a real wake-up call—I'd been going through some tough times and had been hitting the bottle way too hard. I knew immediately that this had to stop and I haven't touched a drop of the real hard stuff since. I'd never given a thought to guardian angels, but I know the old man was real and that he led me out of trouble and, whoever he was, I feel profoundly grateful for his intervention.

Strangely, a curious synchronicity also took place. The visiting friend's mother called from England to say that his elderly grandfather had made his transition at the exact time that Jay would have been following the old man around the lake. Whether or not the helpful guide was the spirit of the deceased grandfather remains a mystery, but all concerned felt intuitively that this was a strong possibility.

Betsy Balega, author of *Being Mystic: In Touch with God* related the following story:

My mother had been diagnosed with terminal lung cancer. She decided to make her transition in a nearby hospice. The day before mom passed, she lapsed in and out of consciousness and we were able to have a conversation.

> Suddenly, she made a comment that really surprised me. "The priest was here last night and gave me communion." This sounded impossible, because I already knew that the priest in question only visited patients at the weekend and that he had been at home in the rectory that evening. However, I thought my mom must just be groggy from the effects of the medication and thought no more of it. The next day, she crossed over and the following week, my sister and I were reminiscing and I mentioned what had happened. My sister worked at the hospice in question and told me that mom had not been imagining things; for it was a well-known fact that many patients spoke of this unknown priest, who came calling just prior to their passing. I was speechless, but it gave me a warm comforting feeling to know that my mother had received such a visit and it strengthened my own spiritual beliefs.

Moments of mystical enlightenment often take place in Nature. While walking through a field at sunset, Bede Griffiths had a majestic sensation of creative renewal. The symbolic language of the natural world has provides inspiration for many visionaries, including William Blake, who writes of seeing the world in a grain of sand, and heaven in the face of a flower. A friend shared her own mystical moment of enlightenment:

> I was walking though a meadow after a long dry summer. The rains came early that year and what had been parched scrubland, was suddenly transformed into a lush carpet of verdant green. I marveled at this sight of renewal and found myself contemplating a single blade of emerald green grass that seemed to suddenly stand out on its own and I thought, "I am like this blade of grass and I am part of the continual cycles of nature." The feeling was one of wonder and amazement that still feels just as real as when it first struck me

> with such an overwhelming sense of connection to everything.

William James reminds us, "It is as if there were in the human consciousness a sense of reality, a feeling of objective presence, a perception of what we may call 'something there,' more deep and more general than any of the special and particular 'senses' by which the current psychology supposes existent realities to be originally revealed."[6]

Nature often lifts the invisible veil on a larger and more marvelous universe and fills the experiencer with a profound sense of appreciation and joy. I recall such an experience that took place when I was only ten years old, but I have always retained the wonder of that moment:

> It was a couple of days after Christmas and I had gone to the stables with a friend to ride. We weren't quite sure whether we would be able to go out that day, as it has snowed quite heavily the night before. However, the owner said that it would be fine. I was especially pleased, because my favorite horse was there and I could ride him. We set off to gradually wind our way up one of the paths that snaked around the hills behind the stables. As we got to the top, we paused and I remember just gazing down at the surrounding countryside. The snow was so white that it seemed to dazzle and sparkle in the sunlight. The sky was a bright winter blue that reminded me of a field of cornflowers. I happened to have a jacket on, which was exactly the same color and suddenly, I felt that I had merged into the sky in a moment of supreme joy and happiness in which everything appeared to be completely perfect—and the total perfection of that moment remains as vivid in my mind now as it did all those years ago.

Synchronicity or a meaningful coincidence also binds the visible to the invisible or the physical to the psychic realms. Learning Style Consultant, Gael Belden, describes the following experience:

> I must have walked right past the approaching snake when I entered my house one evening. I was late for my dance class, so I was only inside for a few moments, then turned to leave. As I opened the door, I nearly tripped over the dun-colored snake that was weaving back and forth, as it inched toward the open door. She (I couldn't tell the gender, but it seemed like a she) kind of rose up a little, her tongue flicking the air for signals about my size and my desirability as food, but there was more. She seemed, somehow, familiar. And she seemed curious about me and for a split second, I thought, "She wants to come in". Closing the door behind me, I knelt down and watched her, as she turned toward the spilt water from an overturned dog dish. I thought that she might drink, but she moved across the water easily, unconcerned, her snake-ness connecting the ancient world with what is modern and devoid of the primitive. I was able to notice her markings and later learned that she was a garter snake. She was so large that I imagined her name might be, as Blake so eloquently put it: "dragonish snake," or certainly a messenger. A short while later, my grandson's snake, our beloved ball python, Karma, died. We realized later that she must have been sick. But before she got sick, she escaped from her enclosure. We never liked that she spent her life behind glass, and so on some level, we made a pact with her: we would not notice if she occasionally pushed up the screen roof and escaped, as long as she came back.
>
> We always found her in a corner of a dark closet. Or, she would appear suddenly, terrifying the dogs. However, her last escape was outside and for the first time since she was taken from her home in Asia to be sold to people in the States that

> like to keep reptiles as pets, she moved by her own agency. She crossed the street in front of the house, not once, but twice. She returned after two weeks, but she must have eaten something bad. After she died, in my grief I remembered the other snake, the one who looked like her—the one who seemed to insist on coming in to tell me something. I don't know how we can possibly understand what snakes need to tell us. They eat; they sleep; they shed; and they like to roam around. But sometimes, the other world breaks through the sky parts, and the mystery reveals itself. And one species tries to bridge the gap and communicate with another. One snake died and another lived on. And I am left with wonder and grief and an appreciation of how little we know of how life and death move together. And how connected we are—all of us—creatures and humans to one another.

The luminous symbolism of the halo of light, which is sometimes white or colored like the rainbow, pervades the galaxy and can be seen surrounding the moon, Jupiter, and the earth that are set in a background of star-filled space. For astronaut, Edgar Mitchell, who was onboard the Apollo 14 mission, this voyage into outer space gave way to a mystical moment, as the spacecraft headed for home. He sensed the earth as being the "blue jewel-like home planet suspended in the velvety blackness."[7] This description is very similar to Jung's alchemical vision of the earth, experienced during his NDE that took place several decades earlier. Mitchell then had a profound epiphany, accompanied by feelings of exhilaration and "an overwhelming sense of universal *connectedness*. I actually felt what has been described as an ecstasy of unity."[8] He then had the overwhelming realization "that our presence as space travelers, and the existence of the universe itself, was not accidental, but that there was an intelligent process at work. I perceived the universe as in some way conscious."[9] Upon returning to earth it took Mitchell a while to integrate the magnitude of his sudden leap of intuitive understanding, but the course of his life changed dramatically, as he left NASA to found the Institute of Noetic Sciences, an organization dedicated to the study of consciousness and the intuitive "inner knowing" of the mind and spirit that reflect a new and expanded vision of reality.

For many ancient cultures, the earth possessed subtle powerful forces that gathered in concentrated areas, known as sacred sites. These geographical regions provided a portal to higher states of consciousness, enabling early people to experience a normally invisible *otherworld,* and the resulting wisdom was passed down the generations, through rituals and oral stories. Such powerful vortexes often contain commemorative monuments, including the formation of stone pillars at Stonehenge in England and the Great Pyramid at Giza, where natural radioactivity appears to provide a *psi* mind-altering property. Paul Devereux writes, "It seems to me that a characteristic of radiation-*psi* is a sense of time-slip—the percipient is momentarily lifted out of his or her space-time and a view of the past (or possibly future) flashed into awareness."[10] He also reminds us that ancient structures were built with materials from the natural world, in order to construct a pathway to the spirit realms, where rituals of healing and fertility would take place. These thresholds remain open, as thousands of years later; we still seem to access similar altered states while visiting these ancient shrines. Intuitive and radio presenter, Hillary Raimo, describes what took place when visiting the sacred site at Teotihuacan in Mexico:

> The journey began at the base of a mountain that led straight up through miles of cliffs and jungle to the Tepozteco Pyramid, an ancient worship place to honor the god Ometochtli-Tepoztecalt. The spirits of the place were tangible and you could feel them circling in the misted air around you.

> There was an altar a short way up the mountain that we had brought offerings for. We simply touched the belly of the stone and thanked it for calling us here. Immediately, we noticed the pathway was covered with scarab beetles, and they would be our constant companions for the entire journey, as we headed up on what would be a two mile hike up into the clouds and jungle to what seemed like another world existing outside of time and space as we know it—a place where magic and mystery live. I faced my biggest fears, as the narrow ledges and steep staircase challenged everything I thought about myself. There is a legend about this place that says once you pass the gates of Tepoztecalt, you are reborn. Rebirth is the best I can do to describe this moment. When I stood at the top of the Pyramid of the Sun, I felt a complete merging of Self. The feeling of wholeness was incredibly humbling. I felt a complete remembering at that moment. I saw all my past lives swirling around me from times long ago. I felt lifted, and most importantly ALIVE!"

Hillary then traveled on to the United Kingdom and made a trip to Stonehenge:

> The power of being here physically was overwhelming. Words really cannot describe how it changes you. You come home to your life, and you have a different perspective, a broadened experience base to compare your previous belief systems. I feel deepened and my consciousness has expanded. The secrets long held by secret schools and mystery schools are available to us all as we evolve and deepen.

For Hillary, as with many that experience expanded states of consciousness, the most significant aspect is not so much an emptying of previous thoughts and belief systems, but rather the sensation of refilling the entire body and spirit in sensations of déjà vu, hinting that one has already existed in other lifetimes or alternate dimensions of being.

The concept of reincarnation and memories of previous lives features in religious traditions, including Hinduism, Buddhism, and Taoism. The ancient Greeks had similar beliefs, acknowledged in both Platonic philosophy and that of the Orphic Mystery cult. Child psychiatrist and psychologist, Ian Stevenson researched over 3,000 cases in which children gave meticulous details of past lives and detailed his extraordinary finding in, *Twenty Cases Suggestive of Reincarnation, Unlearned Languages,* and *Children Who Remember Previous Lives.*

One of the most compelling recent stories of reincarnation involves the testimony of a young American boy, James Leininger. Just before his second birthday, James began to have disturbing nightmares and recurring memories of a previous life, as fighter pilot, James Huston, killed when he was shot down by enemy aircraft in the battle for Iwo Jima. The child recalled many details of his earlier incarnation that included his name and the name of the aircraft carrier, and he also identified fellow comrades. His father, Bruce, was highly skeptical and doubted each piece of evidence until it could be fully corroborated, but as his Christian belief system was shaken to the core, he writes, "And I had a kind of revelation. James's experience was not contrary to my belief. God, I thought, gives us a spirit. It lives forever. James Huston's spirit had come back to us. Why? I'll never know. But it had. There are things that are unexplainable and unknowable."[11] As James grew older, the nightmares ceased, but he continues to have many memories of his former life.

The dream world is one that we all experience every night, as we enter the archetypal realm where the past, present, and future merge into one. Sometimes, dreams can have prophetic qualities that strengthen beliefs in a spiritual or *other* realm of consciousness. Jade Ashcroft describes her experience:

Earlier this year I had a very traumatic experience in which I suffered a miscarriage and was rushed into hospital and surgery within one hour of my admission. Obviously, this kind of thing is every mother's worst nightmare, and up until the point where I was in the room with the A&E doctor, the whole experience didn't seem like I was actually taking part in it. While the doctor was talking to me, I had this vague recollection of a dream I had written down months earlier in which I had been in the same room, with the same doctor, and in the same predicament. I had dismissed the dream as being a warning for a friend of mine, who had also suffered a miscarriage. When I regained consciousness, it was really difficult to discern between the physical nurses on the ward and the half-luminous beings walking around me. This is not the first time that I have had visitors from other realms, but they were particularly close to me at this time. When I was left by myself on the ward, I could hear my granddad speaking to me, and lots of other family members who passed away a long time ago. In that suspended state, they came so close to comfort me and guide me through my personal grieving process, and to remind me of my reasons for staying on the earth plane. Since this experience, and the not so gentle reminder of how little precious time we do have, not only has my belief in the spiritual world been strengthened, but I have also been blessed by the presence of others sharing the same goals and the will and determination to keep on bringing light into the darkest recesses for as long as I am physically able. It is hard to put into worlds just how profound an effect that whole experience brought into my life.

A dream narrated by another lady, illustrates an example of synchronicity in which the barriers of time and space dissolve. These meaningful 'coincidences' possess a psychic element, beyond that of causality, in which both inner and outer events exist simultaneously and so a person can experience reconciliation and the transition of another, through direct contact with the collective unconscious:

> I had been involved in an acrimonious divorce for about two years and by that time I was involved in another relationship and had moved to a different town. At the time, I was taking my ex-husband back to court for his failure to comply with our property settlement. I woke up one morning after having a weird and intense dream. In the dream, I felt myself being pulled into a vortex madly spinning—it was unlike any feeling that I have ever had before and it felt very physical. I felt like I had been dreaming about my ex-husband all night and I remembered that at one point, we were both sitting on a perfectly rounded mountain overlooking the ocean, as feelings of complete peace washed over us. I almost told my partner about the dream, but then decided against it. I went running with a friend that morning and I talked about my ex-husband the entire time. I felt so 'full' of him. When I returned home, my partner was waiting for me with a message—my ex-husband had been killed in a plane crash the previous evening. My feeling is that while I was sleeping and my ex-husband was making his transition, I shared the experience with him and we were together in that same place at the same time.

Similar dreams occur far more frequently than perhaps we would believe, and sometimes, they predict future events that manifest in the present moment. One lady told me of how one night, she awoke to see a vision of her daughter, who told her that she had come to say goodbye and that she loved her very much. The following day, the lady in question learned that her daughter had died the night before. Another woman described how upon hearing that her father had suddenly passed away from a massive coronary decided not to tell her mother, who was away from home and in poor health, for fear that the shock may bring on serious medical consequences. Instead, she told her mother that he was seriously ill and that she should prepare herself for the possibility that he may not recover. Her mother listened to this news and then told of a dream she had the night before in which her husband visited her and gave her a kiss and a hug. The dream was so vivid that upon awakening, she expected to see her husband lying in the bed next to her. When she learned that he had made his transition, she realized that the dream was his way of saying goodbye to her. A friend relates a similar incident:

> I had a friend who was suffering from terminal cancer and had the following dream. I was with his daughter, who had come to visit me and we were sitting talking, when the phone rang. It was my friend, John, and I was really surprised to hear from him, and he said, "I can't stay long, because I'm getting ready to leave." I realized when I woke up that he was letting me know that he was about to pass on, and he did so, a few days later. This dream was very important to me, because I knew that we had communicated on another level that transcended the fact that he was in another country at the time and was lapsing in and out of consciousness.

There are also many accounts of 'calls from the dead,' when the phone rings and the voice of a deceased relative or loved one can be clearly heard. Such experiences that cannot be rationally explained usually occur only once, but convince recipients that they have experienced genuine after death communication. One lady relates:

> After my father died, I was suffering from inconsolable grief. My mom had passed away a couple of years before, and when

> dad went, I felt so alone. One day the phone rang, and as I answered, I just heard his voice, saying, "Hello, it's Dad," and then the line went dead. I've never had this type of experience before, and at first, I just felt stunned. But after I thought about it for a while, I was convinced that it was my dad and that he was just letting me know that he was okay and still there in some form. I still miss him an awful lot, but this 'mysterious' call did comfort me and make me think that perhaps death is not the end.

Throughout this exploration into the archetypal quality of mystical states of consciousness, the NDE has been used as a model, as there are so many accounts of these profound journeys into an alternative realm that imbue survivors with another way of seeing or contemplating consciousness and leave the imprint of transformation. The story of my inspirational friend and mentor, Reuben Beckham, demonstrated to me how life changes are the most positive outcome of an NDE. Reuben, who had previously been fully emerged in the corporate world, changed his whole mode of being to become a dedicated spiritual counselor to the dying. For sixteen years, following his near-death journey, Reuben selflessly helped hundreds of people make their transition with grace and dignity, in a state of peace. His presence at the bedside of the dying brought comfort, love, and a strong assurance that physical death is only a threshold to eternal life and he often described seeing the aura of a dying person leave the body at the moment of death.

Reuben's message was simple, yet powerful, and he kept repeating it until a few days before he crossed back into the light in the late summer of 2009. He reminded people of the wisdom gained from his NDE, as he saw other souls returning home to God. He spoke of his life review and how up until that point, he had really not been particularly interested in others, but his awakening led him to realize that we touch thousands of people, simply by being alive, and that the real meaning in life can only be found in love and relationships. His glimpse of the 'other' side revealed a beautiful and wondrous place that filled him with exhilaration and joy, as he merged with the light. He emphasized that we are all unique living souls that can become catalysts for change, as we carry the 'light' within us and in this reality—we are all one.

Reuben was a quiet unassuming man, who had an extraordinary presence and the final words of his last speaking engagement were simple, yet powerfully evocative, "We don't love one another enough. We don't remember that love is the most powerful energy in the universe. We need to open up our hearts and minds and express love more often—for love changes everything."

The dying process of a loved one places us in a heightened state of awareness, as along with the miracle of birth, it is one of the most profound experiences that we can share with another human being. During this detachment from the ordinary world, alternate dimensions are revealed in many deathbed visions that are clearly defined by the feelings of elation experienced by the dying.

Shortly before my mother's death, I was privileged to share her visions of visitors from other realms, who started to make their presence felt in the six weeks prior to her death. One morning, she woke up excited and animated and told me about departed family members, who had come to her the night before. "They were all urging me to leave with them, because they are going to take me to a wonderful place that has the most beautiful garden." These visions continued night after night and my mother excitedly continued to recount these extraordinary encounters. One morning, I told her, "You are free to go with them whenever you are ready to do so." She replied, "No, I'm not quite ready yet." Sometimes, my mother appeared to be talking to her father, who seemed to be very close by, and she would get agitated and upset when his presence appeared to leave for a while. Some family members believed that she was just suffering from hallucinations or dementia and brushed off these interactions, but I knew of many cases of end-of-life visions and so encouraged her to fully describe these comforting experiences. She became so unusually vibrant and alert at these times and was certain of the existence of these otherwordly guides, as she prepared to transition from earthly life.

A colleague relates how shortly before her father's death, he told her of recurring dreams in which he was being urged to leave on a journey, as a voice told him that someone was waiting at the gate for him. All his life, he had described himself as an agnostic, but also related how he was no longer afraid of crossing over, because he had experienced a further dream in which he was 'shown' that death was nothing to be afraid of or worry about.

I witnessed something very similar when I went with a friend to visit a young woman, who was terminally ill in hospital. When we entered the room, all we could see was a shrunken emaciated figure, suffering the terrible ravages of disease. But suddenly, I had the oddest sensation and felt I was in a cathedral, as the room appeared much larger with a high ceiling and was bathed in a golden light. A choir of angels stood around and behind the bed, and as I looked at the woman, she became radiant with a luminous glow, and I remember thinking, "She is the most beautiful woman I have ever seen." As we left, my companion told me that he had experienced the very same sensations. Something very holy and sacred took place that day, and when I heard the young woman had died shortly after, I had an image of her surrounded by love, beauty, and peace.

Life coach and radio presenter Kelly Hudson relates her profound experience at her grandmother's passing:

Late one evening in September of 2005, I spotted my mother

was online and sent her an instant message asking her what she was doing up so late. She responded by saying that she and my cousin were at the nursing home with my grandmother, who wasn't expected to live through the night. I was especially close to my grandmother, and this was the news that I had been dreading since I was young. But when it finally came, the experience was not what I had been expecting. Instead of heart-wrenching pain or inconsolable sorrow, I felt a peace and serenity settle over my spirit like a warm blanket on a cold night. My grandmother had been missing my grandfather terribly in the four and a half years since his passing. They had been married young and spent their entire adult lives together. Grandma had been diagnosed with cancer earlier in the year, and she had decided to forego any treatment, preferring to let nature take its course. She thought it was time for her to go and was looking forward to being with my grandfather again.

To this day, it still amazes me that my mother, not a technically minded person, decided to take her rarely used laptop to the nursing home with her. Because I lived in another state and there wasn't time to get there, it turned out to be a decision that would allow me to be as present as possible during my grandmother's transition—a decision for which I shall remain eternally grateful. The wonder of technology allowed me to pass my thoughts and feelings to my grandmother through my mother and cousin. It allowed the three of us to be together to comfort and support one another, and to be completely present. I was able to tell my grandmother that I loved her and that it was okay for her to leave. I was also able to thank my cousin for supporting my mother, who was losing her only living parent, and I was able to offer my love and support to my mother, as she felt on the verge of being orphaned.

Not long after we connected with one another, my mother

remarked on a song, which was heard playing in my grandmother's room. It was some song from the 1920s that my grandparents used to dance to. I commented that maybe it was a sign that my grandfather was there, waiting to welcome my grandmother home. But then another memorable song came on, and another and I asked my mother to check the bedside controls and see what station the radio was tuned in to. None of us were aware of a station that solely played music from this era— especially without a DJ or commercial breaks. My mother discovered that the bedside controls were off, and that the music wasn't coming from the bedside speakers, but rather from the overhead speakers in the room. I asked her to go and check at the nursing station and see if they were piping music into my grandmother's room. While she was out of the room, my cousin commented on how peaceful my grandmother looked, and we agreed that the familiar music was likely bringing her comfort. My mother returned and announced that the nurses had said that the public music system was turned off in the rooms after 10:00 p.m. and only played in the hallways, and that it was just set to a classical music station. At that point, we knew the music was just for us—or mostly for my mother, to help her understand what I already sensed: that my grandmother was not alone during this process of transition, and that the husband she loved was waiting for her. The music continued to play for hours, as the same set of songs were repeated over and over again, until my grandmother took her final breath and left this place for one that I believe is better. And then, the room was silent.

During my grandmother's passing there was no pain, no sorrow, and no empty ache. The blessing of having been present through technology and the energy of love washed all of that away. The experience of hearing my grandparent's favorite songs play until she peacefully slipped away provided a joyful knowing of the reality of death: that it is merely a transition to a new kind of life. I view the experience as a final gift from the grandparents I love so deeply, and will treasure it always.

When my father was making his transition, I had been sitting with him all day, and then went home to freshen up and have a rest, as his passing wasn't expected for at least another twenty-four hours. My younger son, Toby, volunteered to stay with his grandfather for the remainder of the night, and a few hours later he described a sense of complete peace entering and enveloping the room. He felt so relaxed, as opposed to the anxious state that he had been in all day, and wondered what on earth was happening. Then he sensed a strong presence and believed it was his grandmother, who had passed away six years previously. He found himself calling out, "Nan is that you?" and then he saw images on the TV screen go haywire and blur into what he described as being "a rainbow of many colors." He walked over to my father's bedside and noticed that he looked very calm and serene, and was breathing peacefully. He then took some holy water that one of the nurses had brought in earlier and anointed his granddad, feeling intuitively that the peaceful presence had come to escort him on his transition. He kissed my father goodbye and returned home knowing he had witnessed something quite extraordinary that affected him very deeply.

A short while later, I was awoken by the phone ringing and switched on the bedside lamp, but nothing happened and I sat there in the darkness, as the hospice nurse told me that my father had passed away. In the last few days that I had been keeping a vigil at his bedside, I had asked my father to send me a sign, if he could, just to let me know that he was alright and as I replaced the phone, the lamp suddenly came on and filled the room with light. I sat there feeling the overwhelming sadness of losing his physical presence, but was assured that he had indeed sent me the sign I was waiting for. Jung believes such a synchronicity reflects archetypal energies emerging into consciousness. In the above example, the bedside light failing to work and the announcement of my father's death appear to have no causal connection. What links these two events is an illuminating sense of 'meaning.' The symbolic interpretation of darkness surrounding such news, followed by the illumination of light, signified to me that my father had moved through the darkness of death and into the eternal light.

The above example and numerous similar stories, demonstrate that many of us experience profound synchronicities and sense the presence of archetypal energies when fully present with the dying. Aniela Jaffe writes, "From the common bond, the archetype, we understand that emotion may be present in the person who perceives the event, or it may be connected with the happening that is extra-sensorially observed. Emotion is only a symptom pointing to an archetype, and, in cases of synchronistic events, to the 'organizing' factor in the unconscious."[12]

An open forum for disclosing such psychical manifestations is often barred by fear, even though hearing such uplifting narratives can alleviate anxiety over death through the repetition of experiential affirmations of rebirth. Although not all deaths are peaceful due to unresolved issues that make letting go far more difficult, we can prepare ourselves for this ultimate journey by becoming more receptive and entertaining archetypal dimensions of such testimonies, which echo beliefs embedded in most mainstream religious traditions.

Countless stories of after death communication with loved ones indicate that departed spirits seem very accessible at this time and teachings from *The Tibetan Book of the Dead* reiterate the concept that the soul of the deceased is very nearby following death. In a 1993 survey, conducted by the National Opinion Research Center, four out of every ten people interviewed reported some form of after death communication, and a 1994 Gallup Poll revealed that 49% of those questioned, stated that they were open to such a phenomenon occurring. Spirit communication manifests in various forms that can include: sensing the presence of a loved one, smelling their perfume or scent, or becoming aware of subtle messages that could only originate from the deceased.

One lady recounted receiving a message that brought her great comfort. Her daughter had severe problems due to alcoholism and had been on life support several times, but managed to pull through. However, her ravaged body finally gave out and she passed away, leaving her mother distraught and in deep mourning. One day, sometime later, this lady went to a music concert that was uplifting and joyful. Suddenly, in the vacant seat next to her, she sensed her daughter's presence telling her that she was alright and had moved on to a better place.

Following the tragic death of her son, Pisti, Betty J. Kovacs came to the stark realization that grief became a catalyst to envisioning the reality of a vast, loving universe. She describes her moving and poignant experiences in *The Miracle of Death* and firmly believes that her awakening to a deeper spiritual understanding of life was found in the mythic, symbolic, and mystical dimensions of her mind. The powerful visions that she and her husband, Istvan, shared opened a door to the powerful language of images, metaphors, and symbols, leading them on a journey to a 'new' way of seeing that transformed their lives. In the dreaming state, Kovacs also describes an apparition of her deceased son:

> I longed for Pisti to be present in the material world of time and space. I longed for the known world, the familiar world—with all its limitations. It was true that I wanted to make room in myself for "immensities of the universe," but tonight it seemed to me that my relationship to these immensities could only exist through my love for the individual forms here in

> my time and my place. I knew Pisti's essence existed even though he was no longer in the body. I had experienced his presence, his love, his consciousness, but now, this evening, I felt such a need to see him, to see his earthly form. I had trouble sleeping, and when I did sleep, I had strange, confusing dreams. Finally, in the early morning I dreamed Pisti came home. He walked into the kitchen where I was making breakfast. I could see him clearly. He was wearing the white Tibetan shirt he loved, jeans, and his old, dirty Nikes. I asked him why he was wearing his old shoes when I had bought him new ones before he died. He smiled and asked me in return, "Am I real enough?" We both laughed at his joking response to my need as we embraced each other. I was prepared to feel empty space, but much to my surprise, he was solid and I was not.[13]

One lady, Carol, told me that when learned her ex-mother-in-law, Jean, was on hospice care and not expected to live for more than a few days, she attended her spiritual study group and added her name to the list of people in transition, praying for her to be surrounded by love and light. The power of prayer offers a method of direct communication with a higher power for all, even if supplicants have no religious convictions. Prayer instills a sense of interconnectedness to all fellow beings and to something greater and more powerful than the self and in many religious traditions, this medium provides a means of intercession for the well-being of the living and the dead.

Following the meeting, Carol returned home exhausted, and crawled into bed. Within moments, she felt a presence in the room. She switched on her bedside lamp and saw that in front of her, stood a pearlescent figure that was solid in appearance, because she couldn't see the wall behind the image.

> I was startled by this manifestation, and my immediate

> reaction was to scream. Immediately, the figure collapsed, as if withdrawing from the veil it had pushed through to visit me. I never took my eyes of this manifestation until long after the silhouette of its shadow had started to fade, and then once again, I was looking through where it had made its presence felt and could see the wall across the room. I knew this apparition had been Jean. When I woke up in the morning, I made a call to a friend of mine who knew Jean and confirmed that she had made her transition the night before. I then enquired to the exact time of death and discovered that it was during the period that we had been praying for her.
>
> It's a strange and fascinating thought that the person with whom I had by far the most difficult relationship with ended up giving me the greatest gift I had ever received. I knew with certainty that this manifestation confirmed that we do survive death of the physical body and for this concrete evidence, I will always be grateful. On a personal level, this after death visitation also provided me with the knowledge that I had grown enough to feel compassion and sincerely pray for someone that had caused me such a lot of grief during my life.

Apparitions that have a *pearlescent* quality often emanate as white in color, symbolizing pure light, and they often represent the deceased or foretell that a person is about to transition. Pure light has scientifically been proven to contain the entire color spectrum, although it appears colorless to the spectator, until reflected through an object. White is associated with heralding death, but also symbolically hints at new life. Jaffe suggests, "If we allow our imagination to play with these thoughts we marvel at the analogy that colors are hidden in light, images and consciousness in the unconscious and—who knows?—life in death."[14]

I clearly remember my mother telling me how a fatal epidemic of a childhood disease had swept through her home town when she was young. Her best friend had been taken seriously ill and later died. During the night of this little girl's death, my mother had woken up to see her sitting at the end of the bed in a shimmering white dress. She smiled and told my mother not to worry, because she was happy in her new surroundings. This vision was so vivid that my mother retained the image and message it conveyed for the rest of her life.

Following my father's transition, I also had a very vivid dream after death communication. In the dream, I realized that although I had informed everyone that my father had died and had received condolences from many people, I had made a terrible mistake. My father was not dead; he was very much alive. In fact, he was standing at my side waiting for me to take him out to lunch, something we often did together. We went to a local restaurant and began to order. I appreciated his physical presence so much and placed my hand on his arm noticing the texture of the jacket and feeling the solid material. We had such an enjoyable time together and upon awakening, I felt convinced of the reality of the dream and my father's presence.

Thanatologist, Mo Hainer, told me of a family experience, following the tragic death of her grandson:

> After my grandson died, my daughter and her husband scattered his ashes in the ocean as the sun was going down. It was a beautiful sunset and the light expanded into a bright yellow as it hit the horizon. They took a photograph of this beautiful scene and when it was developed, it was possible to see my grandson's face reflected in this light. Interestingly enough when the picture was turned upside down, the image of his face was even clearer.

While many see apparitions of loved ones following death, there are also instances when a presence manifests that is completely impersonal. Stories of ghostly sightings that capture the imagination are universal and appear in myths, legends, literature, and religious traditions. Tibetan Buddhists celebrate the compassionate Feeding of the Hungry Ghosts, who have their own realm in the Wheel of Life, symbolizing the futility of fulfilling earthly desires. Taoists believe that ghosts or spirits that cannot find sustenance in the afterlife return to prey on the energy and fear of the living. Rituals are practiced to sustain these entities, so that they may move on. Part of the *Garuda Purana*, an ancient Hindu holy text is recited during cremation of the deceased in order to guide the departing spirit, and in ancient Rome, the yearly festival of Lemuria made offerings to ghostly or spirit beings.

In the Christian trinity, the spirit or breath of God is embodied in the Holy Ghost, often symbolized by a dove, which was seen hovering over Jesus at his baptism in the River Jordan. (Matthew 3:16). This aspect of the trinity is often referred to metaphorically, and through both the alchemical properties of purifying water that enables spiritual rebirth, and the transformational element of fire, depicted in "the tongues of fire" that descended over the disciples on the morning of Pentecost. Also seen to assume the invisible and visible qualities of cloud and light, the Holy Spirit "overshadows" the Virgin Mary, enabling her to conceive a son, Jesus, and is also likened to "a sound from heaven like the rush of a mighty wind" (Acts 2: 2-4). The Egyptian goddess, Isis, also held the power of the wind and reflected divine feminine qualities of love and compassion. This feminine influence manifests in the Holy Spirit and is believed to imbue some Christians with supernatural abilities, including the gifts of healing, prophecy, and wisdom.

Non-Christians also embrace the concept of a Holy Spirit. Muslims believe this divine manifestation is a reflection of God that emanates through prophetic messengers, including Muhammad. For the Navajos, an unknown, mysterious, holy power is present in all of creation and many diverse mythologies imagine the existence of an eternal spiritual essence that permeates everything and can be found within each individual.

The original meaning of the word *ghost* is closely associated with the *spirit* or *soul,* but acquired the meaning of a disembodied spirit. Ghostly sightings date back to pre-Christian times. Pliny the Younger, a poet, writer, and lawyer in ancient Rome described a house in Athens, said to be haunted by the ghost of an old man whose hands and feet were shackled in chains. After a receiving a proper burial, the ghostly presence was never seen again.

Continuing human curiosity and fascination with ghostly entities and apparitions has found its way into the collective creative imagination. In Shakespeare's *Hamlet,* the plot revolves around the 'shade' of Hamlet's murdered father and in *Macbeth,* the murdered Banquo returns as a ghost. Many other writers, including Oscar Wilde, Charles Dickens, and Henry James have also been inspired and captivated by images of supernatural entities.

A 2005 Gallup Poll revealed that approximately 32% of Americans "believe in the existence of ghosts," and these sighting continue to be avidly reported. Many sightings are recorded in 'haunted' houses that seem to hold an energetic memory of violent or tragic events. The presence of archetypal energies appears to occur during a weakening of individual consciousness, when the concept of time and space change dramatically. Jaffe writes, "This phenomenon has been scientifically investigated, but it has also been recorded by sensitive human beings, or by the people, and represented in legends and tales."[15]

Dr. Chris Clogston, narrates her ghostly experience while staying in an old English manor:

> In 1994, I traveled to England to attend a five-day residential course on Grail literature. The site of the course is Hawkwood

College, and is a many-roomed manor that was reportedly built on, or was somehow connected to, an older monastery on the property that was no longer there. The site was beautiful and lush, with greens of plant life that I don't see in sunny, dry, southern California. It rained every day I was there, and the drippy foggy mornings were very atmospheric.

During the course, I was staying in a single bedroom that had a sink and vanity mirror on the far end of the room, opposite the bed. On the second night, I was awakened by the sound of my hairbrush hitting the floor. I had placed the hairbrush, my toothbrush, a tube of toothpaste, and a container of lip balm on the mirror shelf, just above the sink. Sitting up in the bed, I was facing the sink and mirror directly and I watched while each of my other items, one by one, flew off the ledge and landed in the middle of the room. The items didn't fall from the ledge, as if slipping and then obeying gravity; these items flew, as if propelled by a flick of a finger or the sweep of a hand.

As I was about to leave the bed to investigate, I heard the sound of footsteps on the creaky wooden floor and these footsteps headed directly for my bed. Completely startled by the sound, I just sat there while the footsteps came right up to the side of the bed. Near my left ear, I heard an adult male voice say, "Help me!" This was followed by a whooshing sound that moved towards the door, and then I heard and experienced nothing more. Sleep was definitely difficult for the rest of that night!

The next morning, I kept trying to find out indirectly from some of the other attendees if they had experienced anything unusual the previous night, but no one had (and I didn't want to say that I'd had an odd experience).

I finally confided to another American taking the course, and she informed the owners of the venue. One of them stopped by my table during the evening meal and said that I'd had an encounter with a ghost they were familiar with, a monk who had died at the monastery, hundreds of years ago. I was assured that he "liked" me or was "attracted" to me in some way, because he didn't "visit" everyone, but was choosy. Great, I was chosen.

Was I visited by a ghost? I didn't see anyone, but I did hear a voice. Being a scientist, if I was told that I had experienced auditory hallucinations (the footsteps and the voice) coupled with a sagging mirror shelf, I could probably accept that. It's a lot of rational explanation for the event, but I would probably be okay with it. However, physician Vincent Lam observes, "Certain complex experiences…are part of the mystery of being human, the wispy territory in which we exist somewhere between our ambitious science and our daily frailties. In the mysterious gap between our knowledge of biological mechanisms and our everyday experiences as people, we find that things occur that are not easily explainable, but are no less real for that."[15] I would take Dr. Lam's commentary for my own.

Manifestations of psychic phenomena in various guises are far more common than many of us would imagine, forming part of the fabric of our personal stories and collective timeless myths, and legends. In our 'civilized' technological world, we still crave answers to the same existential questions pondered upon by ancient philosophers, and we continue to express wonder and awe at the possibility of 'magical' or otherworldly states that reveal glimpses of an archetypal connecting portal between science and mysticism. Heightened spiritual, psychic, or mystical experiences remind us of the vital breath or 'spirit' that originates from the Latin *spirare*, which not only gives life an animate vitality, but reiterates the concept of an immortal soul, by which humans are distinguished.

For some, integrating mind-blowing catalysts and spiritual

epiphanies that dismantle prior beliefs and herald profound changes in lifestyles can pose traumatic challenges and long periods of adjustment. The American Center for the Integration of Spiritually Transformative Experiences (ACISTE) is a nonprofit organization, dedicated to enhancing the well-being and needs of those who have had near-death or similar spiritually transformative experiences, through research, education, and support. Programs include: peer support groups, workshops, training of mentors and therapists, and online information designed for community building, discussion, and learning. They can be found at www.aciste.org . The International Association for Near-Death Studies (IANDS) also has local chapters and group meetings throughout the United States and in many other countries.

Difficulty in entertaining the reality of mystical and psychic phenomena stems from sole identification with the body, as we become entangled in the everyday rush of life. But if we truly wish to *awaken*, we need to invite the sacred into our lives and appreciate the fine golden alchemical thread that gives shape and form to the mystery of creation and stimulates our creative imagination to voice the timeless, symbolic, and archetypal language of the soul that can fulfill our collective *immortal yearnings*.

Notes

1. C. S. Lewis, *Letters to Malcolm: Chiefly on Prayer* (Orlando: Harcourt, 1991), 64.
2. Fritjof Capra, *The Tao of Physics*, 8.
3. C. G. Jung, *Memories*, 183.
4. T. S. Eliot, *The Wasteland, Prufock, and Other Poems* (West Valley City: Waking Lion Press, 2009), 78.
5. Ernest Shackleton, Fergus Fleming, and Frank Hurley, *South, The Endurance Expedition* (New York: Penguin, 2004), 212.

6. William James, *Varieties of Religious Experience*, 64.
7. Edgar Mitchell, *The Way of the Explorer* (Franklin Lakes: New Page Books, 2008), 15.
8. Ibid., 16.
9. Ibid., 2.
10. Paul Devereux, *Place of Power: Measuring the Secret Energy of Sacred Sites* (London: Blandford Press, 1999), 194.
11. Andrea Leininger, Bruce Leininger and Ken Gross, *Soul Survivor: The Reincarnation of a World War 11 Fighter Pilot* (New York: Grand Central Publishing, 2009), 255.
12. Aniela Jaffe, *Apparitions: An Archetypal Approach to Death, Dreams and Ghosts* (Irving: Spring, 1979), 194.
13. Betty J. Kovacs, *The Miracle of Death*, 97.
14. Aniela Jaffe, *Apparitions*, 82.
15. Ibid., 117.

6th Books investigates the paranormal, supernatural, explainable or unexplainable. Titles cover everything included within parapsychology: how to, lifestyles, beliefs, myths, theories and memoir.